MARX AND THE MARXISTS
THE AMBIGUOUS LEGACY

SIDNEY HOOK

Chairman, Graduate Department of Philosophy
New York University

AN ANVIL ORIGINAL

under the general editorship of

LOUIS L. SNYDER

D. VAN NOSTRAND COMPANY, INC.

PRINCETON, NEW JERSEY

TORONTO   LONDON

NEW YORK

To the memory of

BENJAMIN ZINKIN

whose predictions came true

D. VAN NOSTRAND COMPANY, INC.
120 Alexander St., Princeton, New Jersey (*Principal office*); 24 West 40 St., New York, N.Y.
D. VAN NOSTRAND COMPANY (Canada), LTD.
25 Hollinger Rd., Toronto 16, Canada
D. VAN NOSTRAND COMPANY, LTD.
358, Kensington High Street, London, W.14, England

Library of Congress Catalog Card No. 55-11286

PREFACE

This volume of exposition, comment, and readings is offered as an introduction to the study of the theory and practice of Marxism. Obviously it cannot be comprehensive in scope or exhaustive in its analysis. Some currents of thought, for example, syndicalism and guild socialism, which have had only peripheral relations with the main streams of Marxist tradition, have not been considered because of the short compass of the work. I have sought only to lay before the reader the chief issues which have divided Marxists from non-Marxists and Marxists from each other.

The development of Marxism as a movement has resulted in some peculiar paradoxes which make it difficult to retain traditional conceptual formulations. Where Marxism as a movement has triumphed, as in the Soviet Union, its socialist ideals have failed or have been betrayed; where it has failed as a movement, as in the West, its ideals have made considerable headway. It seems as if history itself has been guilty of lèse-Marxism.

Events of the last twenty-five years or so have shown how important a knowledge of the ideas and movements discussed in this book is to an intelligent appreciation of political affairs. It is safe to say that had Roosevelt and Churchill and their advisors been better informed of them they would have been better prepared for the Soviet strategy of the cold war. The wages of ignorance may very well be the loss of freedom.

The most a book of this kind can do is to arouse the interest of the reader to a point where he is curious to find out more about the subject it treats. Whether it is successful in this respect each reader, of course, will judge for himself.

New York,
April, 1955

SIDNEY HOOK

TABLE OF CONTENTS

Part I

MARX AND THE MARXISTS

— 1 —

THE CONTRIBUTIONS OF KARL MARX

1. On Understanding Marx. Karl Marx is one of the most influential figures in human history. Judged by the number of those who have regarded themselves his followers, and of the organizations set up by them, he has inspired the greatest mass movement of all times. This movement transcends national, racial, and continental boundaries. Only in Anglo-Saxon communities has he had a comparatively small following, to some extent because of the use made of his ideas elsewhere. The result is that in England and particularly the United States, he is often condemned without even being read. On the other hand, in some regions of the rest of the world, a new religion has arisen which proclaims that History is God and Karl Marx its chief prophet.

The increasing complexity and interrelations of modern civilization make it practically certain that the fashion in which Marx's ideas are interpreted will have a very great bearing upon the future of the Anglo-Saxon world, especially the United States. That is one sufficient reason why every reflective person should have some familiarity with his doctrines, their evolution, and their current impact upon the stormy political life of our era.

In many situations it is not so much the actual past which determines the present as what people imagine the past to have been. Similarly with the ideas propounded by a great thinker of the past. Save as a rule in the natural sciences, it is not what a man actually has said or meant so much as what he is interpreted to have said or meant which influences the present. Of few figures

11

is this truer than of Marx. These varying interpretations are affected by current needs and interests, and explain why from the fact that a man calls himself a Marxist one can hardly be more confident about his actual beliefs than about the actual beliefs of one who calls himself a Christian. Nonetheless, although it is difficult it is not impossible to determine with some fidelity what Marx really taught and believed. Any hypothesis about the actual meaning of his doctrines is an hypothesis about a matter of historical fact and must be tested by the same fundamental canons of evidence as we bring to bear upon other historical questions.

In Marx's case this is rendered difficult by the circumstances of his life and the occasion of his writing. He was not an academician interested in ideas for their own sake but a revolutionary activist who developed his ideas in an effort to influence the course of events. He was a fierce controversialist and polemicized against individuals who held contrary positions, so that sometimes he stresses one point and, at other times, when this point seems overshadowed by events or eclipsed in argument, he emphasizes its opposite. Nowhere is there a systematic exposition of all his leading ideas and of their relation to each other. He wrote at a time when precision was not regarded as a great virtue, when statistical and probabilistic conceptions of scientific law were in their infancy, and when the social sciences pretentiously modeled themselves on the physics of the day. Marx's terminology often reflects his Hegelian heritage. Almost all of his basic formulations seem ambiguous. Honest critics have charged him with flagrant inconsistencies and a fundamental incoherence, while uncritical admirers have accepted every word even when his conclusions appear contradictory. All these difficulties are aggravated by the fact that Marx has become a political symbol evoking emotive reactions rather than intellectually discriminating ones.

2. Life.   Marx was born in 1818 in the little Rhenish town of Trier which boasted of its origins as a distinguished Roman outpost of early times. On both sides of his family he was descended from a long line of Jewish rabbis. For social reasons, Marx's father became converted to Protestantism and his son grew up without any consciousness of himself as being Jewish. After a conven-

tionally brilliant career at school, Marx attended briefly
the University of Bonn and then the University of Berlin
where he developed strong intellectual interests in law,
philology, and theology. Upon the completion of his
doctorate he was made editor of the *Rheinische Zeitung,*
which was shortly suppressed because of its advanced
liberal views. In 1843 Marx married. He then moved to
Paris where he plunged into a study of French communism and political economy. While in Paris he met Fried-
rich Engels and forged a lifelong friendship with him.
Engels, son of a wealthy manufacturer, shared, helped
develop, and popularized Marx's ideas. He also relieved
the burden of crushing poverty on Marx's family. Exiled
from Paris, Marx went to Brussels where he joined the
Communist League and on the eve of the Revolution of
1848 wrote the *Communist Manifesto.* He took a lively
part in helping to organize the Revolution of 1848 in
Western Europe, was banished from Brussels, arrested,
tried and freed in Germany, and compelled to leave
France again. He finally found political asylum in London, where he spent the rest of his life in research, writing, emigrant squabbles, political journalism of the
highest level, and in organizing the First International
Workingmen's Association. He published comparatively
little during this period aside from the first volume of
Capital, although he left behind the draft of several
other volumes.

Fame and acknowledgment came slowly to Marx, and
when he died in 1883 few outside the circle of his political followers were aware of his work and stature. The
most paradoxical thing about his theories is that they
fail to explain plausibly the impact of his own life and
doctrines on the history of society. There would have
been a socialist movement without Karl Marx. But its
form and history bear the stamp which only his personality and ideas could have given it.

3. **Marx's Intellectual Development.** Marx's characteristic ideas ripened in the course of an intense intellectual development during a period when, although
politically and industrially Germany was still among the
most backward countries of Western Europe, its thinkers
were bold and extreme. At the University of Berlin he
came under the influence of the Hegelian philosophy
which interpreted the world as a dynamic and spiritual

process that progressively revealed itself as a reasonable order. What occurred latest in time was the best in quality. To the searching eye of dialectic, anything that was truly real would be found to be both necessary and rational. At any given time, despite surface appearances, "God's in his Heaven, All's well with the world." The evil of the part is essential to the good of the developing whole. Truth lies only in the completed whole; short of it, each age has its own partial truth.

In Hegel a Universal Consciousness or Spirit took the place of the God of traditional religion. World history was marked by the stages of its progress towards a state of affairs in which the implicit necessities of existence appear as an explicit freedom in consciousness. The "spirit of the times" informs the whole of a culture, gives it a dominant style of thought and feeling, relates ideas and events, and then makes way for another pattern in which it is continued and transformed. No cultural phenomenon could be adequately understood except in its context within the pattern.

The "Left-wing" Hegelians emphasized the element of process in Hegel's thought rather than its system. To them Spirit was not a disembodied great soul or a bodyless mind or a logical abstraction but the very life of a culture, the expression of its organized energies. They were dissatisfied with the notion that the "Spirit of the times" had an autonomous history or that it had a causal influence on the rise, growth, and decline of cultures. Far from explaining events the "Spirit of the times" seemed itself to require explanation because it varied from place to place and period to period, to be able to do something in one country, such as abolish slavery, which it could not do in another.

Three outstanding Left-Hegelians contributed to Marx's emancipation from Hegelian orthodoxy. D. F. Strauss, with particular reference to religion and the rise of Christianity, regarded Spirit as the unconscious mythmaking power of the community or the collective mind. Bruno Bauer reduced the Spirit to individual consciousness and explained religious myths and dogmas as inventions of clever storytellers with a purpose. He taught that at any definite moment the "Spirit of the times" is nothing but a complex mass of interacting feelings, desires, and thoughts of individual persons, some more gifted and persuasive than others. Ludwig Feuerbach completed this cycle of thought and attributed the works of the Spirit to the presence of needs, wants, and lacks in the life of man. All other worldly religions and philosophies are projections of human needs or their compensatory fulfillments. Outside of nature and society, there was neither Consciousness nor Spirit. "Anthropology (the study of man) is the secret of theology." Men create gods in their own moral image and this image blossoms from social roots. For a number of technical reasons, as well as because of the misleading associations of the word "materialism," which suggested crass egoism and the cult of pleasure, Feuerbach regarded himself as a naturalist and a humanist.

Marx accepted, with some important modifications, the basic philosophy of Feuerbach, especially his critique of existing religion as a projection in distorted form of human needs and ideals. But he disagreed with Feuerbach in important respects. The nature of man was not only social but historical. Therefore, nothing cultural could be explained by human nature as such but only by the concrete needs and aims of man under specific historical conditions. Secondly, Marx did not follow Feuerbach in his call for a new religion of humanity based on the ideal of love but, together with Arnold Ruge and younger figures among the Left-Hegelians, turned to a critique of political institutions.

These Left-Hegelians believed that just, as in the past, men have worshipped religious abstractions which expressed in a distorted form the actual role of moral and social ideals in their experience, so men were—especially in Germany—in the grip of political abstractions. They hypostatized the state, law, the monarchy as institutions sanctified either by theology, metaphysics, or the eternal natural law. In reality these institutions were patterns of organized power in political life with a determinate history which had arisen to meet the needs and interests of special groups. Marx went further. By analyzing the politics of his time he came to the conclusion that they were rooted in a clash of interests which in turn were the outgrowth of the material and social conditions of society. The most important of the latter were the conditions under which human beings earned their living—the mode of economic production—which determined the form in which wealth was created and distributed. These economic institutions were not natural or unalterable but historical. In the past they had ruled men as if they were uncontrollable natural forces. Instead of bowing to a historical and economic fatality which in reality was nothing but the consequences of their unconscious, unplanned, collective activity, human beings should now intelligently contrive, within the limits of natural necessity, their social life and historical future. In this way they would realize themselves as free and harmoniously developed persons. The necessary and sufficient condition for the existence of the community of free and equal persons is the collective ownership and democratic control of the chief instruments of production.

According to Marx, man's religious emancipation could be achieved and secured through political emancipation. This entailed the complete secularization of culture in which religion would be a purely private matter. Political emancipation in turn required man's economic emancipation, the subordination of the aggregates of economic power to the public welfare. Historically this meant that freedom of conscience, won during the Reformation, could be consolidated only by the political freedoms won in the American and French Revolutions. These were to be ultimately secured, not abolished, when the democratic collectivity had as much power to control its economic life as its political life.

Although Marx added to his philosophy certain doctrines which were to threaten its universalism, he never abandoned, at least in his own mind, the standpoint of a democratic and naturalistic humanism. He had a strong belief in the dignity of man. For him this consisted in striving to master one's own fate and not submitting to the dogmas of church, the tyrannies of state, the blind operation of economic institutions, or the decrees of political parties.

Marx's temperament was Promethean; his intellectual tradition was Greek and scientific rather than medieval and literary; his ethical ideal a society "in which the free development of each is the condition for the free development of all." Ultimately the test of all institutions was the extent to which they made possible for all persons the full and free enrichment of their personalities. This belief in freedom, equality, and individual personality distinguishes Marx radically from all totalitarians who invoke his name. (*See Reading No. 1.*)

4. **Socialism.** Marx was converted to belief in the desirability of socialism before he worked out the theories with which his name is associated. His own doctrines took form in the course of his reflection on the conditions under which, and the means by which, a socialist revolution could succeed and socialism be introduced.

The term "socialism" already in Marx's day was used in various senses. Most often it meant a system of society in which the chief instruments of production, distribution, and exchange are *common* property, leaving personal property, articles of use and consumption, private. When is property common? When it belongs to the state? In this case the Egyptian and Oriental despotisms of the past in which the state owned or absolutely controlled the existing instruments of production would have to be called socialist societies. Is property common when it is nationalized by any government? In that case it would be just as possible for those who work in nationalized industry to be as exploited as those who work in other forms of industry. Ownership of a railroad, for example, may pass from private to public hands without making any difference to the workers' hours, conditions, and rewards of work. Under certain circumstances these may become even worse: for they may be deprived of the right to strike by government decree and in effect kept at forced labor.

That is why the most comprehensive definition of socialism is a society in which there is *democratic* common ownership of the means of production. The force of "democratic" here is ethical. It refers to the process by which decisions are made, the goals towards which the process is directed, the choice and preparation of vocations, the integration of useful work for society in education and the influence of education on work, and above all the ultimate responsibility of those who legislate for the community in economic as well as political affairs to the citizens of the community. As conceived by Marx as well as by some of the Utopian Socialists, a belief in socialism entailed a belief in what today would be considered a fraternal democracy—an equality of concern on the part of the community towards all citizens, with equal rights and powers of all ultimately to determine who shall govern or administer the community. Without such a belief, expressed in institutional practices, there would be no way to distinguish between a collectivized *free* society and a collectivized *slave* society.

Marx believed that what was desirable and historically possible could be significantly determined only when they are related to the actual. The advent of socialism depends upon the gradual emergence of the objective conditions of its feasibility. These are bound up with development of the economic system. Man is omnipotent only in his dreams. He can control nature only by bending nature's means and remake society only with the materials with which that society provides him.

Marx called himself a "Scientific Socialist" as distinct from a "Utopian Socialist." He himself has been called a Utopian Socialist and in some respects he undoubtedly was. But by his "scientific socialism" he meant not merely that he could give adequate reasons for his advocacy of socialism, but that he knew how, when, and under what conditions, socialism could be realized, and especially how it could be helped into the world when it announced its presence as an historical possibility.

This concern with the theory and practice of social revolution, with means and conditions, led Marx to take the democratic ends of socialism so much for granted that he failed to consider the appropriateness of these means and conditions to what was supposed to follow them. Socialism was conceived as a rationally planned collectivized economy in which all social and moral problems would automatically be settled. With memories before him of books full of ridiculous details concerning the socialism of the future, Marx scoffed at the imaginative byplay. Buoyed up by the heady spirits of nineteenth-century optimism with a dash of Hegelian bitters, he assumed that the future would take care of itself, and that society and events would make and remake better men. For all of Marx's appreciation of man as an active creature, he counted without man's dimensions of depth and complexity. Here Marx lost sight of Hegel's insight that there is a tragic element in all human experience in a developing world. After all, if even angels revolt in the City of God who can be sure of human behavior in the City of Man?

5. Historical Materialism. From Hegel and from

critical studies of the Hegelian philosophy of law, Marx learned that the culture of a period is interrelated and differs from other cultures by a dominant tone or style or set of values which pervades all of its chief expressions. He sought to find the key to its systematic structure and development which would explain, say, why the culture of the Middle Ages differs from that of the nineteenth century, and how each arises, flourishes, and disappears. The theory of historical materialism is Marx's answer to the question. (*See Reading No. 2.*)

By a *materialistic* conception of history Marx means any theory which seeks to explain history by empirical laws whose predictions and descriptions are in principle verifiable by observation of the behavior of men, things, and the institutions which relate them. Denying the adequacy of physicalistic or racial or psychological theories, he asserted that, broadly speaking, the economic structure of society and its changes were the independent variables of which all other cultural changes were a function. Or more simply put, the economic structure of society determines the life of any society in historic times. It is "the basis" or "the foundation." As it changes, sooner or later it carries the whole of culture with it. Its course may be somewhat influenced by other aspects of culture but never seriously deflected. It changes gradually for the most part, but at certain times suddenly. Sometimes the theory of historical materialism is referred to as the economic interpretation of history. But there are various economic interpretations and not all of them can be fathered on Marx despite the ambiguities of his language.

In the interest of understanding, two central notions must be clarified.

(1) What does Marx mean by the term "economic"? (2) What does it mean to assert that the economic factor, or any factor, "determines" a culture or that it is "the most important" or "basic" or "foundational" cause, or the "anatomy" of a given society?

Only when some coherent meaning is given to these notions can we tell whether the key propositions which contain them are true or false, and to what degree. To some critics Marx's theory appears nonsensical—no theory at all; to others, completely and clearly false; to still others, including the writer, an intelligible hypothesis which plausibly explains some things but fails to explain others. To most of his declared disciples, on the other hand, the theory appears true no matter what it means.

(1) The term "economic" is used in at least four distinct senses. (a) It is sometimes used to characterize motives like a desire for wealth or money, or for the social status and power which wealth or money make possible. The "economic interests" of a group usually presuppose the presence of such motives even if they are not explicit. (b) It sometimes refers to the presence or absence of land and the raw materials like iron, coal, and oil necessary for production. (c) More often, it means the techniques, forces, and powers of production, including not only tools and instruments but skills and know-how. (d) Finally it means what Marx calls the *mode* of economic production or the *social relations* of production. These are the institutional rules or processes which govern the production and distribution of wealth like the systems of slavery, feudalism, capitalism, and socialism.

There is a great deal of confusion concerning these senses of the term "economic," particularly the meaning of the *mode or social relations of production.* Some critics have characterized it as a piece of mystifying metaphysics designed to conceal the absence of clear thought on Marx's part. It is not something psychological like an economic motive or physical like the conditions and forces of production. What, then, is it? The clue is to be found in that Marx sometimes speaks of "property relations" as a "legal expression" of the relations of production. This indicates that they are *social* and are not reducible either to psychological or physical relations, although without the latter they could not exist.

Why, then, does Marx not speak of legal relations of production or simply property relations as the basic determining factor of culture? Because he is interested in explaining the character and development of the whole culture-complex as effects of the relations of production. In this culture-complex are included the legal codes, day-by-day legislation, and court decisions which we ordinarily designate as the *laws* of a culture. But the existence of systems like slavery, feudalism, or capitalism is not determined by law in the ordinary sense of the term. They are institutional arrangements which control the activities of men in the production and distribution of wealth without depending on any explicit law but on the basic mores which have developed to a point where they appear socially natural. For example, English law and French law are quite different, although both countries are capitalist. And by calling them capitalist Marx meant that the dominant system of production is the production of *commodities* for a market by workers who are formally free to work or not, and who are themselves not the owners of the instruments they use. These commodities are produced for purposes of *profit* to those who own the instruments of production and not in the first instance for the use of those who produce them. When production becomes unprofitable it soon ceases. It is therefore the quest, and ever-renewed quest, for profit which, according to Marx, leads to the expansion of commodity production.

This capitalist mode of production obviously differs from slave, feudal, and socialist modes of production. One may call these modes of production *legal* relations. They then must be distinguished from the corpus of laws which, together with other aspects of the culture-complex, are determined by the basic legal relations.

Every mode of economic production if permitted to develop independently evolves in conformity with certain laws comparable to the evolution of an organism from a seed. It is in terms of its organization and development that other major changes in culture are to be explained. For example, according to this view, changes in the forces and techniques of production as well as changes in the norm of motivation do *not* develop independently. The effects which are often attributed to technology should be attributed to the operation of the mode of economic production. Thus Marx would deny that it is economic techniques which produce effects like monopolies and unemployment. These are consequences of the use of such techniques *in an economy devoted to the quest for private profit*. Man, to be sure, is naturally an inventive animal. Marx defines him, after Benjamin Franklin, as a tool-making animal. But whether his inventiveness takes a theological or technological form is determined, in the main, by the system of production under which he lives, and by the struggles, values, and allegiances which develop in consequence of it. So claims Marx.

It is clear, then, that historical materialism is not a technological theory of history as it becomes if the *forces* of production are considered the motor force of social change. Many Marxists, including Engels, often speak of the forces of production determining history, and Marx himself occasionally lapses into such expressions. But whoever asserts, whether Marxist or not, that man's tools and techniques are the final determining factor in history is demonstrably mistaken. For example, consider a prospector working (i) for himself, (ii) as a slave, (iii) on shares, (iv) for wages paid by a private employer, (v) for wages paid by the community. He may in each case be working alone and with the same set of tools. But in each case the mode of production he illustrates will be different. That under given historical conditions a particular mode of production will lead him and others to use highly developed tools rather than a simple pick and spade does not alter the fact. It confirms it. For it will show that the growth of technology is to be accounted for by changes in the *mode* of production, which in time is caused by the demand for more and better goods.

Marx held that the industrial techniques and processes which are employed in the mode of production are consequences of its selective needs. In this respect, Marx claims, it is like an organism which does not use everything which is potentially food but only what its own internal structure can assimilate. Discoveries in science, which received its greatest impetus under capitalism, may have potential economic effects, but they are used or not in production only if they fit into the pattern of profitability which is the mark of the system. Since it is obvious that many scientific discoveries have been technologically applied for purposes of war, independently of their cost and bearing on profit, Marx is compelled to interpret wars as if they were always the result of the existing mode of production and waged to defend that system. Normally the pace of technological inquiry and application increases or slackens with the business cycle and not vice versa. "Machinery," Marx once wrote, "is no more an economic category than is an ox which draws the plow. It is only a productive force."

What Marx is saying is that the history of politics and the history of art, religion, and science are not independent histories but different aspects of the history of society which is fundamentally the history of the ways in which men earn their living. He carries this so far as to hold that man who makes history has no original *human* nature. Man's nature is limited by his biological structure, but his biological drives may take an indefinite variety of forms, depending upon the society in which he lives. Marx denies that man is an egoistic hedonist as Hobbes, Bentham, and Stirner taught. He repudiates "the economic man" of contemporary political economy as the perennial human type. "Economic man" did not exist in the Greek and medieval worlds. Although man is limited, he is complex. He is selfish and unselfish, rapacious and cooperative, bold and submissive. But the prevalence at any given time of one set of motives over another, which may be inferred from the standards of what is socially approved or disapproved, is explicable, Marx believes, not by man's original nature but ultimately by the economic structure of his society. In consequence, although men's biological impulses have been relatively constant since they emerged from the animal state, their motives and ideals will be different in a feudal society from what they are in a capitalist society and from what they will be in a socialist society. Even in the same society at different stages of its economic development, different aspects of human nature will come to the fore. In the early period of capitalism—because of the need of accumulating capital—sobriety, saving, and thrift were considered social virtues; subsequently when capitalism entered a phase of decline and greater consumption was required to keep the wheels of production moving, these former virtues were condemned as niggardliness and hoarding.

(2) Before we consider the validity of these large claims for the pervasive influence of the mode of economic production, we must determine what Marx meant in asserting that it was the decisive or basic or most important factor in history. That it plays some role no one denies. So does almost anything else. The question is: how much?

In theoretical science expressions like "chief," "basic," or "most important" cause are not found. But wherever human beings act, or are prepared to act, such expressions are inescapable. For they indicate what must be changed and to what degree, or what would have had to be changed, to obtain a certain result. It would be absurd to ask: What is the chief or most important cause of the functioning of the body? It is not ridiculous to ask what is the chief cause of tuberculosis, cancer of the lungs, or the decline in the death rate. In any historical period at any given time an infinite number of social elements are interacting with each other. Taken together they tautologically explain what is happening in the social system. But some things have a greater weight than others in explaining some effects short of the operation of the whole system. What Marx is saying is that, if we make a list of the outstanding events in human history or the outstanding features of any society, an empirical study of the facts will reveal, if not in each case, then in the vast majority of cases, that we must assign the greatest weight in our explanation to what he calls the mode of economic production.

Marx is sometimes interpreted as asserting that everything in society and history is the result of the development of productive relations. This would be syntactically meaningless for it would then be impossible to distinguish economics from anything else. If the occurrence of x causes a change in y the effect cannot wholly be explained in terms of x. The sun's rays may cause a piece of wax to melt, but unless the wax existed when and where it did and unless its characteristic traits were other than a stone, its melting would not have occurred. Whatever the mode of economic production is, at the time it acts it can neither create nor wholly determine the antecedent character of the traditions it affects, or the character of the men it influences. And if its changes determine changes in the law, politics, science, art, religion, and philosophy of a period, it does not create these modes of experience. They may *in fact* have the profoundest influence on changes into the mode of economic production. Only empirical investigation can tell when one or the other set of changes initiates the process of change.

It is possible, then, to show that despite the use of ambiguous, vague, and rhetorical language Marx makes sense. But does he make good sense? We shall return to this question in the next chapter.

6. Social Development.   Change is a pervasive phenomenon and nowhere more obviously than in the affairs of men. Partly under the influence of Hegel, and later of the anthropological evolutionary theory of Lewis Morgan,

(today primarily only of historical interest), Marx conceived of the succession of societies as following a definite and unbreakable pattern from simplicity to complexity, especially in its economic structure. Each society considered from the point of view of its economic structure is marked by a characteristic attitude towards the instruments and forces of production. Some societies spur productivity. Others do not. But sooner or later, according to Marx, a point is reached in every society that is not a socialist society, in which the existing economic structure definitely hampers the full use of the productive forces existing within it, not to speak of actualizing the possibilities of new productive forces. When this state of affairs is reached, great masses of human beings suffer want and privation. Those classes in the population which have most to gain from removing the restrictions placed upon the productive forces become politically revolutionary and in time a new social order is born. The productive forces are then liberated until in turn the inner dynamic of the new economic structure runs down. It is obvious that Marx is projecting as true for all history, except primitive and socialist societies, a schema which seemed to apply to the nineteenth century when overproduction of commodities resulted in closing down of industrial plants, and human beings hungered in the midst of a potential plenty. (*See Reading Nos. 1 and 4.*)

In this connection Marx makes two claims which were to be of tremendous importance subsequently. The first is that "no social order ever perishes before all the productive forces for which there is room in it have developed." The second is that "new higher relations of production never appear before the material conditions of their existence [forces of production, skills, and techniques] have matured in the womb of the old society itself." These sentences stress the economic continuity of society and deny that society can stride from one stage of society to another without going through the intermediate stages of development.

7. **Class Struggles.** History is made by men and not by impersonal social and economic forces acting from the past. The latter only register the effects of what human beings have previously done. But the living generation always experiences them in the form of traditions, institutions, and legal relations which in some respects are

as compelling and independent of their wills as are the forces of nature. We are born not only white or black but high or low in the social scale, with this nationality or that, inheritors of one religious faith or another.

Human beings belong to an indefinite number of classes—national, religious, racial, vocational. But when Marx uses the term "class" he refers primarily to the *economic* group defined by its position in the process of production: slave or master, serf or feudal lord, worker or capitalist. Wherever private ownership of means of production exists there is an objective opposition of interests between classes with respect to the division of the fruits of production. This opposition at times becomes acute and erupts into open conflict. But whether latent or overt, it exercises a pervasive influence on the behavior of individuals in most of their other class associations.

The most conspicuous expression of class conflicts is to be found in politics to which, according to Marx, economics is always the chief key. Underlying the conflicts of political slogans, principles, and personalities, there is always the unremitting pressure of conflicting economic interests. These mount in intensity until, after many uneasy compromises, they end in the victory of one of the contending classes. In the *Communist Manifesto* Marx suggests that the struggle may sometimes lead to the doom of both. But he does not develop the suggestion which is out of tune with the main emphasis of his thought. (*See Reading No. 1.*)

8. The Theory of the State.   Class struggles, although basically caused by clash of economic interests, are also political struggles. The existing state power is always in the background ready to intervene and it must be reckoned with. Current forms of property relations may have the force of tradition and of habitual use and wont behind them, but whenever they are seriously challenged they rely upon the sanctions of extra-economic power to sustain them. The state, for Marx is distinct from the government. It is composed of those institutions —the courts, police, and army—by means of which disputes concerning economic interests, not decided by ordinary methods of negotiation, are ultimately settled. A dominant economic class may not at any given moment be the dominant political class, but unless it becomes such, its economic interests and the functioning of so-

ciety as a whole are subject to continuous frustration. When the struggle becomes hot, the state appears nakedly as the "executive committee" of the ruling class. It must be captured by the new class which in time clothes the state once more with a rhetoric that describes it as neutral or above the battle or as the instrument of the general interest.

The pattern of class struggle and the role of the state in that struggle are clearly described in the history of mankind from the decline of primitive society to the present. The state, according to this view which was shared by many socialists of the nineteenth century, consists of more than the administrative machinery necessary to take care of required community needs. It is the apparatus of coercion visible to all eyes in the form of separate bodies of armed men standing outside the population. Not until the economic exploitation of man by man disappears, an exploitation which, according to Marx, is the source of all other forms of exploitation, can the state disappear. Such economic exploitation will necessarily come to an end when the instruments of production are socialized—a large assumption, as we shall see. Since in such a society there is no special class of owners, inasmuch as all citizens are *both* owners and producers, by Marx's definition it is a classless society. There will, of course, be all sorts of other group divisions made more fluid than today because presumably the division of labor will not be so sharp, even if it does not altogether disappear. But it is assumed that since these divisions will not lead to organized and systematic human exploitation, they will therefore not require a special apparatus of coercion. Once socialism exists, there will be, so to speak, "traffic rules" regulating social intercourse, there will be traffic "policemen" administering the rules, but no clubs or fines or jails to enforce them. Apparently Marx believed that everyone will take turns at policing traffic, at governing community affairs, at physical labor, and at going fishing.

Irrespective of how literally Marx is construed as anticipating this rosy and optimistic picture of a classless society, it is indisputable that he believed it would be characterized by a higher standard of living, by greater political and cultural freedom, and by far less coercion of any kind than has been attained, or is attainable, in all previous class societies no matter how democratic or liberal. In passing, it should be observed that Marx's sanguine expectations were not much different, if less extreme, from those of the Utopian Socialists of the nineteenth century whose methods of realizing socialism he scorned. For example, William Godwin in his *Political Justice* speaks of a future day in which "there will be no war, no crime, no administration of justice, as it is called, no government. Besides there will be neither disease, anguish, melancholy, nor resentment. Every man will seek, with ineffable ardor, the good of all." Marx contents himself with the belief that society and government will function without a state. There is no evidence that he gave much thought to the problems this vision opens up. How socialism is to be achieved, once the objective historical situation made it possible, was his main concern. Before considering his theory of social revolution, his critique of capitalism as an economic system must be briefly expounded.

9. **Economic Theory.** Marx developed his economic theory many years after he had formulated his theories of history, classes, and the road to socialism. His economic theory was designed to show that the historical development of capitalism produced conditions which paved the way for a socialist society. He predicted certain fundamental tendencies in the evolution of capitalism like the centralization of industry, concentration of capital, periodic booms and depressions, and growth of monopolies. These predictions have been recognized as valid by many economists who are neither Marxist nor even socialist. But Marx's attempt to derive them from his theory of value, adopted from Ricardo, is much more questionable and has met with little acceptance by modern economists.

Marx defined capitalism as a system of society in which the instruments of production are operated for the private profit of those who own them by means of the labor of workers who are neither slaves nor serfs but freemen. Profit is the first and last goal of production in such a system. How does it arise?

Marx assumes that the value of a commodity is determined by the amount of labor-time necessary for its production—not, however, any amount of labor-time, for that would make a commodity produced by a lazy man or one working with antiquated tools more valuable than a commodity produced with modern tools. The labor-time must be socially necessary. What is socially necessary varies with the prevalent skills, intensity of effort, and technological conditions of production at any given time. The worker sells his labor power on the market as a commodity. Its value is determined like that of any other commodity, viz., by the socially necessary labor-time required to produce it and reproduce it. The worker receives in exchange for the time he works a sum of money equivalent in value to the means of subsistence necessary to sustain him and his family. But labor-time, according to Marx, is absolutely unlike other commodities. It creates more value than its own market value, i.e., more value than it itself is worth. If the capitalist sold a commodity merely at what it cost him to produce it, i.e., the costs of overhead, raw material, machinery, taxes, wages of superintendence, and wages paid to the worker, he would make no profit and would not long remain in business. There would be no point in tying his money up merely to give himself the job of manager; indeed many owners do not even manage their own plants and yet draw profit therefrom.

Marx rejects the customary explanation of the origins of profit and asserts that (a) only labor is the source of value; (b) that surplus labor-time, i.e., what is expended over and above the time necessary to create the value equivalent to its cost of subsistence, is the source of surplus-value; and (c) that profit, as well as rent and interest, is derived solely from the surplus-value created by the workers. Machinery, new inventions (except as forms of labor), and the vicissitudes of the market do not add value to anything and therefore cannot be the source of profit.

Since the worker produces more value than he is paid for, Marx refers to the capitalist process of production as just as much a system of exploitation as the systems of slavery and feudalism in which it was apparent that the slave or serf performed work for which he was not paid. The mystery of capitalist production is that the worker is ostensibly paid the full market value of his labor-power. The secret of the mystery, according to Marx, is that he is paid only the value of his labor-power but not the actual value produced by his labor-power.

The drive for profit is the soul of capitalist production. The latter thrives and develops by finding new ways and opportunities of increasing surplus value—the source of profit—by prolonging the working day. When labor is too strong to permit this, rationalization, speed-up, and other methods of increasing productivity are introduced, most notably by improving industrial tools or techniques or inventing new ones. Under the spur of competition, capitalistic production must expand with a proportionately greater investment going into plant and machines than into labor. This process is punctuated by periodic crises resulting from the fact that more commodities are produced than can be sold on the market, not because there is no need for them, but because of the inadequate purchasing power of wages. The result is—so long as the system of capitalist production is not interfered with from the outside—ever larger concentrations of industry and capital which are in effect monopolies, a relatively dwindling working force, growing armies of unemployed, and widespread distress. The rich become richer and fewer as they devour each other in the process of becoming economically bigger. The poor become poorer and more numerous; the workers become less skilled because they are continually being replaced by complex machines which require only attendants to push buttons and levers.

Capitalism on this theory cannot stabilize itself. It must expand or die. In the course of expansion crisis succeeds crisis, sometimes relieved and sometimes worsened by war, until the workers rise, take power, vest ownership of the instruments of production in the community, and operate them in a new social economy planned for the use and benefit of all. Mankind is liberated from "the fetishism of commodities," from the blind rule of the products fashioned by its own hands. With the help of science and technology all the resources of the community, material and human, are planfully employed to further human welfare. The age of plenty dawns.

Marx's economic theories tell us nothing about the day-by-day behavior of prices, the changes of interest rates, or the rise of new industries. Nor are they designed to do so. His interest was to lay bare the laws of capitalist *development* and to show that its own immanent processes lead to a necessary expansion of the productive facilities of society to a point where the system can no longer function. It is killed by its very success—or, more accurately, renders itself powerless and creates the forces which kill it.

10. **The Road to Socialism.** If men make their own history, then, although social and economic institutions may break down, new ones will not arise of themselves in their stead. A transition from capitalism to socialism must be effected by political action. Unless conditions are ripe for it, socialism cannot succeed, and attempts to introduce it will be disastrous. But a situation may be ripe and still not develop properly. Many a ripe fruit is left to wither or rot on the vine. What is required to transform the socialist potentialities of a capitalist system in decline is political intelligence and resolution on the part of the working class. It, and it alone, must constitute the organized mass base of the socialist movement.

Why must it be the working class and not peasants or farmers or the professional classes or benevolent individuals from any class? Marx's reply is, first, the members of the working class are more numerous than the members of any other class and have acquired a certain discipline and capacity for organization in virtue of their function in production; second, they occupy a strategic role in society and can paralyze the economy by general strikes; third and most important, the conflicts between all other groups can be composed without altering in any fundamental way the basic property relations of society, whereas the conflict between the workers and the owners of the instruments of production is endemic and breaks out again and again in acute form. It cannot be solved short of transformation of the entire system— by a social revolution carried out in democratic countries peacefully and in non-democratic countries violently.

The working class cannot succeed in its historical task without a leadership to enlighten and guide it. This leadership is supplied by those socialists who have taken to heart Marx's theories. In order to distinguish them from socialists guided by other theories, Marx referred to them as communists in 1848, but later reverted to the use of the term socialists when the German Social-Democratic Party was organized. But even when he was a member of the Communist League, the educational society in whose name Marx drew up the *Communist Mani-*

festo, he differentiated himself from "those communists who were out to destroy personal liberty and who wished to turn the world into one large barracks or into a gigantic warehouse."

The task set for those who agree with Marx is clearly described. They are to participate in the day-by-day struggles of the working class, encourage organization of trade unions, and conduct militant struggles to improve conditions and standards of life. They are not to rest, however, with mere agitation for immediate reforms and better conditions but must press on to politicalize working-class activities and show that every class struggle is a political struggle. They, however, "do not constitute themselves a special party over and against other working-class parties" but strive to unite them in a common front. Further, "they erect no sectarian principles by which to control the proletarian movement." They do not impose a "Party line" but emphasize what is to the interests of the working class as a whole. At the same time they try to draw to the side of the workers discontented elements among other oppressed sections of the population. Finally, they seek to keep working-class parties free of narrow nationalist prejudices and, in an interdependent world with interlocking economies, teach that the fundamental interests of the international working class are of primary concern. (*See Reading No. 1.*)

In summary, Marx conceived of his "party" neither as a conspiratorially organized underground army nor as a group intent upon imposing a dictatorship *over* the proletariat, nor even as a special political party. Its function was primarily to exercise educational leadership. Nonetheless, as the number of his followers increased, Marx actively encouraged them to organize or transform existing working-class groups into Marxist parties. Marx's own political practices hardly lived up to his theories of the relation which should exist between socialists and the working class.

Marx concerned himself only briefly with the strategy of the march to socialism. In different countries the working class would come to political power in different ways. But no fundamental social change can be effected at one stroke. The process consists of (1) the act of political victory by which old state forms are destroyed and replaced by new; (2) socialization of the basic instruments of production and the establishment of a new legal norm for non-personal property; (3) the emergence of the "first phase" of the classless society which still bears some of the traits and stigmata of capitalist society and rewards individuals according to what they produce; and (4) the "higher phase" of the classless society in which individuals will "contribute according to their capacities and be rewarded according to their needs."

These steps or phases are not sharply distinguished from each other and are of importance because of the uses and abuses subsequently made of them by Lenin and Stalin. In one place of his criticism of the Gotha Program, adopted at the unity Congress between two groups of socialists—the Lassalleans and Eisenachers—from which the German Social Democratic Party emerged ("our party," Marx calls it), he writes: "Between the capitalist and communist society lies the period of the revolutionary transformation of one into the other. There corresponds to this also a political transition period in which the state can be nothing but the revolutionary dictatorship of the proletariat."

The phrase "dictatorship of the proletariat" which was later to prove such a fateful bone of contention among those who called themselves Marxists was not used in any major published work of Marx and only twice in his correspondence. According to Marx, even under a political democracy, so long as the instruments of production are owned by a few, in effect a social dictatorship exists. For those who own and control these instruments, by their power to give work or withdraw it, exercise an arbitrary power over the lives of those who must live by the use of these instruments. The state, functioning as an instrument of the dominant economic class, enforces that power. When the workers establish their own state, the situation is reversed. By socializing production, the workers expropriate the former owners. No matter how democratic the political forms and processes by which this is done, it is in effect a social dictatorship by the workers over the former owners.

As Marx conceived it, the political expression of the social "dictatorship of the proletariat" takes the form of a workers' democracy. Engels and Marx both regarded the Paris Commune, in which many parties participated and in which the followers of Marx were a tiny minority,

as a "dictatorship of the proletariat." The political processes of democracy as they exist under capitalism are
broadened so that the people by referendum and recall
have a greater direct influence upon the agencies of the
state. As Marxism as a movement developed, the phrase
"dictatorship of the proletariat" fell into almost total
disuse in every politically democratic country until it
was revived by the followers of Lenin and Trotsky.

11. The Nature of Ideology. Marx emphatically
believed that, although the origin and influence of ideas
and ideals were socially conditioned, they play an important role in human affairs. He considered his own ideas
to be of moment and assumed that their acceptance
would determine in part the prospects of success of the
socialist movement.

Whether men are defined as rational animals or not,
they certainly are creatures who give reasons to justify
their actions. These reasons, for the most part, do not
truly explain their action but mislead others, as well as
those who offer them, about the goals and springs of
their behavior. Marx believed that the social ideas and
ideals which are invoked to explain the behavior of men
and institutions mask the clash of economic interest. A
struggle for acceptance is waged by conflicting social
ideals and whichever set triumphs in the end determines
the ruling beliefs of an epoch. "The ruling ideas of each
age have ever been the ideas of its ruling class." Where
the basic antagonism between classes is openly recognized, the ensuing struggles are accompanied by conflicting ideas concerning the good and bad, and sometimes, the true and false.

Broadly speaking, Marx regards all social philosophies
and theories as either myths or scientifically grounded
doctrines. Myths are of two kinds: ideas which are false,
refuted or refutable by evidence, and ideas which, although capable of rallying and inspiring or discouraging
and demoralizing large masses, are too vague to be
tested. Both classes of myth function as psychological
rationalizations of interests which, if nakedly asserted,
would not so readily be gratified. According to Marx, all
social philosophies which teach that interests are common
in a class society are myths. Further, all social philosophies and theories incompatible with his own and which
purport to give a true account of the structure of society

and its development are also myths. Marx uses the term "ideology" as a comprehensive term for both classes of myth, especially for any explanation which would tend to serve as a justification for the status quo. His own social ideas and theories he regards as "scientific." The fact that they are elaborated to further the struggle of the working class to achieve socialism does not affect their validity. He believed they could stand rigorous examination. To this we now turn.

— 2 —

EVALUATION OF MARX'S CONTRIBUTIONS

Rigorous examination is one thing Marx's ideas will not stand because they were not rigorously formulated. To do justice to his intent they must often be reinterpreted and qualified. They constitute a mixture of the true, the vague, and the false.

At the outset it should be apparent to any sensitive reader that Marx writes primarily as a critic of capitalism, as a man fired with a passionate ideal to eliminate the social inequalities, the poverty, and injustices of his time. Much of what he said makes sense and good sense considered as a description of the capitalist society of his time and as a prediction of the probable historical development of any capitalist system *on the assumption* that nothing outside that system, especially political influences, interferes with its development. Marx's fundamental errors arise from an uncritical extrapolation of what he observed in capitalist societies to all class societies, and from a disregard of the enormous influence which political, national, and moral forces have exerted on the development of capitalism as an economic system.

1. Historical Materialism. Modern historiography, even when it is not avowedly Marxist, reflects the profound impact of Marx's ideas albeit in a diluted form. Marx's ideas have enriched historical writing, made it more realistic and down to earth, and set interesting problems for investigation. Even so Christian an historian as Professor Butterfield pays tribute to the wholesome effect of Marx's approach on historical scholarship. As a rough approximation, Marx's theory of history plausibly accounts at most for the *general* character of nineteenth-century industrial society up to the First World War, for the urbanization of culture, its commercialization, many of the consequences of science upon society, the major political struggles of the period, and the imperialistic expansion of Europe to a commanding world influence.

No matter how charitably interpreted, however, it does not explain the transition from feudalism to capitalism. Feudal societies have existed in many periods and regions of the world. But only in Europe, in a tiny corner of the world, did capitalism arise. It spread elsewhere not by virtue of any immanent law of the development of the social relations of feudalism but by conquest or adaptation (e.g., Japan). There is even less evidence that the transition from slave to feudal societies was universal and that where it occurred it fitted into Marx's scheme. His claims about primitive society, derived mainly from Lewis H. Morgan, have been conclusively refuted by the findings of modern anthropology.

Even for the period of capitalism the theory of historical materialism in most of its customary formulations is inadequate. It seeks to explain all major political and cultural changes in terms of development in the mode of economic production. Such a sweeping claim cannot be established except on a statistical basis after piecemeal investigations of major political and cultural phenomena have been undertaken. It ignores the fact that the economic basis of society at any given time is often compatible with more than one political form, and that therefore the degree of democracy present or absent in any particular country may be explained by other than factors attributable to its mode of production.

The very metaphors of the theory are misleading and can be turned against it. The mode of production is regarded as the "foundation" of society. But a foundation does not completely determine whether any stories will be built on it, the number of stories, their style, function, and use. Nor do foundations develop. They are purposefully built and sometimes purposefully destroyed; on occasions they may be replaced without affecting the superstructure. At most, just as existing foundations may *limit* the possibilities of further construction, so the mode of production may limit the cultural and political possibilities. Its existence may make certain alternatives relatively impossible, but it cannot prevent human beings from *attempting* the historically impossible. The cause of ensuing disaster would then be attributable to the decision to attempt the impossible as much as to the obstacles which doomed the attempt.

Historical materialism in its orthodox form systematically confuses ultimate and proximate causes and forgets that science is not concerned with ultimate causes. It admits, when pressed, that there is a reciprocal influence among various factors, and between economic cause and cultural and political effects. But this is minimized as incidental, and in the most "a priori" fashion the mode of production is declared to be *always* the decisive influence "in the last analysis." Yet independent developments in science which originally had not the slightest relevant connection with the mode of economic production, like the theory of relativity which led to the liberation of nuclear energy, may have a far greater influence on the politics of our era, indeed on the mode of economic production itself, than any immanent law of the latter.

Historical materialism tends to see heroes of thought and action merely as carriers or "expressions" of social forces, ultimately economic, but it cannot account for the fact that an event-making person like Lenin had far greater causal influence on the Bolshevist October Revolution of 1917 in Russia than the state of the forces of production or the degree of development of the relations of production. The existence of states like Ireland and Israel illustrates another type of historical phenomenon which the theory neither predicted nor could plausibly explain in its own terms even *after* the event.

As a monistic theory in quest of total solutions, historical materialism is not intelligible and serves only as an excuse to avoid thought about troublesome questions. As a pluralistic theory which gives greatest weight to the mode of economic production, it is a useful *heuristic* principle with which to approach specific problems. We should applaud Engels' remark in this connection that the proof of the pudding is in the eating. But enough puddings have been eaten to warrant considerable skepticism of the large claims made for it. That the mode of economic production had more to do in determining the major political events from 1750 to 1914 in Europe than any other single factor may be true, although it still remains to be conclusively established. But it is noteworthy that neither Marx nor Engels nor any leading protagonist of historical materialism predicted the rise of Fascism in any of its varieties. Nor is it easy to fit Fascism and other forms of totalitarianism, which are neither socialist nor capitalist, into Marx's analysis.

Without denying in the least the continuing influence of the mode of economic production, it does not seem to have had as great an importance since the rise of totalitarianism as it did previously. Political decisions like the Treaty of Versailles, the New Deal, the long years of appeasement of Hitler, the failure to support the original democratic regime in Spain, the war against Hitler, the appeasement of Stalin, the demobilization of the American army in Europe, UNRRA and the Marshall Plan, the U.S. involvement in Korea, the rearmament of the West to counter Communist aggression, have had a more powerful influence on economic development than the mode of economic production on political affairs. (*See Reading No. 23.*)

2. Historical Development. If it is true, that, as Marx claimed, "no social order ever perishes before all the productive forces for which there is room in it have developed," then it is difficult to see why any social system not destroyed by war or natural disaster, should perish. An indefinite number of possibilities for expansion exist. Slavery would not have disappeared until it had at least become universal. Capitalism might keep on going by opening new frontiers of need requiring new industries for their gratification. Theoretically, human ingenuity under any system can build contrivance upon contrivance to develop productive forces. Historically, there is no evidence whatsoever that in October, 1917, when the Communists took power in Russia, capitalism had run its course. Marx never made a convincing case for his assertion that capitalism *must* be followed by socialism rather than *other* forms of society. There are various alternatives which he ignored, like one which continues private ownership of means of production with extensive social control of its operation or a mixed economy with private and public sectors of production. Both of these alternatives are equally removed from his conceptions of capitalism and socialism and closer to present-day realities in various countries.

3. **Class Struggles.** Although not distinctive to Marx, the concepts of social classes and class struggles are used in his writings in a brilliant way to illumine some crucial periods in modern history. Since Marx's time these concepts have become part of the intellectual tool kit of all empirical historians. It is one thing, however, to recognize the role of classes in political and social life. It is quite another to assume that economic classes, no matter how economic classes are defined, always have an overriding significance in relation to other class divisions—religious, national, or racial. It was clearly to the interests of the working classes in all countries to oppose the First World War. Their chief political parties had pledged themselves to do so before the war broke out. But they rallied to the support of their respective governments with no less patriotic enthusiasm than other classes.

The term "class" in Marx is used in various senses, not all strictly derivative from each other. Sometimes its defining feature is the role a group plays in production, sometimes it is their common mode of life, including culture and traditions, sometimes the source of their income or the level of their income, sometimes their vocation or, in the case of the unemployed, their lack of any. If, as the *Communist Manifesto* declares, "all history is the history of class struggles," it certainly is not true that all class struggles have been economic in any of the above senses. Nor is it true that all history is the history *only* of class struggles; it is just as much, if not more, a history of class cooperation. Antagonisms often remain latent when classes join forces either in meeting a common danger or uniting in a common effort for their mutual benefit. The frequency and intensity with which Marxists have denounced "class collaboration" is eloquent testimony of how pervasive such cooperation is even in areas where one might expect open clash of interests. It proves that "the law of class struggle" is either not a law, since it has so many exceptions, or is of very limited validity.

Here, as elsewhere in Marx, it is not so much the concept of class struggle which is illegitimate but its uncritical extension and the tendency, especially among Marx's followers, to interpret cultural, religious, and intellectual conflicts, as well as scientific development, as corollaries of a struggle for a greater share of social wealth and power. No doubt the latter is often an attendant feature of these conflicts, sometimes a genuinely relevant causal factor. But in relation to vast areas of culture, especially the arts and sciences, and to some extremely significant events, like some of the Crusades or the rise of many nationalist movements or the war against Hitlerism, they are altogether negligible or contributory only to a minor degree.

4. Economic Theory. There are certain standard difficulties in the Marxian theory of value and surplus value which have never been adequately met. First, the conception that all labor, including every variety of skilled labor, can be reduced to a certain amount of homogeneous labor power seems extremely arbitrary. There exist distinctive and irreducible differences between certain kinds of labor. For example, physical labor and reflective thinking which may deduce an important mathematical conclusion without any physical labor at all are as different from each other as colors and sounds. They may have a common *measure* but do not have a common *substance*—"a congelation of homogeneous human labor"—as Marx claimed.

Second, the notion that the use of machinery and all sorts of labor-saving devices add no value to commodities except that of the labor power involved in their manufacture is inherently implausible and cannot be squared with the facts of exchange.

Third, if labor power is the sole source of profit, then equal amounts of capital expenditure with varying proportions of parts invested in machinery, etc., and labor, should show, if the rate of exploitation is the same, corresponding differences in the rate of profit, with a higher rate of profit where the proportion of labor cost to total investment is higher.

Thus, if a million-dollar business has invested $900,000 in plant, machinery, etc., and $100,000 in labor, and a second million-dollar business has invested $100,000 in plant and $900,000 in labor, and if the labor force is working equally hard, then, according to Marx's theory, the rate of profit of the first business should be 10%, and of the second 90%. But, in fact, the rate of profit is approximately equal. Marx attempts to avoid the contradiction by broadening the concept of a business to include the whole of the productive plant of society. He argues that the sum total of the prices of all the commodities produced in society is equal to the sum total of the values of these commodities. This is a sheer tautology. It leaves completely unexplained what determines the price of any specific commodity, including the price of labor power as well as the source of profit.

Much more successful are Marx's predictions concerning the development of capitalist production. He foresaw that capital would grow into larger and larger units and would adopt monopolistic practices. He grasped the revolutionary impact of science on industrial technology. He predicted the growth of the proletariat, periodic cycles of boom and bust, and imperialistic expansion. He correctly saw that the very successes achieved in the accumulation of capital would continually generate new difficulties as capitalists sought ever-new opportunities for profitable investment.

On the other hand, Marx vastly underestimated the regenerative power of capitalism to overcome its own periodic crises, the diversification of forms it has taken, the economic influence of organized trade-union action, the pressure labor could exert through the extension of political democracy on the distribution of wealth and on social security, the rise in the effective purchasing power of wages, the improvement of health and standards of living. Although appreciative of the transforming effects of applied science, he underestimated its importance for the multiplication of new industries. He sensed the significance of the separation of ownership from management in modern capitalism but failed to take into account its consequences—increasing social regulation of industry and greater social mobility. He barely conceived of the possibility that industry could be made an appendage of the state independently of the interests of the owners of the instruments of production and that by a succession of controls on prices, wages, and profits, as well as by currency regulation, deficit financing, taxation, and public banking, the state could profoundly affect the channels of reinvestment, and this not only in times of war.

Marx believed that an "ideal" system of capitalism, i.e., one which developed in relative isolation of the effects of political intervention on the part of the state or of the organized working class itself, could not at one and the same time guarantee sufficient profits to be a spur to necessary reinvestment, provide full employment for all able and willing to work, and guarantee an adequate standard of living above the subsistence level for the masses. He never really proved this even for an "ideal" system. But there never was, nor in all likelihood will there be, an ideal system of capitalism or indeed of any system.

In existing capitalisms at any definite time, profit may not be guaranteed for all capitalists but only for a certain number. But this number may be sufficient to keep production up to a level where most workers are employed while those who are temporarily unemployed receive social benefits. Marx was indisputably right in anticipating periodic economic dislocations where the market still operates in an unplanned economy. It remains an open question, however, whether even in a planned economy some economic dislocations, as well as unemployment hidden by a swollen and inefficient labor force, may not occur.

Today, at any rate, the British, American, and Western-European economies show features almost as profoundly different from those Marx predicted as inescapably involved in the development of capitalism as are the characteristic features of Soviet economy from those Marx expected to follow upon the disappearance of capitalism.

5. **The Road to Power.**   Marx came to an intellectual maturity at a time when democracy, as we understand it, was far from being the rule in the political life of the day. Universal suffrage had not been won in most countries in Europe. Save for several periods in English history, hardly any major political and social gains had been achieved except in the teeth of fierce opposition from those entrenched in power. Marx was skeptical of

the likelihood that ruling social groups would peacefully surrender the reins of power to popular majorities intent upon radically altering the property structure of society. He specifically excepted, however, Great Britain, the United States, and Holland. In those countries, he held that, because of their democratic traditions, the transition to socialism might be effected entirely by peaceful and legal means.

Events have confirmed Marx's anticipations only in part. Until the outbreak of the Bolshevik Revolution and the liquidation of the Russian Constituent Assembly, the development of democratic institutions in Europe was quite impressive. The chaotic conditions after the first World War, together with fear of Communist revolution fanned by the attempts on the part of some Communist parties to capture power by violent means, gave rise to an ever-stronger counter-movement of Fascist violence in Italy, Hungary, and Germany. Communist provocations were welcomed by reactionary groups as a pretext to destroy the non-Communist labor and socialist movements. In countries like England, Holland, Sweden, Norway, Denmark, and France, where democratic traditions prevailed and Communist parties were too weak to attempt insurrectionary overthrow of representative institutions, the march of social reforms and socialist legislation has been almost continuous. The New Deal in the United States marked a momentous shift from a predominantly *laissez-faire* economy to the beginnings of a welfare state and was accompanied by even less civil disorder than that which attended the English reform movements of the nineteenth century.

All this indicates that the Marxian theory of the state is a dangerous oversimplification. The state in democratic countries turns out to be not the executive committee of the dominant economic class but the instrument of any class or combination of classes which succeeds in winning the confidence of the electorate. Sometimes big business, sometimes the farmers, sometimes labor, or a combination of the two, as at the time the Wagner National Labor Relations Act was passed, will be in the saddle.

In this connection we must distinguish between the *substantial* and *functional* conception of the state. The first defines the state by its so-called essence or nature which is to serve as a mere instrument of the capitalist class. Gains won by the workers or farmers are casually explained away as concessions yielded to them under pressure. As if the power to exact concessions by pressure were not the most convincing evidence of actual control over the state irrespective of its mystical "essence"!

According to the *functional* conception, the state is what the state does. Only a painstaking empirical analysis can enable us to discover whose interests at any definite time the executive, legislative, and judicial organs of the state are furthering. The historical record shows that, wherever political democratic institutions exist, democratic changes in social and political life do not lag far behind.

6. The Socialist Society. Because Marx was primarily interested in the critique of capitalism, he gave very little thought to the structure of the socialist system he assumed must succeed it. He was so aroused by the evils of the *status quo* that he never inquired whether the evils of the *post status quo* might not even be worse, particularly if the means used were not checked by their consequences on the professed ends which guided them. He never seriously examined the possibility that the workers might be just as much, or even more, exploited under a system of collective ownership where they faced one big boss, panoplied in the armed powers of the state, as under a system of private or mixed ownership in which there were many bosses often at odds with each other. He assumed without argument that democratic political institutions would necessarily thrive when capitalism had been overthrown and that free enterprise in the life of mind would flourish when free enterprise in economy had been completely abolished. He overlooked the demonstrable truth that under socialism the degree of political democracy which prevails is of far greater importance than the degree of economic collectivism. For without democracy, a collectivized economy becomes at best a tool of benevolent despots and bureaucrats, and at worst, the most terrible instrument of oppression in the history of mankind. Recent historical events have brought home even to followers of Marx that by itself socialization or a change in the legal relations of property does not necessarily affect differences in power, status, or privilege.

The two clearest illustrations of Utopianism in Marx are his belief that the state will wither away under communism and that its rule of distribution will be based only on need. Even if absolute and total collectivism existed under democratic political forms, differences would undoubtedly arise as to how the production of wealth would be distributed among different social or vocational groups. These may be peacefully arbitrated or not. If there is to be no forced labor, the right to strike must be respected. In any event, for these and other reasons, a complex society must always have at command some agencies of coercion to prevent conflicts from getting out of hand, and, in emergencies, to safeguard the public interest.

In a world where it is technically impossible to produce more than enough of everything *at the same time,* the proposal to distribute goods and services in accordance with need alone is unworkable. Needs are indefinite, subjective, and potentially unlimited. Wherever there exists scarcity in quantity at any moment of time there must be an order of priority in distribution based on merit or chance or some other selective principle. It may be technologically feasible so to arrange things that everyone's *basic* needs for food, clothing, and shelter can be gratified irrespective of their capacity to work or even their willingness to work. But this leaves luxuries, everything over and above the basic needs, to be distributed.

And even the concept of "basic needs" is an historical variable. What Marx had in mind was a system of society whose ties of organization approximated the bonds which united a loving family in which the varied needs of individual members are gratified in a spirit of fraternity rather than in accordance with rules of justice. But the whole of society can never become one family, not all families are free of conflict, and even in loving families love is not always enough.

7. The Doctrine of Ideology. That ideas have a history which, to some extent, reflect their times, their social milieu, and the needs and interests of those to whom they appeal, is certainly true. But this by no means confirms the Marxist doctrine according to which ideas of good or bad, of valid or invalid, in every field express in a distorted form the interests of economic classes in conflict. Even if this were true it would have no relevance to the validity of the ideas in question. Otherwise not a single reason offered by Marx for relegating other doctrines to the intellectual limbo of ideologies would exempt his own doctrines from being assigned to the same place.

It will be helpful in appraising Marx's theory of ideology to distinguish between (a) the genesis of ideas, (b) their meaning, (c) their acceptance, and (d) their validity, in order to determine the relevance of social conditions and class conflicts to each distinction.

(a) Very little is known about the genesis of ideas. This is a question of individual psychology. Ideas may be causally determined by any one of a number of things in a person's environment or experience, depending upon his suggestibility, intelligence, traditions, and funded knowledge. A similar environment may provoke the most disparate responses from different individuals. It is true that people with different interests, when aware of them and of the fact that they conflict, are likely to think differently concerning policies and programs which involve these interests. But a vast area of thought in no way involves personal interests and especially economic interests. And even when conflicting economic interests are involved, human beings are not always aware of the conflict and may not think differently about them.

(b) The meaning of a doctrine cannot always be understood merely by an analysis of the statements in which it is expressed in isolation from its context and the way it is used. Key words are sometimes ambiguous and it is often necessary to observe how people behave in order to see what their doctrine means to them. Occasionally differences in social position may influence the way in which statements having a social context are interpreted.

(c) The acceptance of ideas by some groups rather than others will be influenced by their conceptions of the bearing ideas have on their interests—independently of the truth or falsity of these conceptions. Manufacturers of cigarettes will probably be the last group to give credence to results purporting to show that cigarette smoking increases the incidence of cancer of the lungs. It is here that Marx's permanent contribution to the study of the history and dissemination of ideas is to be found —especially ideas concerning social justice, public welfare, the nature and proper ends of man.

(d) The validity or invalidity of ideas, their truth or falsity, is completely independent of any kind of social or economic interest even when such ideas are *about* interests. To speak, therefore, of "class truths" or "class science," whether "capitalist" or "proletarian," or about "Fascist" or "Communist" or "democratic" biology is not only a contradiction in terms but a piece of cultural barbarism.

The foregoing remarks bear not only on the Marxist doctrine of ideology but on most conceptions of the sociology of knowledge which take their inspiration from him.

8. Marx, the Man. In bringing this evaluation to a close, something should be said of Karl Marx, the man. He has been the object of uncritical deification and violent execration. Both testify to the far-reaching influence of his personality and ideas—an influence which does not provide the best perspective for an objective estimate.

There was a strange contrast between Marx's public and private personalities. He was primarily a revolutionist and almost everything he writes shows a rebellious and impatient temperament. Neither poverty nor frustration nor unhappiness in his personal relations led him to renounce what would have been a distinguished conventional career. He chose his vocation on the basis of what he believed to be true about the nature of society and the process necessary to change it. His watchword was struggle. Despite the fact that his mode of life, tastes, and values differed little from the philistines he scorned, he considered himself at war with the dominant institutions of society. He was capable of great love and friendship and personal sacrifice, but these were displayed only in the narrow circles of his family and his immediate political following. He was intellectually imperious towards others, hypersensitive to criticism, and not inclined to brook contradiction. He had the stigmata of the professional fighter in a good cause. He tended to judge people only in the light of their possible use in the political battles of the moment, which he regarded as linked with the continuing struggle for human liberation from antiquity to the present. Marx in one of the earliest of his writings glorified Prometheus as "the foremost saint and martyr in the philosophical calendar" and probably identified himself with him in the romantic fashion current in the nineteenth century.

Marx was a man who lived by his ideas. Absolutely incorruptible, he was sustained by a sense of his own moral righteousness disguised as a feeling of superior insight. He was ruthless towards political opponents and interpreted disagreement with his views as either apostasy, moral degeneracy, or political idiocy. These unlovely traits of character were undoubtedly exacerbated by a life of great hardship. One of his children seems to have died of the effects of chronic undernourishment. For many years the family rations depended upon Engels' largesse and loans from pawnbrokers.

Despite his refusal to appeal to ethical principles, Marx had a passionate sense of social injustice which burns fiercely in everything he wrote. He would have scoffed at the idea that he was in line with the Hebrew prophets, but he sometimes spoke of the laws of History as if they were the decrees of Jehovah punishing a wicked society, and of the socialist revolution as if it were the catastrophic prelude to a new dispensation.

Marx had no pride of race or nationality. He considered himself a European. He was a great admirer of the Greek tragic poets, of Dante, Shakespeare, and Balzac. He was a radical democrat who had no respect for the will of unenlightened majorities, a fierce individualist who would become apoplectic at the notion of party discipline or of loyalty to anything but his own creative insights. He would have been an intellectual firebrand in any society, including the socialist Utopia of his fantasy. It was characteristic that he concluded his introduction to *Capital* with a line from Dante:

"Follow your own course, and let people talk."

3

ORTHODOX MARXISM—KAUTSKY, PLEKHANOV, DE LEON

Karl Marx left a rich and ambiguous intellectual legacy. It was largely ignored by the learned world. Marx's immediate followers were drawn in the main from middle-class intellectuals who popularized and applied his ideas to guide the political and economic struggle of the European working class. What had once been the esoteric doctrine of an outlawed sect became the proudly proclaimed, if imperfectly understood, theory of mass parties. By the time Marx died a powerful German party was already in existence. In France the influence of Proudhon and Bakunin was receding. Under the leadership of Guesde and Lafargue a Marxist party had been formed. Even in England a Social-Democratic Federation had sprung up under the leadership of Hyndman and Belfort-Bax.

The reasoned authority of "scientific socialism" was invoked to strengthen the spontaneous demand for social justice among the workers of Western Europe. But the complexity and ambiguity of Marxist theories required that they be interpreted before they could be applied. Criticisms mounted with the growing strength of Social-Democracy and had to be met. The dominant interpretation of Marxism which emerged—here called "orthodox Marxism"—stressed those aspects of Marx's thinking which were deterministic, evolutionary, and democratic. It held sway until the First World War.

Engels himself, the first and greatest of the orthodox Marxists, both in his theoretical writings and practical pronouncements, pointed the direction of the development. Shortly before his death he wrote: "We, 'the revolutionaries,' the 'overthrowers'—we are thriving far better on legal methods than on illegal methods and overthrow." He did not, however, renounce the right of socialists to take up arms in the event the ruling class itself resorted to violence to nullify a constitutional or a parliamentary victory of the workers and their allies.

It will be instructive to examine the interpretation of "orthodox Marxism" in the writings of three individuals in countries as profoundly different from each other as Germany, Russia, and the United States in order to show how widespread this approach was. We shall briefly consider the views of Karl Kautsky, Georgi Plekhanov, and Daniel De Leon.

1. Karl Kautsky (1854-1938). Until his death Karl Kautsky was indisputably the theoretical leader of international Social-Democracy. His writings were marked by sobriety rather than brilliance, and conscientiousness rather than profundity. His piety towards Marx and Engels did not prevent him from revising or improving upon them in detail, but from first to last he considered himself a faithful disciple. By the time he reached middle age he was called "the old warhorse of Marxist orthodoxy." In 1883, the year Marx died, Kautsky founded and edited the *Neue Zeit* which became the leading theoretical organ of Marxism in the entire world. The socialist controversies of the next fifty years were to rage in its pages. Kautsky played the foremost pedagogic role in educating two generations of Marxists. In addition to his monumental editorial and publicistic work, he popularized Marx's economic doctrines, issued the fourth volume of Marx's *Capital,* and made many independent applications of the theory of historical materialism. Among his publications are studies devoted to Thomas More and his *Utopia,* the Anabaptists, the Peasant Wars, the Class Struggles at the time of the French Revolution, and the origins of Christianity. Except for the last they are rather pedestrian, but all throw some fresh light on events which until then had been treated in a narrowly political and religious fashion.

a. Theory of History. Kautsky's maturest work is his massive *The Materialistic Conception of History* (1927). It is the most comprehensive exposition of the subject in any language. In it Kautsky undertakes the systematization and refinement of the theory left in an inchoate state by Marx and Engels. He answers objections, corrects misunderstandings, introduces useful distinctions, and gives greater recognition to the complexity of the historical process than was customary in the writings of orthodox

Social-Democracy. Although the initiating role of human will and action is admitted, the emphasis still falls predominantly on the objective determining economic conditions which sooner or later *compel* men's will to take the historical direction it does. Men are fighting, praying, and loving animals, but the differences in the institutions of war, religion, and marriage depend primarily upon differences in the economic structure of society. If we can predict what the future economy *will* be, we can feel what the future man *must* be. (*See Reading No. 8.*)

In this and other of his writings, Kautsky stresses the concept of historical readiness or maturity. He criticizes revolutionary impatience, even when it is ethically motivated, and deplores attempts to storm the trackless heights of social progress instead of building the road from level to level. He argues not only against socialist revolutionists who would impose a noble dream of the future on an unready people but also against nostalgic revolutionists, who, like the leaders of the peasant revolutions which failed, sought to bring back conditions of the past. Socialism is inevitable, but it will come in its own good time.

At no point does Kautsky deny that the Social-Democratic Party, as a Marxist party, is a revolutionary party. But he distinguishes between a revolutionary party and a revolution-making party. Revolutions are not made or instigated. They happen as spontaneous consequences of a social and economic process which human beings can do little to arrest or accelerate. "We know that our goal can be attained only through revolution. We know that it is just as little in our power to create this revolution as it is in the power of our opponents to prevent it." There is not much point in trying to bring about what must come anyhow. All the more futile is it, therefore, to turn socialist parties into clandestine and conspiratorial organizations.

The great difficulty with the view that the future is inevitable is that futile efforts to avoid or influence the inevitable must likewise be regarded as inevitable. It, therefore, constitutes no basis for practical political decisions in the present or for announcing policies for the future, something no political party can avoid. The social revolution may be inevitable, but how is it to be carried out—by outright confiscation of private property in the instruments of production or by reasonable compensation, en bloc or piecemeal? Kautsky's answer in all such situations was to defend that alternative which furthered the extension of the process of democracy and which promised the most peaceful settlement of the issues in dispute. The class struggle goes on in any event, but how it is waged depends, in part at least, upon the moral ideas the workers bring to the struggle as well as upon the level of civilization and culture attained at any given time in society. In the specific illustration mentioned above, Kautsky favored compensation rather than expropriation as more likely to prevent counter-revolution and violence. He saw that the use of means was not inevitable: he did not see that, to the extent ends depend upon means, ends, too, are not inevitable.

b. Agricultural Program. Marx had included agriculture in the scope of his economic critique of capitalism. He anticipated that the same tendencies towards concentration and centralization which he predicted for industry would hold for agriculture. Mechanization and scientific farming would result in making farms larger and larger until they had to be operated like factories. The small farms would disappear, the farmers would become factory-farm-laborers, and their class struggles against the agricultural barons would bring them to the realization that they shared common interests with the industrial proletariat.

Marx was right in anticipating the important effects of capitalism and science on agriculture, the growth of large farms, and the relative decline in importance of agriculture in the total economy. But he was wrong—and from the point of view of its effect on the socialist *political* program, disastrously wrong—about everything else. The peasants and farmers as a class did not disappear or become proletarianized. Although there was a proportional decline in the number of independent, small property holdings, the absolute number remained so large that the peasants and farmers as a class in almost every country— England is a notable exception—were able to wield a political influence often greater than the working class and sometimes greater than the capitalists. Up to this very day, despite periodic claims that "the farmer is doomed," there is no evidence of the transformation of their economic, social, and political status along the lines

Marx predicted. "The idiocy of rural life," which Marx expected to disappear under socialism, has disappeared in modern capitalistic countries as a result of technological, not social, revolutions.

Kautsky's writings on the agrarian question illustrate the way in which orthodox Marxism held on to its dogmas even at a political cost but then shifted its emphasis to bring the party program more in line with historical events rather than inherited doctrine. Kautsky began with a valiant defense of Marx's position against bourgeois and socialist critics. But as the peasants grew stronger and not weaker, he tempered the hostility of the tone of the socialist program. Gradually he began to take issue in a Marxian spirit with some of Marx's central contentions. He denied that there was a continuous increase in large-scale agricultural production. He questioned whether it had ever reached predominant proportions as a result of economic processes alone. In the Soviet Union it was obviously a consequence of political fiat. Nor was Kautsky as confident as Marx in the universal superiority of large-scale agriculture as compared with small holdings. Social factors other than purely economic ones affect productivity. Where social factors are the same, then the application of modern machinery and agrarian technology would, of course, give greater yields per acre on large farms than on small farms worked by conventional methods. But in a startling departure from Marx, Kautsky, in his discussion of the agrarian revolution in Russia, maintained that "where large and small holdings are worked with the same appliances and the same knowledge, the small holdings always prove to be superior, for the interest of the peasant in the output from his holding is far deeper than the interest of the hired laborer in the working of the large holding"—and this presumably in independence of who owns the large holding, state or land baron.

Kautsky makes other interesting claims, such as that modern large-scale organization of agriculture, because of varying conditions, requires a higher degree of intelligence and independent judgment on the part of the agricultural worker than most branches of large industry require of their workers. Markham's "man with the hoe" can fit in much better on an assembly line than on a modern farm. Finally, Kautsky admits that scientific technology and equipment can also be profitably employed on middle-sized, privately owned farms. (*See Reading No. 8a.*)

The full implication of all these admissions was not drawn by Kautsky. For they open the possibility that, in a democratic socialist economy, agriculture could be left largely in private hands which was too much for his orthodoxy to swallow. But they do explain why, among other reasons, he condemned the enforced collectivization of agriculture in Communist countries as not only a form of barbarous oppression but as economically wasteful. In justice to Kautsky it should be recalled that, although in his early writings on the agrarian question he defends the desirability of the socialization of agriculture, he insists that the *voluntary cooperation* of the peasants and farmers themselves must be a *sine qua non* of the program.

Even the specific form of agricultural socialization which Kautsky advocated differed from that which Marx assumed would exist in a socialist society. To understand Kautsky's program, American readers must bear in mind that European peasants do not live on their farms in the manner of American farmers, but in village settlements sometimes considerably removed from their fields. Kautsky believed that, even in a socialized agricultural system—which his own admissions indicate is not necessary—house, outbuildings, farmyards, and gardens "would still be managed privately by the peasants, being still his absolute private property as they were in the days of common land tenure; fields, on the other hand, would be cultivated collectively by the community."

One of the main reasons apparently for Kautsky's belief in the desirability of agricultural socialization is the necessity of providing the urban population of crowded Western Europe with adequate food, a consideration which certainly does not apply to most American countries, and which might not be of decisive significance even for Europe if international economic cooperation were developed.

Viewed in perspective, what is impressive about Kautsky's discussion of agricultural questions, despite its incompleteness, inconsistencies, and straining for doctrinal orthodoxy, is its flexibility, its sensitiveness to the human elements in the situation, its emphasis on the voluntary and cooperative principle throughout, its open-mindedness to fresh solutions and refusal to swallow the dogma that under all conditions collectivism as a mode of agricultural production is inherently superior to private or mixed forms of agricultural enterprise.

c. Democracy. This temper towards specific programs, especially as he grew older, cut across Kautsky's acceptance of the historical inevitability of socialism. It was exhibited in his lifelong conviction that democracy and socialism are indissoluble. The *form* under which socialization or nationalization of industry is carried out determines its content. Although here and there Marx and Engels warn in passing against identifying a state enterprise as such with socialism, Kautsky makes this central and explicit in his entire discussion. It is the *form* of operation, the type of management, the degree of workers' participation in setting the goals of industry and conditions of work—in short, the activity of free trade unions in a politically democratic society—which determines whether nationalization is a step forward or backward. "Socialism desires well-being and liberty for the working class. Where this aim is favored by nationalization we must be in favor of it, but nationalization which has not this aim in view we must not support." Shortly before his death he wrote that "Democracy is the shortest, surest, and least costly road to socialism, just as it is the best instrument for the development of the political and social prerequisites for socialism. Democracy and socialism are inextricably intertwined."

It was Karl Kautsky who first emphasized the fact, later distorted by Lenin, that it was the middle-class intellectual, revolted by the spectacle of human degradation produced by the Industrial Revolution and fired by the moral vision of a society in which there would be no human exploitation of labor, who brought the ideal of socialism to the proletariat. Neither Marx nor Kautsky glorified the working class as such or attributed special virtues to its members. For the "working class" to them was not synonymous with the "proletariat" or "the industrial workers." It was the proletariat which had the historical mission to achieve economic emancipation, not in order to transform itself into a new ruling class and oppress others but to abolish class rule. Its members were not only the most strategically situated in the struggle for political power, they were also, Kautsky insists, the conscious carriers of a moral ideal. *Potentially* they could achieve political power in virtue of the role they play in production. *Actually* it is only in virtue of their intelligence, discipline, and moral integrity that they can win over the majority of other groups in the working class and ultimately the majority of the population.

Kautsky makes a fourfold distinction among those designated by the loose and overall cover term "working class." First, there is the wage-earning proletariat, the moral elite, proud of its working skills, politically sophisticated, and aware of its historic responsibilities. Second, there is the *lumpenproletariat* for whose members one may feel compassion but who have been so demoralized that they often serve as willing tools of reaction. Third, there is a great mass which Marx characterized as "the undeveloped figure" of the proletariat. Like the proletariat they are serious wage earners; but their political maturity is on the level of the *lumpenproletariat*. The latter beg for alms; *they,* however, beg for work. They collaborate with employers, are grateful to them, and see them as benevolent wage-givers rather than as exploiters. Finally, there is the labor aristocracy, the skilled proletariat interested only in taking advantage of the monopoly of their skills for personal gain, indifferent to the welfare of the unskilled and unemployed, caste ridden, racially chauvinistic, faithless both to labor and capital. Towards them Marx and Kautsky express contempt. They are *verbürgerlicht,* bourgeoisified, petty capitalists *manqué.*

In view of these distinctions it is apparent that the proletariat has hard work cut out for itself—so hard, indeed, that one wonders how it can succeed in educating and leading the entire working class as well as all other oppressed groups without succumbing either to the superior might arrayed against it or to the corruptions of its very success. But whether naive or not, feasible or not, the entire conception of the role of the proletariat is pervaded by a sense of the necessity of the proletariat winning moral leadership by *educational* means, not by a coup d'état from above as Blanqui and Bakunin and Nechayev believed. The assumptions on which Marx and Kautsky staked their faith may be illusions, but these illusions testify to their belief in the dignity, rationality, and courage of man.

Neither Marx nor Kautsky ever developed a moral theory adequate to their conception of the superior virtue resident in a proletarian victory. Their theory of history, particularly as interpreted by Kautsky, makes it difficult to see why any special moral justification is required if men's conceptions of right and wrong are merely super-structural expressions of economic interests. For the alleged law which determined the succession of economic interests in history would also determine the succession of moral systems. "Higher" would only mean "later." Implicit, however, in the political judgments of Marx and Kautsky are moral assumptions which cannot be plausibly interpreted in terms of the theory of historical materialism except if the latter is interpreted in such a way as to allow much more than they did for the relatively autonomous historical influence of moral ideals, independently of their alleged origins.

The poverty of Kautsky's analysis of ethical questions is painfully apparent in his critique of Kant and in his implication that the desirability of socialism is a corollary of its inevitability, which hardly differs from the Hegelian use of Schiller's dictum *die Weltgeschichte ist das Weltgericht*. Socialism is inevitable because the victory of the proletariat is inevitable, and this because the class struggle is inevitable, which in turn flows from the inevitable drive to expand productive forces in behalf of the inevitable urge to maximize profit. Here as elsewhere in orthodox Marxism there is present an element of sheer mysticism, a reliance upon inevitable cosmic and social processes which automatically guarantee man's moral ideals, ideals which have surreptitiously been introduced into the factual cosmic and social premises.

2. **Georgi Plekhanov (1856-1918).** If Kautsky was the dean of Social-Democratic orthodoxy, Georgi Plekhanov was its leading professor. After an early beginning as a Populist, he became the founder and foremost teacher of Russian Social-Democracy out of which developed the Menshevik and Bolshevik wings. Kautsky and Lenin, despite the latter's political hostility, refer to him as the most philosophically educated intelligence of the socialist movement. He contributed to the discus-

sion of some of the open problems of Marxism, such as
the role of the individual in history, the place of art in
society, and the nature of its philosophical assumptions.
He specialized in replying to unfriendly critics of Marxism.

In his theoretical approach Plekhanov stressed the
monistic aspect of Marxism, and, following Engels, tried
to link socialism to a world view. His writings show considerable erudition and a feeling for the richness and
complexity of cultural phenomena. But a zeal for doctrinal orthodoxy, even when the doctrines are ambiguous,
outruns his logical discretion or acumen. He confuses
necessary and sufficient conditions, makes admissions
with a cheerful unawareness that they are incompatible
with his main doctrines, and rarely meets fundamental
criticisms squarely.

a. The Individual in History. Plekhanov's theoretical
interest as well as practical political concerns led him to
a consideration of the problem of the role of the individual in history. As a Marxist he took the field against
some revolutionary Russian groups which glorified the
activity of individual terror against Czarist absolutism.
He has no difficulty in establishing the political futility
of individual violence as a weapon of social overthrow.
The rule of absolutism may be tempered by assassination
but never replaced. But on the main question, whether
the life and actions of an individual are ever more decisive than social forces in determining a great event so
that in the absence of the individual the event in question
would not have taken place, Plekhanov is evasive and
far from satisfactory. What he does show is that the
occasions of heroic action, the conditions under which it
takes place, are not made by the hero. This is true and
an obvious retort to such a position as Carlyle's. But it
is irrelevant to the question which is not: Does the hero
or outstanding individual make *all* of history or create
the condition of his activity? The question is: Does he
ever remake or redetermine it? Would the pattern of
historical development have been substantially the same
if he had never lived?

Russian history, because of its absolutist character,
seems to provide prima facie evidence that some of the
far-reaching actions carried out by its rulers, especially
Peter the First and Catherine II, would not have been

undertaken at that time or age, and possibly not at all, had they not occupied posts of power. The denial that the individual ever plays a redetermining role in history in contradistinction to other factors, to the extent that they can be distinguished, leads to the view that no leader is ever indispensable in the achievement of a great historical event, good or bad. If it is believed that the multiplicity of factors involved in the historical process can never be distinguished, and relative weights assigned to them, then no causal judgments can be made in history, and the doctrine of historical materialism, which sees the cause of all historical development in changes in the mode of economic production, would be either meaningless or false.

Plekhanov asserts that he does not regard the individual as a negligible force in history. A great man is an accident and "sometimes the fate of nations depends on accidents which may be called accidents of the second degree." This concession shatters the monistic theory of history, but Plekhanov seems unaware of it. Accidents of the second degree are not chance events, he insists. They are themselves caused. Quite right, but then the question reads: Are the causes of the existence of great men—these accidents of the second degree—economic rather than biological, psychological, religious, or what not? To this Plekhanov replies that "in the last analysis" the *effects* of a great man's activity cannot be explained except in terms of the social forces of his time. (*See Reading No. 9.*) This is an *ignoratio elenchi,* an answer to a quite different question from the one at issue. It simply ignores the question of what explains the *existence* of the great man. Napoleon's influence, to be sure, was limited by his social environment, a truism which holds of anybody's influence. But what explains the *difference* between a great man's influence and that of a mediocrity? The social environment may *select* a great man. But it cannot *produce* him.

Plekhanov's orthodoxy and monism compel him to believe that the social forces of a period not merely select but produce great men, and that the history of any period would pretty much have been the same no matter what individuals had existed. The very history of Marxism, and its effect upon history, from Marx to Lenin and Stalin gives the lie to this.

b. Art and Culture. In his discussion of questions of aesthetics, Plekhanov applies the theory of historical materialism not to test its validity but merely to illustrate its claims. According to Plekhanov the history of art in its most significant respects can be correlated with the history of economic development, not in detail, but in broad outline, to show that the mode of production explains the rise, variation, and disappearance of art forms, the vicissitudes of their appreciation, and the shifts in the norms of aesthetic excellence. Although he asserts that he does not seek to establish a direct connection between art and economics, his criticism invariably shows evidence of oversimplification, gratuitous stress on economic factors, and unwarranted generalizations. For example, in considering primitive art he asserts that the conception of "the beautiful" is derived from the conception of the "precious" and that what is regarded as the most precious is always a fact or factor in the immediate *economic* environment of the tribe. He is justified in denying that the biological nature of man is sufficient to explain the varying content of aesthetic experience, but he is not justified in assuming that "the precious" is always "the economic." Even primitive man may find aesthetic delight in religious, military, or sexual occasions and objects of satisfaction. Certain shells and metals, including gold, are considered precious even when not useful. Or they are considered more precious than other objects which are more useful. In some cultures certain decorative patterns of form and color are preferred which are not derived from the patterns and forms of useful or "economic" objects.

Plekhanov's discussions of modern art are less objectionable as long as he remains on the plane of description. As soon as he offers causal explanations he goes astray. He will admit the influence of certain obviously noneconomic psychological and religious factors on a work of art but then maintains that these influences "ultimately," or "in the last analysis," can be traced back in time to economic causes which are decisive. He not only fails in actuality to trace these non-economic influences to economic causes but overlooks the fact that even if he succeeded it would not establish their relevance. It is as if one were to argue that the "ultimate" or "decisive" cause of the death of a victim of a hit-and-run driver was not the drunkenness of the operator nor the speed of the vehicle which struck him down but capitalism because whiskey and automobiles are commodities. Since causes themselves have causes and these have causes without end, the quest for an "ultimate" cause or a cause "in the last instance" would either end in a "first cause" (a theological notion) or in an infinite series of causes— the totality of existence—which would explain nothing specific because it would explain everything.

c. Democracy and Dictatorship. If theoretically Plekhanov's shortcomings were typical of the entire Social-Democratic movement of his time, in practical politics his orthodoxy stood him in better stead. In one of the earliest of his writings he stresses the absolute indispensability of a developed capitalism within Russia as a condition precedent to introducing socialism. The attempt to build socialism in a backward country is doomed to failure. If socialism is imposed by force, he wrote in a prophetic vein as early as 1884, it will inescapably lead "to a political deformity after the image of the Chinese and Peruvian Empire, a renewed Czarist despotism with a Communist lining."

Nonetheless, because the Russian Social-Democrats were struggling against a political despotism which denied them even the rights of agitation, Plekhanov was neither clear nor consistent in his conception of the "dictatorship of the proletariat" and contributed to obscuring the democratic presuppositions of the Marxist movement. He sometimes interpreted the concept as if it would be legitimate to sacrifice democratic processes in the interest of the proletarian power. This would make the extension of democratic privileges to non-proletarian groups contingent upon how strong the proletarian government would be. Even parliamentary majorities might be disregarded after the revolution. On the other hand, he sometimes made the fulfillment of the proletarian interests dependent upon the extension of democratic rights to the entire population. Before he died, however, all traces of ambiguity vanished from his position, and in 1917 he became an outspoken opponent of any and all varieties of Marxism which did not wholeheartedly affirm, once political despotism had been overthrown, the centrality of the democratic process. But by that time his political influence was near the vanishing point.

3. **Daniel De Leon (1852-1914).** Daniel De Leon is important not so much because of the character of his own independent contributions to Marxism but, among other reasons, because he is the best American exemplification of orthodox Social-Democracy—and this in its purest, one is tempted to say its most religious, form. So fanatical was De Leon's orthodoxy that as late as 1911 he was still deploring the union in 1875 of the two German Socialist groups—the Lasalleans and the Eisenachers —as a fusion which had betrayed the purity of socialist principle and aided neither democratic reforms nor socialist revolution. And this despite the fact that even Marx and especially Engels had reconciled themselves to this fusion.

De Leon's emphasis upon the purity of principle and the intransigeance of party or organization, no matter how small, was fortified by a fervent belief, which sometimes sounds like a pious wish, that the laws of capitalist development would do all the work which was required for the socialist revolution. It was also reinforced by a kind of social evolutionism current in America during the last quarter of the nineteenth century which saw close analogues with the laws of evolutionary biology. Economic classes were compared with biological species and the class struggle with the struggle for existence. "The laws that rule sociology," declared De Leon, "run upon lines parallel with, and are the exact counterpart of, those that natural science has established in biology."

Political action as De Leon saw it was to be nothing more than a form of agitation registering only the extent to which the decline of the capitalist system had educated the working class. It was not to concern itself with immediate aims for improvement or gradual reforms of existing evil. Concern with such things as taxes, housing, social legislation were an abomination. They were snares and delusions hiding from the workers the fact of their ever-growing impoverishment. "The organization of the revolution of our generation must be the most uncompromising of any that yet appeared on the stage of history. It demands the unconditional surrender of the capitalist system and its system of wage slavery: the total extinction of class rule is its object. Nothing short of that—whether as a first, a temporary, or any other sort of step—can at this late date receive recognition in the camp of the modern revolution."

According to De Leon socialism would come all at once and at one blow—but not a modest one. Conditions would inescapably become so intolerable that the political representatives of the working class would secure a majority in Congress. They would then adjourn *sine die* and turn over the effective rule of the nation to the great trade unions organized not along craft but industrial lines. Representation would shift from a geographical to an occupational basis. In a certain sense De Leon can be regarded as the first who projected the idea of political rule by industrial unions which subsequently developed independently in Russia in the form of Soviets. (*See Reading No. 10.*) As bitterly as he opposed socialists who sought to win reforms for the workers and gradually introduce socialism (Half a loaf is not better than none because half a loaf is always a stone!), De Leon also attacked the syndicalists who rejected political action for direct action. The socialist movement must cling to the civilized standpoint of legality so long as no violent opposition to the mandate of the people materializes. Until that time, socialists, i.e., those who were organized in the Socialist Labor Party, were to purge their ranks of reformers; expose the Socialist Party as advocates of sops and palliatives instead of total revolution; attack the incitements of the Industrial Workers of the World to direct action as provocations that would unleash a reign of terror; and, finally, refute the claims of pure and simple trade-unionism, especially of the American Federation of Labor, to improve the conditions of the workers as pure and simple deception. De Leon called for the organization of dual trade unions which would commit themselves to the program of total socialism. The consequence was that the Socialist Labor Party dwindled in size and significance. The weaker it became, the more assured and strident were its claims to Marxist orthodoxy.

De Leon is distinctive for other reasons besides his orthodoxy and sectarianism. The failure of Marxism to take hold in the United States labor movement has sometimes been attributed to the character of its language, to its foreign and technical jargon. De Leon, however, wrote clear, simple prose and in an authentic American idiom spiced with indigenous American wit and humor. His popular writings are doctrinally orthodox but he never argued merely from authority. He sought wherever possible to cite materials from American history to illustrate Marxist doctrine. For example, he made noteworthy use of Madison's paper in the *Federalist* to expound the theory of historical materialism. Nonetheless, his writings and ideas had no impact whatsoever upon the main American labor movement. His failure proved that Marxism in its orthodox form was no more palatable to the American worker in a folksy idiom than in transliterated German.

De Leon differed from most other American socialists in the high place he gave to organizational loyalty and discipline despite the fact that, in his view, organizations could do little except proclaim the inevitable. "The principle and organization are one," he asserted. Any difference with him on organizational matter, any opposition to his leadership, was construed as disloyalty to socialist principles and met with prompt excommunication. Forgetting the function of ideas as instruments of social change, he preferred to have a doctrinally pure organization to a politically effective one. His doctrines, however, taken all in all come nearest to representing a *reductio ad absurdum* of orthodox Social-Democracy in their apotheosis of history, over-emphasis on determinism, fetishism of slogans and organization, than the ideas of any other leader of a revolutionary organization. In a letter to Kautsky, Marx confessed to a certain suspicion of "Yankee socialists" as "crotchety and sectarian." The reference was not to De Leon, but the fortunes of orthodox Marxism in America seem to have confirmed Marx's hunch.

4

REVISIONISM—BERNSTEIN AND JAURÈS

The seeds of orthodox Social-Democracy fell on barren soil in the New World. In some regions of the Old World, especially Germany, they flourished. The German Social-Democratic Party grew, in the course of a few decades, to be so powerful that it was not unreasonable to hope, once Bismarck's proscriptive measures against it had been lifted and equitable electoral reforms introduced, that it would win an absolute majority in support of its program. Meanwhile it grew by leaps and bounds in membership, in number and variety of its organizations, in newspaper outlets, even in its real estate holdings.

The character of the Social-Democratic Party gradually changed with its success. The necessities of everyday adjustments to events, the support it received from other elements in the population, its close collaboration with the trade unions which far from provoking social disorder soon acquired a vested interest in industrial peace, its local triumphs in winning political concessions —all conspired to transform the avowedly revolutionary German Social-Democratic Party into a democratic socialist reform party. The more reformist it became in practice, the more tenaciously did it cling to the fierce revolutionary rhetoric with which it had burst upon the world.

To this must be added certain cultural traditions, developed in the course of the nineteenth century, which contributed to dampening propensities to revolutionary zealotry. The Germans were great "respecters" of authority, sticklers for the letter of the law, with deep veneration for the trappings of royalty. As Germany grew in strength and status in the world arena, most of the population, including some elements among the workers, took a vicarious pride in its military achievements. Bismarck's measures of terror and welfare had failed to prevail against the Social Democratic Party. After the repeal of the anti-Socialist laws an unlimited vista of peaceful gains stretched before the German working class. The tendency to come to terms with the environment, to consider it not as something to be completely transformed but reconstructed piecemeal, gradually became dominant.

1. Edward Bernstein (1850-1932). Edward Bernstein was the man who boldly recognized the disparity between the professions of the Social-Democrats and their practices, and called upon them in the interests of clarity to speak as they acted. His writings stirred up a great and continuing controversy not only in Germany but in every quarter in which orthodox Marxism had any influence. When Bernstein first penned his critical observations of current Marxist thought, he claimed to be defending the real and living Marx against his embalmers—almost in the same way as William of Ockham, whose razor cut the throat of medieval Aristotelianism, claimed to be conducting the operation in the name of the true or real Aristotle. In time, however, unable to convince many that he had read Marx aright, Bernstein abandoned the claim to having inherited the mantle of Marxism and argued for the validity of his position rather than for its Marxist authenticity.

The spirit and direction of Bernstein's revision of orthodox Marxism are best expressed in a famous sentence from his chief work published at the turn of the century. "What is generally called the goal of socialism is nothing to me, the movement everything." (*See Reading No. 11.*) What Bernstein meant by this was not that he was opposed to the ideals of socialism but only to an apocalyptic conception of them, to a view which anticipated their sudden introduction into history after a violent revolution which more likely than not would hardly live up to socialist ideals. To become arrested in a verbalistic fixation upon the final and total triumph of socialism resulted either in political insincerity, if it had no practical bearings on conduct, or in adventurism, if it encouraged ultimistic and impossibilist demands. One who takes health, physical and mental, as a goal may strive to reach it at one bound or through a series of quick, short exercises. Or he may talk about it or long for it without it making much difference to his conduct.

In either case health is considered as if it were something separate and apart from the process of daily living. Properly conceived, ideal health is found in the proper functioning of the organism as a whole in its day-by-day tasks. In the course of this functioning one grows healthier without ever enjoying or worrying about absolute health. In other words, health designates a process rather than a limit of a series. Similarly with respect to the goal of socialism. According to Bernstein it was unimportant whether the socialist movement would ever reach its declared goal, the classless society in which the principle of fraternity would also serve as the principle of justice and in which science would be so highly developed that the principle of the division of labor would no longer be valid. Important only was the fact that the socialist movement was continuously enriching the lives of the workers—increasing the scope of their participation in politics and industry, getting more and better housing, building cooperatives, raising their standard of living, insuring their greater security, transforming education from a leisure-class good to a common good accessible to all the gifted, and therewith developing their self-respect. Socialism was a way of life to be experienced and enjoyed in the here and now, not glorified as the end of history.

Bernstein called attention to the fact that the reforms achieved as a result of the pressure of trade unions and the Socialist Party had altered in some ways the grim economic prospects of capitalism as predicted by the orthodox Marxists. He inferred from this and other social phenomena that the workers could gain both more allies and more victories by the extension of democratic methods than by preaching and practicing class war. Class struggles were endemic to the economic system. But they need not take a violent form. Bernstein in effect made the socialist *program* subordinate to the democratic *process* and the interest of class a means of furthering the good of the community.

Bernstein's writings provoked bitter polemics in the German Social-Democratic movement and he narrowly escaped expulsion at the hands of those who felt that he not only had profaned the terminological and doctrinal pieties of the Party program but that he had blunted its fighting edge. There was some truth to this but not in

the sense that Bernstein's doctrines affected militancy—
the edges of the German Social-Democratic Party had
already been rounded by prosperity—but in the sense that
he was undermining its sense of historical mission. It
was difficult for mystical notions to withstand the corro-
sive acids of his common-sense empiricism. What saved
Bernstein from expulsion was not so much that he had
been a close friend of Engels and an intimate of all the
elder statesmen of the Party but the support of the leaders
of the German trade-union movement. They were freer
of *parti pris*. They felt that Bernstein was giving an
honest account of what the socialist movement in Germany was in actual fact, and believed that the policy he
was urging would make easier the accommodation of
grandiose ideals to the workaday yet satisfactory world.

During his years of exile in London, Bernstein had
acquired from the English intellectual atmosphere a certain impatience with abstractions not applicable to, or
testable by, events, and an irreverence towards history as
the arbiter of values. This was reflected in his consistent
efforts to purify the doctrinal legacies of Marx from
their Hegelian influences. He condemned the dialectic
as a kind of abracadabra, defended the critical point of
view of the French rationalists rather than the tendency
to offer historical explanations of events in such a way
that they were merely rationalizations of what happened.
Most important of all, Bernstein denied that the ethical
appeal or justification of socialism could ever be derived
from the necessities of economic development and the
class struggle. There were right ways and wrong ways of
fighting for socialism, and they could not be deduced
merely from the economic consequences of human action
or from the strategies of political power. A compromise
which resulted in less human suffering, and prepared the
way for its further mitigation, was to be preferred to a
victory attended by greater human suffering.

Without denying in the least the relevance of a scientific study of the nature of capitalist economy and society
to the socialist program, Bernstein contended that the
socialist movement, its élan, enthusiasm, belief in the
possibility of progress, and commitment to a different
mode of production and distribution of goods and services, rested on *ethical* principles. The development of
capitalism made socialism possible and not desirable.

What made socialism desirable was the demand for justice, the desire for freedom, an acceptance of the underlying fraternity of all peoples, and an equality of concern for all individuals to develop their personalities to the fullest. Bernstein believed that Kant must supplement Marx. Otherwise ethical terms in the mouths of Marxists were the purest cant. The hardships and self-sacrifice endured by socialists in their struggle for a better society could be explained, according to the revisionist approach, neither by the pressure of material forces nor by self-interest.

No one *dies* for a cause, as many a scientific Socialist has done, out of enlightened self-interest, particularly if he puts no stock in a hereafter, but only because he regards some things as more precious than life itself. Just as the socialist movement, urged Bernstein, should recognize that in actuality its politics were reformist not revolutionary, so it should recognize that among the mainsprings of its activity were ethical imperatives continuous with the ideals observable in the long and uncertain history of human emancipation from ignorance and oppression.

Although Bernstein was denounced as an "opportunist" and "backslider," he defended democratic and socialist ideals more courageously and consistently than many of his more orthodox Marxist critics. He was always critical of German foreign policy and was one of the first in the Social-Democratic parliamentary faction to refuse approval of war credits after the First World War broke out. He was a man of incorruptible intellectual honesty, never trimming the truth for the cause of his Party, always prepared to reexamine his own first principles as well as to criticize those of others. He was tolerant of all theoretical differences and much fairer to his opponents than they were to him. His point of view, but unfortunately not his resolution and fearlessness, gradually became the official point of view of German Social-Democracy during the Weimar Republic. Bernstein's fate was that many who seemed to agree with his revisionism espoused "reform" not so much on ethical grounds as on narrow practical grounds. It seemed easier, less exacting, less disturbing to their comfort and philistinism to be democratic, to take a middle course, to go slowly. But when the life of democracy was at stake in the Weimar

Republic, when the middle course was not easier but more exacting, when faith and ardor and heroic courage were required to save the decent and sane traditions of society against fanaticism, many fell away from Bernstein's socialism. He himself died a few weeks before the Weimar Republic was destroyed between the hammer and anvil of Fascism and Communism. Had he lived he would have been among those who defended its democratic institutions to the last.

2. **Jean Jaurès (1859-1914).** An even more outspoken figure of socialist revisionism was Jean Jaurès, the great French socialist leader cut down by an assassin's bullet on the eve of the First World War. Although he often called himself a Marxist, he declared that "Marxism itself contains the means by which it can be supplemented and revised"—a sentiment that usually prefaces a critique of orthodoxy. Jaurès never concealed his opposition to orthodox Marxism, and, for all his acknowledgment of indebtedness, on occasions he was more sharply critical of Marx and Engels, especially about tactical questions, than Bernstein. Bernstein, in the main, asserted that Marx's insights had been rendered invalid by the development of events. Jaurès asserted that some of these insights were mistaken even at the time they were made.

Jaurès' socialist inspiration was originally derived from non-Marxist sources—German philosophical idealism and French Utopianism. Although he accepted historical materialism as a tool of historical inquiry, he rejected philosophical materialism of all varieties. The universe is more than an organization of matter or energy moving blindly without direction from one state to another. The fact that it has given rise to human ideals, to passions of love and justice, indicates that it is informed by a spiritual principle, for nothing can be actual which is not already potentially present. This principle animates all things and, despite apparent conflicts, accounts for the developing order and harmony in nature and society. Without this unitary and unifying spiritual element the universe would long since have dissolved in chaos.

Jaurès derived the desirability of socialism from man's rights as a man to be a person and be considered as one. In affirming his own individuality, the workman "claims everything that belongs properly to a man, the right to work, the right to the complex development of his faculties, to the continuous exercise of his free will and reason." What Marx showed was that the historical evolution of property made it impossible for society to guarantee all of these rights unless the dominant form of property became social. Socialized property is to be vested not alone in the state or nation but in the many associations of which the worker is an active member—cooperatives, trade unions, local communities—which will guarantee him his rights as a person and by their plural and complex forms of social property protect him from the tyranny of any particular group or of the nation itself.

Jaurès was a socialist humanist more anxious to find a basis for common faith and action in a political opponent than a disguised class enemy in a critical Party comrade. His goal, which he sometimes confused with the goal of history, was the liberation of entire humanity from political despotism, religious superstitions, and economic exploitation. Since the proletariat was the class which suffered most, the amelioration of its lot was the most pressing concern. But the principles by which its lot was to be improved were binding upon *all* classes. Consequently, although class struggles are an undeniable fact, class cooperation and class collaboration, based on objective principles of justice, could and should be used to achieve social reforms. Often a minority voice in his own Party, and often denounced by orthodox socialists like Guesde and Bebel in the Socialist International, Jaurès defended socialist support and participation in bourgeois governments if thereby reforms could be won and great impending evils avoided. In this respect he went much further than Bernstein.

Because of his humanism, Jaurès was a radical socialist but not a Radical Socialist.[1] He believed that democratic principles were valid in all spheres of life. Economic democracy, he argued, was a corollary of political democracy. And by economic democracy he meant much more than the principle of collective bargaining. "If labor is

---

[1] The Radical Socialist Party in France is a party wedded to the support of capitalism and bases itself primarily on peasant and small business groups.

to be really free the workers should be called upon to take part in the management of the work. They should have a share in the economic government of the shop, just as universal suffrage gives them a share in the political government of the city." By the time Jaurès gets through spelling out the nature of the workers' economic government, it is clear that he expects them to have as much power, directly or through their representatives, as Boards of Directors.

Universal peace, according to Jaurès, is a necessary condition of a humanist civilization. Therefore, conflicts should be settled by negotiation and arbitration rather than by force. This applies not only to conflicts between nations but *within* nations. Jaurès' sharpest and most cogently argued polemics were directed against the cult of force and the syndicalist myth of the general strike which had some influence in socialist ranks. He scoffed at the idea that socialism could be imposed on a nation by a revolutionary minority. He employed his formidable historical erudition to show that successful social revolutions in the past "would have come to nothing if it had not been for the will of the immense majority of the nation back of it." With rather dubious validity, he infers the presence of majority will not from the registration of consent but from the historical events themselves. More persuasive was his contention that social revolutions in the past merely transferred political and legal power to a class already strongly entrenched economically, whereas the socialist revolution would require a far greater social transformation. All the more necessary was the present need for a revolutionary majority. "In 1789 the Revolution had only a negative work to perform in the domain of property, that is to say, it abolished, it did not create. . . . The Socialist Revolution, on the contrary, must not rest content after it has abolished capitalism; it must create the new forms under which production is to be carried on. . . ."

Like contemporary humanists, Jaurès argued that, if human beings are to settle their problems adequately, and not just talk about them, they must be properly informed. The entire birthright of human culture and modern science must be available to them. Therefore, a sound universal education must accompany universal suffrage. If that education is to be genuinely liberal, it must be free from any kind of authoritarianism. Therefore, education must be completely secular. Church and state must in our age be clearly separated. In this way natural, limited, and imperfect man becomes progressively humanized by invoking eternal ideals in an historical process which spirals upward through phases of ever-growing social cooperation and ever-diminishing conflict.

As much as Bernstein, Jaurès criticized the deification of "the great day" which would witness the sudden end of capitalism and the dawn of socialism. But whereas Bernstein insisted that there was no guarantee that day would ever dawn, Jaurès was confident it would. He merely substituted for the orthodox doctrine of the inevitability of sudden revolution the notion of the inevitability of gradual revolution. The emphasis, however, of both revisionist thinkers fell upon the present, not the future. It was far more important "to live always in a state of socialist grace, working each hour, each minute" to remake the world closer to our socialist ideals than to hug the consolation that history was on our side. Like Bernstein, Jaurès believed that trade unions, cooperatives, benevolent associations, all the manifold activities of the working class, should be schools for socialist living. Instead of counterposing social reforms to social revolution, the first would be the means by which the second would come to pass.

Jaurès was a great conciliator, so much a man of good heart and good will that he sometimes attempted to reconcile the irreconcilable. An ardent Dreyfusard, he saw in Dreyfuss' persecutors individuals who were merely ignorant rather than wicked. Despite his philosophical training, he showed a greater aptitude in applying socialist ideals to practical affairs than in clarifying theoretical issues. He was sympathetic to any doctrine which brought people to the socialist movement if only it aided the unity of that movement which he saw threatened by sectarian fixations on purity and orthodoxy. He wrote a gentle satire on those who would rather be Left than right, but he sometimes went to great rhetorical lengths to appease them.

In the great debate between Kautsky and Bernstein, Jaurès characteristically sided with both, but more with Kautsky than with Bernstein. "When I approve fully of Kautsky by the same token I am approving par-

tially of Bernstein." With the exception of a maladroit
defense of the Marxist theory of value (which Jaurès
defends as compatible with Bernstein's belief in the
possibility of continuous improvement in the workers'
standards of living), Jaurès' professions of orthodoxy
turned out to be quite Pickwickian.

This is clearly demonstrable with reference to the
theory of historical materialism which Jaurès often declared to be no more valid than the theory of historical
idealism. (*See Reading No. 12*.) He sometimes claims to
believe that the mode of economic production has ultimately the strongest causal efficacy in determining all
cultural phenomena. He then asserts that it is very hard
to distinguish between political influences, the impact of
science, and economic forces as causal factors, and that
to separate them in the quest for an explanation of what
causes what (which is precisely what is required by the
theory of historical materialism) is merely an artifice of
thought. More significant is his emphatic assertion that
law, democracy, philosophy, science, and art, although
limited by the operation of economic factors, have their
own independent logic and history of development. This
last proposition is as flat a denial as anyone can wish of
historical materialism which teaches that non-economic
phenomena do not possess an independent history. To be
sure, Jaurès, like the orthodox Marxists, after recognizing
the reciprocal interaction of plural social and cultural
factors asserts the "ultimate" domination of the economic
factor. But he then turns the table on the theory of historical materialism by claiming that the operation of the
economic factor is an expression of the primacy of the
human spirit. Although the mode of economic production is allegedly dominant, it does not always in fact
determine cultural events. Indeed, "precisely because
democracy, the church, science have their own logic,
their own internal structure, their particular force of
development, *we* should act directly upon them, in order
to encourage them if they work in an economic direction
desired by *us;* or to oppose them if they work in an
opposite direction" (italics supplied).

Jaurès' greatest published work is his *History of Socialism from 1789 to 1900,* the first few volumes of which
are a history of the French Revolution. In it he describes
with brilliance and originality the influence of economic

factors on political events without making the excessive
claims which mar the writings of orthodox Marxists.
Perhaps of greater significance than his published work
was Jaurès' life work. He was the most eloquent tribune
of French democracy and of peace lovers everywhere
from 1890 to 1914. His last words—a speech on July 25,
1914—call on the workers of Europe to stop the First
World War. When they were published on August 1, he
was already dead. An epoch came to an end with his life.

— 5 —

LENIN

Had the Russian Revolution of October, 1917, not
occurred, the name of Lenin would hardly have been
known outside of Russia. Nothing in Lenin's history
before the year 1917, which witnessed the military and
social collapse of Czarist Russia after three years of war,
provided evidence of the event-making role he would
play in world history. As a Marxist theoretician he was
comparatively undistinguished. He did not anticipate,
even as late as a year before it happened, that he and
his group would be masters of a great empire. And he
was completely surpised by the larger historical consequences of his own actions.

Lenin's genius was primarily political and practical. It
was rooted in a native shrewdness and guided an iron
resolution of purpose not always apparent in the amazing
tactical flexibility which marks his career. Nonetheless,
his readiness to act boldly and ruthlessly depended upon
a certain characteristic emphasis he gave to Marxist doctrines long before his small group was poised to strike
against the democratic regime which followed the collapse

of absolutism. Confronted by the opportunity to take power—an opportunity which his doctrinal intransigeance helped create—Lenin's political instincts were not check-reined by any dogmas about the primacy of economics to politics. Convinced by the ease with which the centers of political power had been seized, Lenin's doctrinal emphasis on revolutionary organization and revolutionary will became so pronounced that before he died he left behind him a corpus of teachings which constituted a far greater deviation from the traditions of orthodox Marxism than the Revisionism he so scathingly excoriated.

1. The Communist Party as a Weapon.   Marx relied upon the development of capitalism to bring the working class to a consciousness of its *existence* as a class. The economic dislocations of capitalism resulting in insecurity, unemployment, and hunger would act as a whiplash to rouse the working class to opposition and string it to a realization of its hopeless *position* as a class so long as capitalism prevailed. Marx assumed that there would always be at hand thinkers like himself who would then educate the working class to a consciousness of its *mission* as a class, who would make explicit the integrating ideal of a socialist society. The Socialists were to be the teachers of the working-class movement—providing spokesmen and responsible leadership—in open, public fashion. They were not to be manipulators controlling the working class from above or behind by secret factions.

We have seen that orthodox Marxists displayed persistent tendencies to interpret historical materialism in such a way as to view politics as a simple reflex of economics. From this they inferred that the political activity of the working class could not sensibly go beyond the confines of economic possibility and that, although one might talk about social revolution, one could not take the notion seriously as a guide to action until capitalism was on the very verge of collapse or had actually collapsed.

In Russia an extreme form of this tendency expressed itself in a current of thought known as "economism" or "Tail-endism." It taught that the working class would spontaneously develop a political socialist outlook concomitantly with its economic struggles. It therefore stressed the primacy of the economic struggle. Lenin took the field against it and argued that belief in socialism, and political activity to achieve it, do not arise as a spontaneous consequence of the workers' experience. Such belief and activity depend upon socialist propaganda and agitation brought to the working class by socialists. Political consciousness was not an automatic by-product of laws of economic development. Otherwise how explain the existence of Catholic trade unions or pure and simple trade unions like the A.F. of L.? Political consciousness is a relatively independent factor. Its presence cannot be inferred from the *economic* class struggle. Nonetheless it contributes powerfully in determining the outcome of the struggle for socialism. Political consciousness is to be instilled into the masses by a revolutionary *doctrine* (loosely called "ideology") disseminated by a revolutionary *organization* which must prepare for the conquest of power, win mass support for its program, and strike when the situation is ripe. This element of *voluntarism* in Lenin's thought was at first muffled but became stronger before and immediately after October, 1917. By the time Lenin died, it reached a pitch where it burst violently through the entire framework of historical materialism.

Lenin never believed that capitalism would automatically break down. Its successes, by generating cumulative difficulties, ripen it for the transition to socialism, but unless plucked in season it can renew itself sufficiently to live indefinitely with large patches of rot. "There are no absolutely inextricable positions or crises," he once declared. For all his worship of history, he knew that history does nothing by itself. It never bestows power. Power must always be taken. And the preparation for the taking of power is the never-to-be-forgotten task of the revolutionary organization, animating all it teaches and all it does. In effect Lenin substituted the conquest of political power, the destruction of the existing state and all its works, for socialism as the goal or end-in-view of the socialist movement. Socialism as a form of social organization and as an ideal of fraternity can only become an end-in-view *after* political power has been won.

Nor did Lenin believe that poverty and social distress cause communist movements to arise—one of the shibboleths of liberalism. Without a revolutionary organization to fan the spark of resentment into a blaze—to nurse it, direct it, extend it in all directions—the fire of rebellion dies out, leaving an arid area which inhibits the spread of other flames.

The organization which is to lead in the struggle for political power is the Communist Party (the name itself was first used after the October Revolution). Armed by Marxist theory, it knows what the true interests of the workers are better than the workers themselves. The necessities of effective organization require that the party be bound by an iron-clad discipline. Its membership cannot include sympathizers, those who merely vote for it on election days, or benevolent well-wishers who desire to make the best of the world they live in and the world they fear will replace it. It must consist only of those who are totally dedicated to the cause, a party of professional revolutionists, hierarchically organized, and centrally controlled. Although Lenin sometimes characterized the structure of the Party as one of "democratic centralism," it actually meant that the exercise, degree, and occasion of democratic activity on the part of the membership was determined by the central source—the bureaucratic and self-perpetuating directors of a paramilitary machine.

Commenting on this conception of a revolutionary party, at a time when he did not share it, Leon Trotsky denounced it as a Jacobean, conspiratorial perversion. "The organization of the Party takes the place of the Party itself; the Central Committee takes the place of the organization; and finally the dictator takes the place of the Central Committee." (Because Lenin's faction won a temporary majority at the 1903 Convention of the Russian Social-Democratic Party on this question of Party structure, it acquired the name of *Bolsheviki*, the Russian word for majority.)

At first Lenin's conception of the Party was advanced only for Russia where, because special conditions of political despotism prevailed, socialist parties were forced to work underground. But subsequently, after the October Revolution, Lenin universalized this theory of organization for all countries of the world including "the freest" and "most democratic," and made its acceptance mandatory for all Communist parties affiliated with the Communist International. (*See Reading No. 14.*)

2. **The Communist Party Line.** Since revolutionary theory provides the guide lines of organizational action,

it becomes necessary to insure the Party against any doctrinal differences in its ranks which might weaken its cohesiveness and striking force. Lenin required not only discipline in action but conformity in thought to the Party line on all important issues. The Party, i.e., its leadership, is the judge, of what constitutes an important issue. Anyone was free to criticize so long as he resigned from the Party or was expelled. Lenin argued that the very phrase "freedom of criticism" was defective and expressed an inherently false, if not hypocritical, notion. Criticism must be subordinated to the truth. Intellectual freedom in the Party meant not the right to express different views but only the right to express the truth as the Party council determined it on the basis of its scientific philosophy. "Those who are really convinced that they have advanced science would demand not freedom for the new views to continue side by side with the old, but the substitution of the old views by the new views. The cry 'Long live freedom of criticism' that is heard today too strongly calls to mind the fable of the empty barrel [which makes the most noise]." And in Lenin's eyes the Party which oriented its course in the light of Marxism could legitimately claim to have the truth, or to be closer to the truth than any other group.

Until the Communist Party took power this doctrinal fanaticism had no effect except upon those who accepted and retained membership. Its fateful consequences to others began to unroll when the Communist Party was in control of the state apparatus and exercised its dictatorship in the name of the proletariat and in defense of the revolution. Criticism of the Communist Party line on any matter the Party declared important was now interpreted as an attack not merely on the monolithic unity of the Party but on the security of the state and the safety of the revolution. In consequence *all* members of the community who voiced criticisms of the Party line in any field were automatically suspected of objectively aiding the counter-revolution. (*See Reading No. 14a.*)

3. **Dialectical Materialism.** For most Marxist political parties the party line was merely its *political* program. The justification of that program and the larger conceptions of the nature of man and the world were outside the scope of political concern. They were just as much matters of private belief as one's personal religion

or lack of it. Lenin was the first Marxist, whose way was prepared for him by Plekhanov, to insist that dialectical materialism was an integral part of the Marxist faith and also directly relevant to its revolutionary program. According to Lenin no one could consistently accept dialectical materialism as a world view without embracing communism in social philosophy as well as the Communist theory of social revolution. Conversely, no one could consistently be a Communist without embracing dialectical materialism.

According to this philosophy all things in the world are interrelated by a dialectical necessity. It follows therefore that a false belief in any field must sooner or later result in a false idea about the nature of social reality. False ideas lead to mistaken actions, particularly in the field of politics. Since the Party knows the truth about the nature of society and is the master strategist in the political struggle, it cannot be indifferent to what is thought and believed in any field whatsoever. Further, every truth is found within a context of some social system, every social system is a class system, and every class system is riven by conflicts. The present class conflict, according to Lenin, must be fought under the leadership of the Communist Party. He therefore concludes that in every description of fact or theory there is also an element of evaluation. "Materialism" differs from "objectivism" in that the former recognizes and the latter denies the implicit reference to a class and Party standpoint in all truths. From this it follows that, strictly speaking, there are no objective classless truths about anything valid for all human beings. To be truly objective a truth must show the spirit of Party (*Partinost*).

Lenin's philosophy is inconsistent with itself and false to his own behavior. According to him ideas are "images" of things, yet his own ideas were images of nothing existing in past or present but were daring plans of action or anticipations of what was to be. His philosophy confuses materialism with realism and is based on a misconception of the nature of scientific method. Its notion of class or Party truths is logically on all fours with the belief in racial or national truths and open to the gravest objections. Here is not the place to discuss its technical philosophical inadequacies. Its implications for practice were

to become apparent in all their enormity under the
regime of Stalin.

4. **Triumph of Political Will.** By 1905 Lenin was
quite clear that the Communist Party was not only a
revolutionary party but a revolution-making party. His
emphasis on the revolutionary will to power was still
tamed, however, by belief in historical materialism. The
development of economic conditions must set the stage
for political action. Otherwise there would be a relapse
to the adventurism of Blanqui and the demagogism of
Bakunin. During this period Lenin did not differentiate
himself from other Marxists who maintained that because
of its backward economic condition Russia was ripe only
for a politically democratic revolution but not for a
revolutionary dictatorship which would start with a political revolution and end with a socialist one. He specifically
disclaims any sympathy with the "semi-anarchist" idea of
a socialist revolution. "The present degree of economic
development of Russia (an objective condition) and the
degree of class consciousness and organization of the
masses of the proletariat (a subjective condition indissolubly connected with the objective condition) make the
immediate, complete emancipation of the working class
impossible."

And as if to remove any doubt, he adds, "Whoever
wants to approach socialism by another path, other than
political democracy, will inevitably arrive at absurd and
reactionary conclusions in the economic and in the political sense."

The military collapse of Russia in the First World War,
the February Revolution of 1917, and the land hunger of
the peasants gave Lenin an opportunity to wrest power
from the moderate Kerensky regime. (At the time of his
arrival from exile Lenin had declared this regime to be
the freest in the world and characterized "by the absence
of oppression of the masses.") He then began the drive
towards socialist transformation hoping to be overtaken
by socialist revolutions in the West.

This was a giant stride away from the basic Marxist
position which asserted that "no social order ever perishes
before all the productive forces for which there is room
in it have developed." There was obviously plenty of
room for the development of productive forces in the

Russian economy of 1917, certainly not less than in that of the United States of 1917, which was decades ahead of Russia in industrial development and which nonetheless has more than doubled its productive capacity since then.

At first Lenin and his associates rationalized their conquest of political power by a pseudo-Marxist gloss. He claimed that if the world economy were considered as a whole it would be apparent that capitalism had exhausted all of its possibilities of expansion. It was, however, marked by unequal economic and political development. World capitalism, according to Lenin, would break down "at its weakest link" which Russia was supposed to be. Trotsky discovered a "law of combined development" which enables backward countries to telescope social development and skip phases of industrial development. These were completely *ad hoc* doctrines advanced to justify a political action which a special conjunction of circumstances made possible. They could just as well justify a socialist revolution in Spain or Turkey, which were still weaker links in the capitalist chain, or a socialist revolution in the Russia of 1905 which Lenin had denounced as anti-Marxist adventurism. If valid, these doctrines would also have held for the period of Marx and Engels. Since they believed, albeit mistakenly, that capitalism had exhausted its possibilities of development in their own time, it would have made nonsense of their earlier predictions that the socialist revolution would come first in industrially advanced countries. As pious Marxists about the past, Lenin and Trotsky had accepted these predictions as justified.

More important still, the basic assumption that there was no room for further expansion of capitalism on a world scale in 1914 turned out to be false whether measured by the indices of productivity, employment, profit, or real wages. The development of capitalism in Russia or elsewhere may have been undesirable but it certainly was not impossible. What was decisive was not any objective laws of economic development but the fanatical voluntarism of the Communist Party in a period of social crisis—and the ineptitude of its opponents.

The Bolshevik conquest of power was preliminary to a more far-reaching abandonment of orthodox Marxism. Lenin and Trotsky counted on socialist revolutions in the

West which would enable an international Communist
state to plan a global socialist economy in which Russia
would be the most backward segment. When the revolution failed to occur, the Communists set themselves to do
what every variety of Marxism had hitherto declared
theoretically impossible, i.e., to build a socialist economy
even though the necessary economic presuppositions were
absent. Both in industry and agriculture these presuppositions were created by radical political measures, operations more comparable to building new foundations for a
house than plucking ripe fruit from a tree. If socialism
be defined as collective ownership of the instruments of
production, or, as Lenin once put it, "Electrification plus
Soviet power," then the Communists undoubtedly succeeded in their task. But their very success refuted the
theory which presumably guided them. Marx had decisively been proved wrong by those who had most
vehemently declared themselves his orthodox disciples.

5. The Dictatorship of the Party. Lenin, as we
have seen, embraced a dictatorial conception of Communist Party organization. So long as such a party came
to power as a result of the *freely given* consent of the
masses, it was possible to reconcile it with a variant of the
democratic process. At first Lenin declared that the aim
of the Communists was "All Power to the Soviets" which
presumably represented the will of the masses. But as
soon as Lenin believed that the Communists would be
unable to capture the Soviets, he frankly acknowledged
that "All Power to the Soviets" was nothing but a political slogan to be used or discredited in relation to the
exigencies of winning power. In July, 1917, he declared
the slogan "All Power to the Soviets" to be "quixotic"
and a "mockery" and the Sixth Congress of his Party
formally agreed on its abandonment. This was tanta-
mount to a clear declaration that the Communists would
attempt, if necessary, to seize power behind the backs of
the Soviets.

After Kornilov's abortive revolt against Kerensky,
Lenin again proposed the slogan "All Power to the
Soviets," suspended it when rebuffed by other working-
class and peasant parties, and returned to it only when
the Communists won a majority in the St. Petersburg and
Moscow city Soviets. Trotsky candidly admits that the

slogans under which Communists carried out their insurrection meant merely "All Power to the *Bolshevik* Soviets."

According to Marxist political theory what is called the social and economic "dictatorship of the bourgeoisie" is compatible with different kinds of political systems. Capitalism is capitalism whether under a parliamentary democracy or a political dictatorship. Similarly, the social and economic "dictatorship of the proletariat" is compatible both with representative democratic institutions and with a *political* dictatorship. Despite the theory of historical materialism, it is interesting to observe that, when capitalist countries lose their democracy and fall under political dictatorships, Communists do not regard this transition as an *inevitable* outcome of economic development but as a consequence of political weakness or betrayal on the part of democrats.

Why, then, must the social and economic "dictatorship of the proletariat" necessarily take the form of a *political* dictatorship based upon terror and "the rule of force uncurbed by law"? Neither Lenin nor any other Communist theoretician offers any explanation in terms of their own Marxist doctrine except the statement that it is a measure of defense against the likelihood that those who do not enjoy the fruits of socialism may in the future revolt against it. This is very much like justifying shooting down an individual guiltless of any illegal act *now* on the ground that at some indeterminate time in the future he *might* break the law. (*See Reading No. 14d.*)

A more plausible explanation is suggested by the necessities of seizing power instead of winning it democratically. Despite an elaborate semantic by-play with terms like "leadership" and "dictatorship" and "democracy," it is clear that Lenin did not regard majority rule as a necessary condition of democracy as he conceived it. "If the proletariat is to win over the majority of the population, it must first of all overthrow the bourgeoisie and seize the powers of the state."

The proletariat in whose name Lenin speaks obviously does not constitute the majority of the population. It does not even constitute a majority of the workers. It consists of those who support the program of the Communist Party. The "victorious proletariat" remains a minority even among the working masses until it seizes power.

Only then, says Lenin, can it "gain the sympathy and win the support of the majority of the working (though non-proletarian) masses." In summary, the Communist Party *first* seizes power. *Then* it strives to win the support of the majority of the workers, and ultimately the support of the majority of the population. Since it alone counts the votes, controls the newspapers, and commands the police, it alone determines the conditions which define majority support.

It is clear that "the dictatorship of the proletariat" means nothing else than the dictatorship of a minority Communist Party *over* the proletariat, as well as over every other class. Lenin is scornful and impatient of those who counterpose "the dictatorship of the Party" to "the dictatorship of the class" because by definition—his definition—the Party, like a parent with respect to its child, knows what is best for the workers and always acts in the best interests of the workers, even though, like children, they may not know it.

Of course, not all parents know and act for the best interests of their children. And those that do, do not expect to keep them in permanent tutelage. Some day the children will grow up. In justice to Lenin, it should be noted that he believes that some day the workers, too, will grow up. This far-off day will be marked by the final withering away of the state, the party, and the police. Until then the Communist Party absolutely controls the state and with it the destinies of the workers. That is why on occasions Lenin admits that the dictatorship of the proletariat is "substantially" the dictatorship of the Party. Long before the directing role of the Communist Party in the whole of Soviet life and culture was explicitly stated in the Stalin Constitution of 1936, Lenin declared: "In the Soviet Union, the land where the dictatorship of the proletariat is in force, no important political or organizational problem is ever decided by our Soviets and other mass organizations without directives from the Party."

The conception of the dictatorship of the Party over the proletariat, confirmed by the whole history of the Soviet Union, marks an absolute break with all the democratic traditions of Marxism. From it there follows, together with Lenin's views about the internal nature of the Party, the outlawry of all other political parties of the working class, all dissident factions within the Party, the dictatorship of the Party leadership over the Party, and the grim outlines of a totalitarian control over the whole of society.

6. From Heresy to Conspiracy. In his earlier phase, when Lenin was still operating broadly within the Marxist tradition, he often wrote as if his views were to be understood as having a restricted application to Russia, i.e., to the exceptional situation of a culturally backward and politically despotic country. But after he broke with the main democratic heritage of Marxism, Lenin insisted upon the universal applicability of his key doctrines. Acceptance of them was made a condition for admission to the Third (Communist) International one of whose tasks was to see that they were properly taught and carried out in all countries. "Exceptionalism" was denounced as a political deviation of the first magnitude.

Since the end-in-view of all Communist parties on Lenin's theory is the capture of power and the exercise of the Party dictatorship, commensurate means must be taken to insure victory. To win over mass organizations their strategic posts must be occupied. Infiltration into the key positions of trade unions, cooperatives, and citizens' groups must be skilfully planned especially in sensitive areas. Sympathizers and fellow-travellers are to be groomed to show a false face to the enemy. Popular issues are to be exploited to fan discontent with the *status quo* into raging hostility. Social-Democrats are to be isolated and denounced as the chief enemy of the working class. Gradually a powerful striking force is to be built up and held in readiness until the appropriate time for action arises. Wherever possible, legal forms are to be used to the uttermost, but at the same time a secret underground of hard-core professional revolutionists must be established. "In all organizations without exception (political, industrial, military, cooperative, educational, sports) groups or nuclei of Communists should be formed . . . mainly open groups but also secret groups."

Fearful lest Communists in democratic countries might interpret this as applying only to countries which lack a functioning Bill of Rights and permit no legal opposition, Lenin underscores the universality of this injunction. "In all countries, even the freest, 'legal,' and 'peaceful' in the sense that the class struggle is least acute in them, the time has fully matured when it is absolutely necessary for every Communist Party to combine legal with illegal work, legal and illegal organizations."

Since the final step in the process of taking power involves an act of armed insurrection, and since the organs of defense of existing society may catch wind of what is afoot, Lenin cautions Communists that "illegal work is particularly necessary in the army, navy, and the police." Great emphasis is placed upon the necessity of auxiliary organizations to serve as transmission belts for Party influence.

As far as Western Europe and America are concerned, what we have here is the most striking transformation of an open, heretical social movement into a conspiratorial political one. The distance between such movements may be measured by contrasting the behavior of the revolutionists of Marx's time who openly and honestly proclaimed their aims no matter at what cost to themselves, and the evasions, subterfuges, and deceptions of Communists since Lenin's times. They have developed into a fine art the techniques of using the freedoms granted them in a democracy to forever destroy it.

The psychology of Communist conspirators cannot be grasped without a knowledge of their ideology. They are not, at least at the beginning of their careers, criminally base, but inspired by a resolute fanaticism to do what they imagine is the work of History. They care little for human life because they are prepared to sacrifice their own upon command. They are unmoved by human compassion because they regard it, like genuine pacifism, as a sign of weakness and hypocrisy. They are untouched by love of country because to them it seems an anachronism and because the Soviet Union is their true, and voluntarily chosen, country. They are rarely moved by argument and evidence because their hearts and minds are encased in the triple-plated dogmas of Marxist-Leninist-Stalinism which enables their substitute for religious faith to triumph over experience. Initially drawn to Communism by a laudable desire to diminish social injustice and human distress, they soon become corrupted by the means they employ. Their capacity for total sacrifice wedded to their belief in total solutions is the source of both their intransigence and danger.

7. Amoralism. One of the outstanding difficulties in most forms of Marxism is that it is unable to explain the actual behavior of Marxists, and the role which ideas and ideals play in human experience. Men are sometimes seized and made over by a vision of an Ideal in a manner quite different from what we would expect in view of their education and environment. Some visions intensify the powers of normal perception to discriminate between fact and wish, to recognize alternatives of action, and to weigh the moral costs of choice among them. Other visions blind the individual to the differences between compulsions of existence and the compulsions of will. He then pursues his way oblivious to the variety of paths which lie before him.

Lenin's vision of Marxism was one which actually did not guide him in political action. It blinded him to the differences between the driving forces of production and the driving force of his own will. But the belief that he was a Marxist in possession of the sure keys to the future contributed to concealing from himself and his followers the fact that he was actually choosing between historical possibilities rather than carrying out historical necessities. He was redetermining history and not following its alleged laws. In relation to their professed goal this made the actions of Leninists not unintelligible—since they believed that the historically inevitable had to come to pass through their own efforts—but insensitive and indifferent, and in the end unintelligent in the light of socialist ideals. Since the end was guaranteed by History, by the law of the class struggle, *any* means, *any* method was justified if it was successful. For it could then be claimed that it was deducible from the law of the class struggle. The human costs could be disregarded with an easy conscience as a price History and not the Leninists imposed upon mankind. By worshipping at the altar of historical inevitability they shed all moral responsibility.

This amoralism was manifest almost at the outset of Lenin's career as a Marxist. In one of his earliest criticisms of the Populist socialists who stressed ethical considerations, he wrote: "One cannot therefore deny the justice of Sombart's remark that in Marxism itself there is not a grain of ethics from beginning to end: theoretically, it subordinates 'the ethical standpoint' to the principle of causality'; practically, it reduces it to the class struggle."

Stung later on by the accusations of amoralism hurled against him by innocent victims of Communist terror, Lenin attempted to vindicate the concept of a Communist morality. He repudiates a superhuman, supernatural morality but, instead of affirming a humanist one, frankly declares: "We say that our morality is entirely subordinated to the interests of the class struggle of the proletariat. . . . For the Communist, morality consists entirely (*sic!*) of solid united discipline and conscious mass struggle against the exploiters." (*See Reading No. 14b.*)

Morality, then, consists in using any means—literally any means—which will succeed in battle. Since success depends upon following the leadership of the Communist Party, the acid touchstone of morality is any behavior which strengthens the Party. No broader norms of conduct bind Communists. This is no speculative deduction, but a summary of Communist practices. Whether employed by the state or school, whether active in mass organizations or holding positions of trust, Communists are expected to follow Lenin's instructions to Communist cells boring from within trade unions and resisting efforts to dislodge them. They are to withstand all attempts to remove them and "agree to all and every sacrifice, and even, if need be, to resort to all sorts of strategems, artifices, and illegal methods to evasion and subterfuges . . . to remain in them, and to carry on Communist work in them at all cost." (*See Reading No. 14c.*)

8. **Illusionism.** Lenin maintained that the end-in-view, the conquest of political power, was a means to the all-embracing and sanctifying goal of the classless society. But he nowhere recognized the continuity between ends and means, and that the shape of the future is moulded not by our *words* about ends but by our day-by-day *deeds*. His failure to relate his means to the Communist goal was in part due to his vagueness about the goal. One had a right to expect a clearer notion of the nature of human society for which Lenin was prepared to destroy so many lives—including his own. But one looks in vain in his writings for a clear pattern of Communist society as distinct from the transitional period which

follows the overthrow of capitalism. Here he follows
Marx's description of the achievements of the Paris
Commune emphasizing equality of wage payments and
direct election and recall of all government officials by
the workers. (*See Reading No. 13a*). Here, too, his
means defeated his professed end, for the methods by
which Lenin took power made all government officials
puppets of the Communist Party and in no way responsible to the workers. Even the initial wage equality introduced after the October Revolution was soon abolished to
spur productivity. Since work and bread were soon
denied to all opponents of the regime, the principle of
wage equality, even if not abolished, would have had
very limited application.

Insofar as Lenin's reflections on the classless society
of Communism is concerned, especially on what would
replace the state, his discussion reveals a terrifying simplicity. A communist society is a planned society in which
production is completely socialized. Individuals will work
according to their inclinations and capacities and be rewarded according to their needs. The state, consisting of
special bodies of armed men or special punitive institutions, will have disappeared. How, then, will conflicts and
disputes among men be settled in the absence of courts,
police, or other agencies of the state? If men were to
develop angelic natures under Communism there would
be no likelihood of any conflict, although there have been
rumors of conflict even in heaven as the legend of Lucifer
suggests—as well as of disobedience in the classless
Garden of Eden!

Lenin is realistic enough to admit that even under
Communism there will be "excesses," as he calls crimes
of violence. But in the absence of the state, outbreaks of
violence, which are only one species of a whole class
of conceivable conflicts and crimes, will be settled in the
same way as the crowd today settles "excesses." "This
will be done," Lenin tells us, "by the armed people itself,
as simply and as readily as any crowd of civilized people,
even in modern society, parts a pair of combatants or
does not allow a woman to be outraged." In other words,
justice will be done on the spot. The laws of the state
will thus be replaced, as James Marshall was the first to
point out, by lynch law. If a crime is committed we are
to forego the calm search for evidence, the orderly proc-

esses of arrest, indictment, conviction, and punishment —all of which require special agencies of the state—and entrust the administration of justice to the armed mob. It is not surprising, therefore, that before he is through Lenin confidently predicts that not only will the state wither away under Communism but "excesses," too, "will inevitably begin to wither away." In the end, under Communism, men may remain armed, but they will acquire angelic dispositions incapable of committing "excesses" against each other and the community.

Lenin had become so obsessed with the capture and retention of political power that the goals of socialism became not principles of control but semantic fetishes. Santayana in his *Life of Reason* defines a fanatic as a person who, having forgotten his aim, redoubles his efforts. In this sense Lenin is one of the most self-deceived fanatics of history.

— 6 —

LEON TROTSKY—FOR THE DEFENSE

It would be unfair to conclude this criticism without examining the eloquent defense of the Leninist version of Marxism made by Leon Trotsky (1879-1940). In a sense Trotsky is as much the author of that version as Lenin himself. Until the outbreak of the First World War, Trotsky was a critic of Bolshevism, particularly of Lenin's organizational theory and practice. At the same time, long before Lenin, he had developed the theory of permanent revolution according to which, despite its economic backwardness, Russia would combine her democratic revolution against semi-feudal Czarism with a socialist revolution against capitalism. (*See Reading No. 15.*) The

proletarian dictatorship thus established would be a preface to the world or, at least, a European socialist revolution. By October, 1917, Trotsky had accepted, not without misgivings, Lenin's organizational doctrine, while
Lenin had adopted Trotsky's perspective of a socialist
and world revolution, to be sparked by the Communist
seizure of power.

The versatility of his talents and the range of his
achievements—as military man, writer, orator, historian,
critic and political thinker—justify the characterization of
Leon Trotsky as the Leonardo da Vinci of Bolshevism.
For reasons of space and because his position was in
essentials indistinguishable from Lenin, we shall consider
briefly only his interpretation of history and his defense
of Communist morality.

1. Theory of History. Trotsky's defense of the
Bolshevik October revolution is expressed in many writings but nowhere with greater skill than in his monumental *History of the Russian Revolution*. It is a frankly
partisan account. Nonetheless it contains sufficient empirical evidence to make Trotsky's own leading contention
dubious. As we have already seen, both Lenin and Trotsky contended that there was nothing un-Marxist in
seizing power in a backward country because of the
peculiarly late character of Russian capitalism—which
turned illiterate peasants into "hands" of a giant industrial plant overnight—and because of the breakdown of
world capitalism as a whole. In their political activity,
they made no secret of their belief that the revolution
depended not so much on the complex of social and
economic forces but on the character of the Communist
Party and its resolution. But the more the Bolsheviks
relied upon their will and political opportunism, the more
they insisted that the October Revolution was inevitable
and that its inevitability was ultimately derivable from
the character of the existing mode of economic production. Trotsky speaks often and with mystic fervor of
"that mighty obedience to natural law which characterizes
the development of great revolutions." Yet, as his own
History of the Russian Revolution shows, the seam of
historical necessity in his analysis is woven with many
more short-and-broken threads of contingency than his
determinist account provides for.

Thus, he seems to agree with Lenin's claim, just before

the Bolsheviks carried out their *coup d'état,* that "The success of the Russian and the world revolution depends upon two or three days struggle." It would be fantastic to assert, however, that the success of that struggle was inevitable or that it was determined by the character of the mode of economic production either in the first or the last instance, whatever "the last instance" may mean. It was determined by the revolutionary leadership of Lenin and Trotsky together. Trotsky gives *malgre lui* a detailed historical proof that Lenin, whose existence and presence in Russia at the time were obviously not socially determined, played a more powerful role than any other force in bringing about the October Revolution, and further that Lenin's role could not have been performed by anyone else, including Trotsky. It is one thing to show that the downfall of Czarist Russia could hardly have been avoided since no special qualities of will, intelligence, or leadership were required to bring it about. It is altogether different to claim that the October Revolution was likewise inescapable. In history, objective social forces determine what may be and what sometimes cannot be but very rarely what must be, unless human effort of heroic dimensions also is considered as a social force. In the latter case we have the unilluminating conclusion that the totality of social forces at any moment determines the totality of social forces at the succeeding moment.

In all of his major historical writings there is observable a conflict between Trotsky's empirical findings and his political voluntarism, on the one hand, and his strenuous profession of Marxist doctrinal orthodoxy, on the other. In a subsequent volume *The Revolution Betrayed* he inquires into the causes of the failure of the Russian Revolution to achieve its original objectives. In field after field he describes situations in which the wrong alternative was taken. This is necessary for his thesis, for in the absence of possible alternatives of social action the very word "betrayal" has no meaning. For example, if the socialists at the outbreak of World War I could not have possibly opposed it, it would make no sense to tax them with the betrayal of socialism. If Stalin had no alternatives of action open to him, he could not have betrayed the Revolution. Nonetheless Trotsky offers a Marxist explanation of the betrayal. It was caused by the rise of

bureaucracy. "The leaden rump of the bureaucracy outweighed the head of the revolution." The rise of the
bureaucracy, in turn, was an inescapable consequence
of the undeveloped forces of production in the Soviet
Union. Indeed, it is an "iron necessity" that bureaucracy
will arise under such economic conditions. And with this
Trotsky pulls the rug from under his own indictment. For
according to him not only was the October Revolution
inevitable, but its "betrayal," once revolutions failed to
materialize in the West, was equally inevitable. His own
evidence, however, shows that neither the October Revolution nor its subsequent development were inevitable.

2. **Ends and Means.** After Trotsky's exile and
shortly before his assassination by one of Stalin's agents,
he undertook the difficult task of replying to the charges
of amoralism directed against the Bolsheviks by socialists
and liberals. Although Trotsky himself became a victim
of the Bolshevik terror, for which he was as responsible
as anyone else, he resolutely defends the system of
terrorism in his brochure on *Their Morals and Ours*—
including the taking and shooting of hostages, the massacre of the Kronstadt sailors after their surrender, and the
liquidations of the secret police. Without mentioning him
by name this pamphlet is also directed against John
Dewey who had headed the International Commission of
Inquiry into the truth about the Moscow Trials. The
Commission had absolved Trotsky from the charges
made against him, but on the strength of his investigation
Dewey contended that these juridical frame-ups followed
from the basic philosophy of Bolshevik-Leninism.

Trotsky's argument restates with some new illustrations
the position he had defended a generation earlier in his
Terrorism and Communism, a reply to Kautsky. (*See
Reading No. 16a.*) The argument rests on two assumptions. The first is that the only alternative to Bolshevik
morality is an absolutist, supernatural morality according
to which some acts are intrinsically right or wrong independently of time, space, human nature, and society.
Those who criticize Bolshevik violence, argues Trotsky,
must believe that *all* violence is wrong, that it is *never*
right to kill. Those who object to Bolshevik deception
must believe that it is *never* right to utter an untruth, that
the truth must always be told no matter what the consequences. These are the positions of Tolstoy and Kant. It

is easy to establish, however, that such absolutist moralities are either inconsistent or unfeasible. Thus, if one refuses under any circumstances to kill, then if we have it in our power to kill a murderer who is about to slaughter others, and if this is the *only* way his action can be prevented, then our refusal to do so makes us not only a moral accessory to the deaths of their victims but increases the number of those killed. Trotsky's defense of terrorism, therefore, is that it is morally justified because it is the only and necessary means to achieve the ends of socialism which are the highest moral ends for man.

The second assumption of Trotsky's argument is that human behavior in society is as much determined by law as the behavior of things and the social law which inexorably determines human behavior is the class struggle. What is morally permissible is ultimately derivable from the inevitable law of class struggle.

It is not difficult to show that the first assumption of Trotsky's argument is false and, in any case, incompatible with the second. The alternative to the standpoint of Bolshevik morality is not supernaturalism. One may be a naturalist, a relativist, or a humanist and reject the principles of Bolshevik morality, as John Dewey showed in a gentle but devastating comment on Trotsky's position. A humanist morality is one which recognizes a plurality of human ends. It justifies any particular action by showing that the consequences of the means used to achieve it realize more of these ends than any feasible alternative. Since ends often conflict, it is sometimes necessary to abridge one end in behalf of the cluster of other ends which are approved after reflection. Truth and kindness are both desirable ends, but few people would refuse, as Kant said he would, to tell a harmless untruth to save the life of a child from a maniacal murderer. By assuming that, if one is not an absolutist, one has no ground for condemning the Bolsheviks, Trotsky completely begs the question.

For the moral argument against Bolshevik terrorism is that their means had consequences precisely opposite to the socialist ends they professed. What were those ends? Trotsky asserts that they were "the increase of the power of man over nature and the decrease of the power of man over man." Were the means the Bolsheviks used—

dictatorship, liquidation, cultural terror—necessary to achieve the ends? The result of the use of the means seems to have been *not* the decrease of the power of man over man but only to increase the power of the Communist Party. Nor, in order to increase power of man over nature, was it necessary, as the history of other countries amply shows, to give power only to the Communist Party or to exercise that power by terrorism without limit. It is apparent that the power wielded by the Communist Party everywhere has resulted in a tremendous increase of the power of a few men over the great masses of other men. It is also true that the Communists have never persuaded a majority of any people that the rule of the Communist Party was necessary to increase man's power over nature and decrease man's power over man. They took power by force and held it by terror; they never won it by persuasion or argument.

Further, human beings recognize that not all values have equal weight in the moral economy. Socialists have always placed primary emphasis upon liberating human beings from oppression, upon decreasing the power of man over man. The increase of the power of man over nature is only one means of decreasing arbitrary human power over other men. But the incontestable facts are that the Communists have used the increase of power over nature as a means of further increasing human power of a few over the many. One need not, therefore, be a believer in supernaturalism to condemn Communist terror. One need only use his eyes intelligently and be moved by compassion for unnecessary human suffering.

Trotsky scoffs at the idea that there are any moral norms which are "obligatory for all." Such an idea is deceitful, he avers. "The norms of 'obligatory morality' are in reality filled with class, that is, antagonistic content." He consequently refuses to condemn *any* action until he knows whether it is an act performed by Communists against non-Communists or by non-Communists against Communists. This is comparable to refusing to condemn the massacre of children until it is known what the politics of their parents are. The class struggle whose highest form is civil war exacts from human beings the behavior necessary for them to carry on the struggle. What is easier than for any individual to regard his conduct no matter how abominable as one of the forms in which the necessary class struggle expresses itself? According to Trotsky's defense of terrorism, it would be either sentimentalism or hypocrisy to assert that a civil war won by massacre of children or other innocent hostages or by the methods of Hitler or Stalin is not worth fighting because it would lead not to socialism but to the kind of society which Hitler and Stalin brought into existence.

Trotsky indignantly denies that Communists believe that their end justifies the use of *any* means. Nonetheless a conclusion very similar to this follows from his position. For the second assumption of his argument in behalf of revolutionary terrorism is that "the liberating morality of the proletariat . . . deduces a rule for conduct from the laws of the development of society, thus primarily from the class struggle, this law of all laws."

Now if there is an inevitable class struggle from which a rule of conduct can be *deduced,* then that rule of conduct is not necessarily related to the ends of socialism— the increase of power over nature and decrease of power over man. For the social law of the class struggle is not guided or controlled by moral ends any more than the biological law of the struggle for existence. On the contrary, the outcome of the class struggle, according to Trotsky, necessarily determines the ends which are to be realized. Man proposes but History—whose law is the class struggle—disposes.

But from the standpoint of moral judgment, the outcome of the class struggle, like the outcome of any other struggle, determines not who is wrong but who is strong, not who has right but who has power. To recognize in the class struggle the law which justifies a rule of conduct is to make the class struggle itself the matrix of moral norms. Might not only wins the fight. Might makes right. The ends of socialism now are completely irrelevant. Trotsky himself admits that " 'lying and worse' are an inseparable part of the class struggle even in its most elementary form." In other words, there is hardly more point in condemning the forms in which the law of the class struggle expresses itself than in condemning the forms in which other laws, natural or social, express themselves. "Stalinist frame-ups," writes the man who was the victim of one of them and who had condoned them against the Mensheviks," are not a fruit of Bolshevik 'amoralism'; no, like all important events in history, they are a product of the concrete social struggle. . . ." Human responsibility is thus once more dissolved in a questionable historical necessity.

There is a certain honesty about Trotsky which distinguishes him from other Bolshevik figures in that he draws consistent conclusion from his fateful premises even when he is not always aware of the implications of the conclusions. If victory in the class struggle is the be-all and end-all of a Communist's conduct, the only moral crime is failure. This well represents the ethics of the Moscow Trials. Since the class struggle can be won only by a disciplined party it is patent "that to a Bolshevik the Party is everything," providing it is the true party which can be determined only by its success in struggle. Just as what Heaven decrees can be interpreted only by the true Church, so what the class struggle decrees can be properly interpreted only by the true Party. Norman Thomas is criticized because "his moral criteria exist outside the party," whereas to a Revolutionary Marxist "there can be no contradiction between personal morality and the interests of the Party, since the Party embodies in his consciousness the very highest tasks and aims of mankind."

Unfortunately his consciousness does not make it so! Whether it is so or not must be objectively established in terms of the consequences of the Party's activities on the ideals of socialism, not in terms of the alleged necessities of the class struggle. Trotsky, like Lenin, after ruling out as irrelevant subjective motives and intentions where the actions of others are concerned, introduces his "consciousness" of his own motives and intentions as evidence that the Party is serving mankind." "Mankind" and "humanity" in the light of the class struggle are merely abstractions. *Classes* are the social reality.

It would be a mistake, however, to assume that Trotsky is prepared to permit the working class a free choice in determining how faithfully the Communist Party embodies the highest tasks and aims of mankind. ". . . If the dictatorship of the proletariat means anything at all, then it means that the vanguard of the class is armed with resources of the state in order to repel dangers, including those emanating from the backward layers of the proletariat itself."

Who is "the vanguard of the class"? The Communist Party.

Who are "the backward layers of the proletariat"? Those who disagree with the program of the Communist Party.

The dangers against which the Communist Party is therefore justified in using the power of the state—including frame-ups, torture, "lying and worse"—encompass the danger that the Communist Party may be repudiated by those whose interests it professedly serves. Trotsky is consistent in subordinating the processes of democracy to the program of the Communist Party. "For a Marxist the question has always been: democracy for what? For which program? The framework of the program is at the same time the framework of democracy."

Although more consistent than Lenin, Trotsky lapses into a more extreme illusionism. He offers as a final summary of Communist morality the maxim: "The welfare of the revolution—that is the supreme law!" In actuality both Lenin and Trotsky made the welfare of the Communist Party the supreme law! But to most socialists of previous generations, it was not the welfare of the revolution which was the supreme law but the freedom and welfare of human beings. Their freedom and welfare were not automatically guaranteed by the march of productive forces but had to be won by means which were actually commensurate with the ends. This meant the moral obligation to be intelligent about alternatives of action and sensitive to their human costs. But the Communists were wedded to a theory of history according to which the ideals of socialism would be inevitably realized by the outcome of history's basic law, the class struggle. This belief did not paralyze their activity, particularly since they read their will into history. It made them callous and indifferent to the means they used. The result was that, although they started out to build an economy of freedom, they ended with a society which became the model of George Orwell's *Animal Farm* and *1984*.

ROSA LUXEMBURG

1. Life and Work. Rosa Luxemburg (1870-1919) was one of the most remarkable personalities in the Marxist movement. She combined fiery revolutionary zeal with keen intelligence and a sensitiveness to the whole spectrum of values in human experience. She regarded herself as an orthodox Marxist in dissociating herself from revisionist currents of thought. She was a more principled opponent of Bernstein than was Kautsky. But hers was a critical and independent orthodoxy which respected principles but did not consider persons or organizations as sacrosanct, not even the founding fathers of Marxism. A controversial but much-beloved figure in the German Social-Democratic Party, she was at times active also in the Polish and Russian socialist movements. During the First World War she was jailed in Germany because of her opposition. Her letters from prison, mainly of a non-political character, are among the small literary treasures of the century.

Rosa Luxemburg's pre-war writings consist of books and articles in which she took an extremely militant position against reformism of all varieties. She vigorously criticized socialist participation in coalition governments, composed powerful polemics against war preparations of any kind, and, without denying the necessity of parliamentary activity, passionately espoused mass action, especially the general strike, as the most effective way by which the proletariat could attain power. Uncompromisingly internationalist in her outlook, she consistently refused to substitute the ideal of national liberation for socialist liberation or even combine the two. The socialist revolution would automatically solve the cultural problems of national minorities in a liberal spirit. In contradistinction to the position Marx and Engels expressed on the Polish question, she regarded the political slogan of self-determination of peoples as a backward step. The social problem came first. National problems would disappear in the United Socialist States of Europe and then of the world.

At the same time she defended and applied in a fresh way the Marxist critique of capitalism and used its conclusions as premises for her rejection of reformism and her demand for a revolutionary strategy. Her *The Accumulation of Capital,* published on the eve of the First World War, argues that capitalism is driven by its own immanent development to expand from country to country, from one region of the world to another. This expansion requires an ever-widening market. Since the internal market is not sufficient to guarantee the continuous reinvestment and accumulation of capital, so necessary to make production profitable, capitalism must engulf and transform the non-capitalist regions of the world. It must do this even to recruit the additional labor power for its periods of boom and Marx is criticized for failure to take note of this fact in his analyses. The necessary striving to become universal breaks down because capitalism can never stabilize itself. By its very nature it needs newer and ever-fresher worlds in order to function. Since these are finite, the collapse of capitalism is declared logically necessary. The precise moment at which this logical necessity is translated into historical necessity depends upon the consciousness of the embattled workers.

When war broke out, Rosa Luxemburg denounced the "social patriotism" of Social-Democracy and called for revolutionary manifestations in *all* countries against war and the social system which bred wars. At first she hailed the Russian October Revolution. Later while in prison she wrote a penetrating, but not unsympathetic, criticism of the theory and practice of Bolshevism. Although not free from inconsistencies, her analysis turned into a grave indictment, and her fears as to how the October Revolution would develop proved uncannily prophetic of events to come.

After she was liberated by the German Revolution of 1918, she organized, together with Karl Liebknecht, the Spartacus Bund. She urged a return to the "spirit" of the Communist Manifesto and a rejection of Social-Democratic orthodoxy as a revisionism no less paralyzing than the earlier revisionism it had criticized. Rosa Luxemburg's own strategy of conquering power called for successive strike actions at factory after factory until sufficient strength had been accumulated by the masses to make resistance impossible. The Spartacus Bund, however, seems to have been more influenced by Bolshevik example than by Rosa Luxemburg's teaching. Against her advice its handful of members rose with arms against the caretaker's regime which had come to power after the Kaiser's abdication. Rosa Luxemburg, as well as Karl Liebknecht who shared her views, abided by the decision of the group. Both met a brutal death at the hands of soldiers while being taken to prison. Since her death Rosa Luxemburg's criticism of Bolshevism has had an increasingly strong impact on the socialist movement in the West, but her other writings have had a negligible influence.

2. Critique of the Russian Revolution. Although prior to the war Rosa Luxemburg had been critical of Lenin's theory of organization, in 1917 she was sympathetic to the program of the Bolsheviks which placed a socialist revolution on the order of the day. She was opposed not to their aim of winning political power but to the way they took power, the way they held power, and the way they justified themselves in doing both. She goes to some lengths to praise their courage and even to plead extenuating circumstances for their mistakes, but she insisted nonetheless that the mistakes were there and that the result was tragic and disastrous. She laid the moral responsibility for these mistakes ultimately at the door of socialists who had lacked sufficient intelligence and moral and physical courage to stop the war and achieve a socialist revolution in the democratic countries of the West. She believed, without proving it, that the logic of the October Revolution had posed a clear alternative between a revolutionary dictatorship and a counter-revolutionary restoration. Without enquiring into the extent to which one form of extremism feeds its opposite, she held that the choice was "either Kaledin [a Czarist general] or Lenin."

This kind of antithesis is always easy to manufacture— the West was to hear it often in terms of the false dichotomy—"Either Communism or Fascism"—believed *only* by Communists and Fascists, and when true made true usually by virtue of that belief. In Rosa Luxemburg's case, however, the conclusion came not so much from an analysis of the concrete scene but from a philosophy of

history according to which the initial democratic reforms
won in a revolution can be preserved only by extending
them. From this point of view a critical period of history
is like a steep incline. Only a social revolution—the
"locomotive of history"—can carry us over the incline.
That is why it must drive full steam ahead. If it falters
and stops, it must roll down to the bottom. Rosa Luxemburg uses a different metaphor to express her belief that
ordinary rules of common-sense political life cannot
apply to revolutionary periods. Democrats who imagine
that they can apply "the home-made wisdom derived
from parliamentary battles between frogs and mice to the
field of revolutionary tactics" have read history to little
purpose and should not try to make it.

Despite the tribute paid to the Bolsheviks in the preface
and conclusion of her brochure, *The Russian Revolution,*
as resolute fighters who have saved the honor of the Russian Revolution and the internationalist socialist movement, the burden of the intervening discussion weighs
heavily against them. (*See Reading No. 17.*) Rosa Luxemburg charges that Bolshevik policies contributed to the
collapse and breakdown of the Russian economy; that
their land program was demagogic and sure to generate
many stubborn and dangerous problems; that their position on the nationalist question gave aid and comfort to
counter-revolution; that their dissolution of the Constituent Assembly was a betrayal of the democratic traditions of Marxism as well as of their own agitational
slogans, now revealed as hypocritical; that their limitations on suffrage and other civil rights made "the rule of
the workers" a mockery; that by substituting the dictatorship of the Party for the proletarian dictatorship they
were really substituting terror for persuasion, thus brutal-
izing public life; that by imposing socialism by decree
they were replacing socialist idealism by opportunism;
and finally and, above all, that they were blind to the
fact that socialism without democracy is impossible.

Of all these charges there is space only to discuss the
last and most important.

3. Democracy versus Bolshevism. Rosa Luxemburg was as aware as any orthodox Marxist of the limitations of political democracy. But as distinct from most
of them she did not denounce "formal" democracy as
a fetish or speak contemptuously about not worshipping

at its altar. She opposed all "fetishes," including the fetish of socialism, and worshipped at no altars and therefore not at the altar of any party. If the democratic expression of the will of the masses seems unwise to socialists, the response should be not repression but education and a renewed appeal to their political experience.

She examines in this connection the reasons Lenin and Trotsky gave for dissolving the Constituent Assembly and declares them insufficient. Those elected to the Constituent Assembly, said the Bolsheviks, no longer represented the true state of mind of those who had elected them a few months before. How did the Bolsheviks know this? If they thought this to be true why did they not call for new elections? If the Bolsheviks really had faith in the masses, as they claim, they could rely on the mood of the masses making itself felt in their representatives. The Bolsheviks complained that the mechanisms of mass control were "cumbersome." Perhaps, but they never complained when the vote favored them.

The corrective to cumbersome procedures, urged Rosa Luxemburg, is reliance on "the living movement of the masses, their unending pressure." Of course, the forms of democracy may be inadequate to its spirit. Then it is up to the spirit to do the work of reformation, not the hangman. What she is plainly saying to the Bolsheviks is that the defects of democracy can be cured only by more and better democracy.

> To be sure every democratic institution has its limits and shortcomings, things which it doubtless shares with all other human institutions. But the remedy which Lenin and Trotsky have found, the elimination of democracy as such, is worse than the disease it is supposed to cure; for it stops up the very living source from which alone can come the correction of all the innate shortcomings of social institutions. That source is the active, untrammeled, energetic political life of the broadest masses of the people.

Lenin and Trotsky, of course, also appealed to the "democratic feelings" of the masses. But unless the mechanisms which register these feelings are specified and carefully guarded from abuses, this is just a phrase. The point is driven home in Rosa Luxemburg's criticism of the Bolshevik limitation on suffrage. Since suffrage is presumably based on "the obligation to labor," the Bolsheviks abridge it by simply depriving their opponents of the right to work. By disfranchising broad sections of society, by placing some outside the law and others outside the economic framework of society, the Bolsheviks can arbitrarily make any claim they please about the democratic feelings of the rest. But even these claims, Rosa Luxemburg goes on to say, cannot be taken seriously in their own terms. For freedom of press and association is denied to those who oppose the Soviet regime and without such freedoms "the rule of the broad mass of the people is entirely unthinkable."

The Bolsheviks felt a compulsion to broadcast professions of democracy because of their propagandistic value, and undoubtedly to interpret their practices to themselves in the best possible light. Sometimes they denied the facts of repression. When they could not plausibly do this, they justified repression as a defensive measure against a suspected aggression in the making. When this wore thin, they defended their organized terror as a retaliatory measure against excesses, real or fancied, on the other side. When the policy of repression became permanent and its pitch tightened with each successive year, they half unconsciously fell back on the techniques of semantic corruption brought to systematic fulfillment under Stalin and later satirized so savagely by Orwell. These techniques identified the normal opposites of words in order to exploit the emotive association of the positive word. Waging war became a method of waging peace; the reign of terror became the reign of freedom; the Party line, even when clearly based on a lie, became a higher truth. Rosa Luxemburg's criticism goes to the heart of the deception in her caustic comment that freedom can never be bestowed as "a special privilege" for the few. Freedom for members of one party only is no freedom at all. "Freedom is always and exclusively for the one who thinks differently."

4. **The Two Sources of Democratic Faith.** Rosa Luxemburg's profound belief in the masses was derived from two sources of very unequal value. The first was her conviction that the laws of historical development would undermine the viability of the institutions of capitalism. Freed from the incubus of the profit system the elemental impulses of the workers would be liberated and

seek new forms of expression. Their intelligence would
be schooled in the vicissitudes of the inevitable class
struggle. Ultimately they would be compelled to embrace
a humanistic world view in consonance with the social
and economic foundations of the new order now being
prepared by the old. The second source of her profound
belief in the masses stemmed from her faith in the validity of the democratic process itself. She was certain that
the actual first-hand experiences of democratic participation and discussion of ordinary men and women in their
daily living and working would broaden their imagination,
make them more reflective, and develop new, complex,
and significant needs.

From the first source there followed her belief in the
automatic breakdown of capitalism, her expectation of
the spontaneity of mass-revolt and its surging development to ever higher levels of revolutionary consciousness.
From the second there followed her insistence that there
had to be a *continuity* between democratic means and
ends, her moral indignation with the engineers and manipulators of mass consent, her awareness that to universal-
ize the pattern of the Bolshevik conquest of power, as
Lenin and Trotsky did, was to betray socialism. From the
first there breathed a revolutionary romanticism and a
mysticism inconsistent with the intelligent and rectifiable
idealism of the second. Happily, in her observations on
the Russian Revolution, Rosa Luxemburg wrote as one
inspired with an insight that went deeper than her
economic analysis, the relevance of which was being outmoded as a consequence of the growing political and
industrial strength of the workers themselves. She wrote
as one who both knew and cared about human beings
and who realized it is the *quality* of the individual experiences which social institutions make possible that is the
final determinant of their value.

The magnitude of Rosa Luxemburg's critical achievement is particularly impressive when one takes into account
the time and conditions in which she penned her reflections on the Russian Revolution, and her scrupulous desire to say everything favorable she possibly could about
the Bolsheviks, whom she exalted because of their opposition to the First World War. All the more devastating
does it read, therefore, as a judgment on Bolshevism in
its purest form.

In the end it must be admitted that Rosa Luxemburg's faith in the workers outstripped the evidence. She absolves them too easily of *their* responsibility for the support of the war and other events she considers as infamies. She saw the workers with the guilt-laden eyes of one nurtured in an easier environment. The fact that millions of Western workers, even if only a minority, have not taken to heart her criticism of the Russian Revolution and have followed Lenin and Stalin despite the fulfillment of her worst predictions ill comports with her historical image of the proletariat. Nonetheless her solemn adjurations to them about socialism and democracy are as valid today as when they were first composed.

> Socialist democracy is not something which begins only in the promised land after the foundations of socialist economy are created; it does not come as some sort of Christmas present for the worthy people who, in the interim, have loyally supported a handful of socialist dictators. Socialist democracy begins simultaneously with the beginnings of the destruction of class rule and of the construction of socialism.

— 8 —

STALIN

Upon Lenin's death early in 1924, Stalin inherited his power after a brief and intense struggle for the apostolic succession. Stalin's rule lasted almost thirty years in the course of which Russian life was completely transformed. Bolshevik theory and practice were further developed. Stalin's ruthlessness and cunning aided by Fascist barbarism and Western appeasement earned rich political dividends. The balance of world power changed in favor

of the Communist camp. Although he probably would
have welcomed the results, it is not likely that Lenin
would have personally approved all of Stalin's methods
in achieving them. Lenin's political testament to the
Communist Party advised that Stalin be dismissed as its
Secretary because he was "too rude" and too peppery a
cook even for Bolshevik stomachs.

Nonetheless, Stalin was apparently convinced that he
was a faithful disciple applying the Leninist version of
Marxism to a new historical period. A definite continuity
exists between their ideas and actions, although it would
be too much to say that Stalin was merely Lenin's heir.
Lenin's life work did not necessitate that of Stalin's, but
without it Stalin could not have succeeded in developing
the repressive features of the Bolshevik dictatorship
into the completest system of totalitarianism in world
history. These developments, both in doctrine and institutions, which already under Lenin represented departures
from the democratic traditions of Marx, carried Bolshevism so far out of the political orbit of Marxism that
a new set of categories and terms seems required to
understand what exists in the Soviet world. (*See Reading
No. 23.*)

Popular conceptions of history, however, scorn lexi-
cographical niceties. The term "Marxism" today is widely
employed to designate the Stalinist version of the Leninist
version of Marx. It is therefore necessary to indicate the
nature of Stalin's doctrinal and organizational contributions. They are neither intellectually profound nor acute.
But they are historically epoch-making.

1. **Socialism in One Country.** A key justification
offered by the Bolsheviks for seizing power in an economically backward country like Russia was based upon
the expectation of socialist revolutions in the West. This
would be a prelude to the emergence of a rationally
planned world socialist economy. When these revolutions
failed to materialize, two alternative paths were open.
One was to hold power and through the Communist International seek to organize revolutions in other countries; the second was to devote energies to building socialism in the Soviet Union while remaining in sympathetic
contact with revolutionary movements elsewhere. Lenin
and Trotsky favored the first alternative, but before he
died, Lenin, on some occasions, seemed to indicate that

the second alternative was feasible. After Lenin's death, Stalin wholeheartedly supported the second alternative. (*See Reading No. 20.*)

Strictly speaking, these two alternatives were neither exclusive nor exhaustive. But politics is often a matter of emphasis, and, politically speaking, the emphasis given one or the other spelled incompatible courses of conduct. Although Trotsky stressed world revolution, he believed that the Soviet Union should move at the same time *towards* socialism and drew up ambitious plans for industrialization. He denied that socialism could finally be established in one country alone. Stalin, on the other hand, believing that the emphasis should fall on building a socialist economy, adopted and trebled Trotsky's program of industrialization. He also carried through collectivization of agriculture *from above*. Its impact had a much greater influence on social relations and daily life than the original conquest of power.

Stalin believed that *if the Soviet Union were left to itself* it could develop a prosperous socialist economy on the basis of its own human and material resources. "What do we mean when we say that the victory of socialism in one country is *possible?*" he asks. "We mean that the proletariat having seized power in Soviet Russia can use that power for the establishment of a fully socialized society there." This is what Trotsky resolutely denied. But Stalin also made it clear that he did not believe the Soviet Union would be left to itself. Long before socialism would be built, Stalin contended, the capitalist powers of the world would be compelled by the nature of their economies to expand or die and that they would choose to expand by making war against the Soviet Union. Lenin had always believed that *sooner or later* war between the two systems was inevitable independently of how far socialism was carried in the Soviet Union. Stalin invoked his authority to prove that, although socialism could be built in the Soviet Union without revolutions elsewhere, the capitalist countries would invade and attempt to destroy the Soviet Union. He could talk in the *manner* of Trotsky, too, without adopting Trotsky's political strategy.

"What do we mean when we say that the final victory of socialism is *impossible* in one country alone, and without the victory of the revolution in other lands? We mean that unless the revolution has been victorious, if not everywhere, but at least in several countries, there can be no full safeguards against intervention or against a restoration of the bourgeois regime."

What, then, was the pragmatic difference between Trotsky's and Stalin's position? Simply this: that where the interests of a revolutionary movement in any country conflicted with the immediate interests of the Soviet Union, Stalin would sacrifice the first and Trotsky the second. Stalin's position had striking effects upon the nature of Communist parties elsewhere. They became border guards of the Soviet Union whose overriding obligation was "Defense of the Soviet Union" to which every internal activity was subordinated if necessary. Thus if a factory manufacturing equipment for the Soviet Union was threatened with a strike, the Communists would sabotage the interests of the workers, no matter how badly they were exploited, to prevent or break the strike in order not to weaken Russia. Originally organized to solve the social problems of their own country by winning political power through legal and illegal means, they became transformed into Fifth Columnists of another country. The early Marxist formula held that the workers had no fatherland except the international socialist commonwealth. The Stalinist formula now asserted that the workers' fatherland was the Soviet Union whose survival at any price, including the ruin of their own countries, took precedence over everything else.

2. The Principle of Inequality. The decision to build socialism in an economically backward country, and at double quick time, necessarily led to an emphasis upon productivity. The primitive state of technology, absence of large units of capital, desire to catch up with and surpass the capitalist countries of the West, contributed to increasing official pressure on the workers to produce more and more. The Bolsheviks, however, were able to provide only the most meager consumption goods and services to the workers and peasants since the major resources were channeled into construction goods industries. They therefore sought to supply incentives to production by introducing devices by which workers had been sweated in the early days of capitalism—speed-up systems paced by shock workers, piece work, and special bonuses to managerial personnel for keeping labor costs

low. These were strengthened by rigorous laws restricting freedom to change jobs, and legal penalties for unexcused absences and lateness. Trade unions became organs of the state, propaganda agencies exhorting the workers to increase their productivity, instead of protecting the workers against their employer—the state. Strikes became a capital offense.

The consequence was an abandonment of the general principle of equality of wage payments proudly introduced at the beginning of the Revolution. The precedent for equality of wage payment had been set by the Paris Commune which Marx and Engels had greeted as an attempt to introduce a proletarian dictatorship.

To be sure, Marx had already observed that even where wage equality existed this could not constitute absolute equality because of the variation in human needs. But socialism was to *approximate* social equality by reducing the differences in income and privileges among men. To encourage greater production, Stalin reintroduced the capitalist principle of distribution in its crudest form—men and women were to be paid strictly in accordance with what they produced. He harshly criticized those who advocated the principle of equality even as a regulative ideal. They were denounced as deviationists, objective enemies of the Soviet state. "We must abolish wage equalization," he declared in 1931. "We cannot tolerate a situation where a rolling mill hand in a steel mill earns no more than a sweeper. We cannot tolerate a situation where a locomotive driver earns only as much as a clerk." Managers, executives, state officials, and foremen were to be rewarded correspondingly more. Before long, differences in earned income in the Soviet Union exceeded differences in earned income in capitalist countries. Differences in social position were accentuated by special privileges extended by the state to a small class while the great masses admittedly suffered from chronic want of food, clothing, and shelter.

Formally, on paper, economic classes had been abolished since everybody owned everything. Actually, since distribution took place according to capitalist principles and since there was no democratic control of how social resources were to be spent, classes reappeared. Commissar and bureaucrat had much more power than did any capitalist or petty state official of old. In sober fact the workers had exchanged a system of many employers—large and small, often competing with each other, whose power was limited by independent trade unions enjoying the right to strike—for one big boss, possessing absolute power, who decreed with unquestionable finality the level of wages and prices as well as the conditions and place of work. Under Stalin, their status changed from one of relatively free workers to what was in effect a condition of forced labor.

Stalin glossed over the patent facts of economic inequality with the rhetoric of juridical equality. Since private ownership no longer exists, no citizen can own anything or exploit anyone: in this respect, the head of a state trust and his servant are equal. An effective comment on the way in which juridical fiction in Soviet society concealed the fact of class difference was made by Leon Trotsky. It holds true for every collectivist society in which democracy is absent, including the period in Soviet history when Lenin and Trotsky were the ruling despots.

> If a ship is declared collective property, but the passengers continue to be divided into first, second, and third class, it is clear that for the third class passengers differences in the conditions of life will have infinitely more importance than juridical change in proprietorship. The first class passengers will, on the other hand, propound, together with their coffee and cigars, the thought that collective ownership is everything and a comfortable cabin nothing at all.

3. The Blossoming of the State.   From the time of the new Stalin constitution in 1936, Stalin openly proclaimed the Soviet Union a classless society, with a complete socialist economy. A few years later he even declared it was moving towards communism. Why, then, was the state not withering away as it was supposed to do in accordance with classical Marxist theory? After all, Stalin himself proudly cited the fact that 99.4% of all who voted supported the government. There was no class enemy within, and the vestiges of capitalism could hardly exist in a generation born under the Bolshevik dictatorship. Did not, then, the existence of an all-powerful state mark the abandonment of Marxism?

Stalin addressed himself specifically to this problem

at the 18th Congress of the Communist Party of the
Soviet Union. (*See Reading No. 21.*) His answer is that
Marx, Engels, and Lenin had discussed the question of
the state "only from the angle of the internal development
of the country." They had failed to consider it in the
light of the situation created when socialism is victorious
only in one country. In the new situation the state is
required to become stronger not weaker, because of the
dangers arising from "capitalist encirclement." Even if
communism were introduced in one country the state
must and will exist. Only when "capitalist encirclement"
is replaced by "socialist encirclement" will the state begin
to wither away.

The term "encirclement" is another elastic term in the
Bolshevik vocabulary whose meaning shifts with time and
purpose. At first Stalin defined it geographically. But
after World War II, when the Soviet Union had become
the strongest power on the Eurasian continents—her
strongest enemies crushed, her armies astride Germany
and Austria, her borders extended farther than at any
time in the Russian past, and beyond those borders her
power recognized as supreme in a cordon of buffer
satellite states—Stalin still maintained that capitalist "encirclement" was a fact. But it was no longer a geographical but a political fact. It really meant that only in a
communist world dominated by the Soviet Union would
the encirclement disappear and the state begin to wither.

Aside from the semantic stratagem with the term
"encirclement," there are several difficulties in the Stalinist revision of Marxist theory. The first difficulty is that
Stalin's defense did not explain the strengthening, instead
of the withering away, of the state in the *internal life* of
the Soviet Union and in every area of that life from the
factory to the family, from the collective farm to the art
studio. Defense against encirclement and encroachments
from without at most justified a large army, which is not
incompatible with an internal democratic regime. But it
left unexplained terroristic measures of internal repression whose pervasiveness and intensity could be gauged
by continuous purges and a concentration-camp population estimated by Dallin and Nicolaevsky as amounting
in some years to fifteen millions of people.

Another difficulty is created by Stalin's claim that the
Soviet Union is already a socialist society and his admis-

sion that socialism can be maintained only where there exists "a higher productivity of labor than in the capitalist system of economy." For the indisputable fact was, and is, that Soviet labor exhibits lesser, not higher, productivity of labor than in capitalist countries. If socialism does not exist in the Soviet Union, then the existence of a powerful state is no problem. For in that case the state is exercising a dictatorship over a class, and since capitalists and kulaks have been liquidated, that oppressed class must be the working class or some large portion of it. This Stalin cannot admit. He must therefore assert that socialism exists, despite the absence of conditions which are its acknowledged presuppositions, and attribute the existence of the state and its monstrous power in the internal life of the country exclusively to the necessity of defending socialism against capitalist encirclement.

The third difficulty in Stalin's explanation is that it failed to explain the concomitant variation between the growth of Soviet power vis-à-vis the rest of the world and the growth of the repressive features in the internal regime. Even on Stalin's explanation one would expect the internal regime of repression to decrease in intensity. But it increased. In Lenin's time, when the Soviet Union was extremely weak and foreign armies were still on its soil, conditions were far less oppressive. Some criticism was permitted within the Communist Party; and outside it considerable cultural freedom flourished in the arts and sciences. All this rapidly disappeared with the emergence of the Soviet Union as a world power. Instead of a process of decreasing coercion, the pattern was one of increasing coercion. This was not merely a correction of the utopian elements in Marxism and Leninism, which envisaged a disappearance of the state. It represented a transformation of the whole concept of a socialist society into one of an industrialized police state, an industrialized serfdom in which workers are tied to their factories with no power to determine the conditions of work, the rewards of work, or the social distribution of the products of their work. The socialist dream of equality and freedom had been transformed into a nightmare of inequality and enslavement.

4. **From Dialectical Materialism to Dialectical Terrorism.** As we have seen, Marxism in Western Europe never regarded the basic world outlook of Marx and

Engels as an integral part of its social and political doctrines. Plekhanov, and especially Lenin, revived Engels'
views on the nature of nature in order to combat developments in modern philosophy which presumably affected the prospects of achieving a socialist society.
Under Stalin the doctrines of dialectical materialism became the official state philosophy and provided the justifying premises for the total politicalization of all culture
including the sciences.

Dialectical materialism teaches that the world is a
developing system of material forces which exist independently of all consciousness, human or divine. These
forces are governed by certain basic laws which explain
the connections of things, their opposition, and their evolution from phase to phase, level to level. "Contradiction"
is an objective feature of nature and history which continually sparks the process of development. At critical
points in the process qualitative new changes emerge.
Applied to the realm of social life these principles give
us historical materialism which "proves" that capitalism
is doomed and communism inevitable.

To the extent that the doctrine is intelligible, it is
logically compatible with any empirical belief whatsoever. But it is the political use to which this doctrine was
put which concerns us. Lenin had already asserted that
all dialectical materialists must, if consistent, be communists and all communists dialectical materialists. Under
Stalin it was alleged that none but dialectical materialists
could have an adequate understanding of the methods
and achievements of science, natural or social. To this
was added the claim that none but members of the Communist Party—indeed, none but those who had the
correct *political* line in that Party, i.e., the line of the
Central Committee—could have an adequate understanding of dialectical materialism. From these propositions
it followed that only the Central Committee of the Communist Party could have a correct understanding of the
world of nature, society, and man. Although not claiming absolute infallibility, the Central Committee asserted
its superior intellectual authority to lay down what was
true or false, valid or invalid, in every discipline of
knowledge—art, astronomy, biology, chemistry, economics, history, literature, music, physics, and, of course,
philosophy. (*See Readings Nos. 22-22d.*) Under Stalin it

issued decrees controlling the work of scholars in these subjects, sometimes prescribing the details of what was to be believed and disbelieved. This was enforced by purges and the familiar instruments of coercion. The arts and sciences became matters for the police. Lenin's doctrine of *Partinost* was erected into an unchallengeable dogma. "Marxism-Leninism shatters into bits the cosmopolitan fictions concerning supra-class, non-national, 'universal' science and definitely proves that science, like all culture in modern society, is national in form and class in content." "Objectivism" was denounced as a heresy dangerous to the security of the state.

The scope and intensity of the controls of the Communist Party varied from time to time. Since there actually was not the slightest logical connection between the principles of dialectical materialism as formulated and the decisions made in their name, the causes for the variations in control and changes of line must be sought not in doctrine but in other things. Sometimes Stalin's ear—as in music—was the decisive factor. In the main, however, political considerations were determining. In one of the writings which appeared under Stalin's name, he seems to exempt the laws of linguistics, as well as of formal logic, from the influence of *Partinost* in order to prepare the way for acceptance of a universal language when communism becomes universal. But at no time has genuine independence been extended to Soviet scholars and scientists to follow the lead of evidence and the logic of analysis. The iron chain of control slackens and tightens but has never been cast off.

5. Nationalism.   Under Lenin the pattern of Communist strategy and tactics in the struggle for political power was Russianized. Under Stalin the entire content of Soviet politics and culture was Russianized. Traditional internationalism, wedded to ideals of excellence rather than to pride in priority, to human and universal values rather than to nationalistic and parochial cults, was stigmatized as the aspiration of rootless and cosmopolitan groups hostile to the Soviet state and therefore to socialism. Russian history was rewritten to glorify the persons and eras of Ivan the Terrible, and Peter the First. The generals of the Czarist armies who had been the mainstay of European reaction in the nineteenth century were described in glowing terms as if they were the precursors

of the general staff of the Red Army. The history of
Czarist aggression was pictured as a process of extending
a progressive culture to people under reactionary native
leadership. Even Engels was rebuked for suggesting that
Czarist Russia was a highly backward country politically
and culturally in the nineteenth century. A hunt began
for Russian "firsts" in inventions and science and was
carried to the most comical lengths. The notion of the
Pan-Slavists that Russia had a special mission to convert
and transform the world was revived in a new idiom and
with a greater fanaticism.

The boast of the Soviet Union has always been that
it is a multinational state in which national antagonisms
have all been resolved, and different peoples work co-
operatively together for a common goal in peace and
equality. Stalin took credit for formulating the Soviet
nationalities policy. But neither his formulations nor his
treatment of minority cultures can be reconciled with the
declared Soviet policy. The very claim that "Soviet culture is national in form and socialist in content" already
indicates that the national element in culture has only a
formal and extrinsic place. The form of a free culture
develops integrally with its content. To insist in advance
that a culture *must* be socialist in *content* means to impose norms and directions on the cultural life of a people
—its art, song, folklore, religion, and literature—instead
of leaving them to the spontaneous expression of its
carriers. In effect freedom of minority cultures in the
Soviet Union has meant little more than freedom to
praise Stalin in all languages except Hebrew.

The history of minority cultures in the Soviet Union
has been a history of continuous repression of their cultural traditions as "nationalistic" deviations. Entire
cultural and national groups, like the Volga Germans, the
Kalmucks, and the inhabitants of the Crimean and Che-
chen-Ingush Autonomous Republics, have been liquidated
and the others curbed by Moscow. Jewish cultural institutions, including a once flourishing press, theater, and
scholarly centers, have been completely abolished. It is
obvious that where the right to differ is absent, there
can be neither ethnic nor cultural freedom.

Formally the Soviet Union is a federation of different
socialist republics with theoretical right to secession. But
this right is as academic as all the other civil rights

enumerated in the Stalin Constitution. The leaders of all the constituent Soviet republics, whether of Party or government, are appointed or removed by the Kremlin. The word of the Kremlin on any subject is law in every Soviet republic down to the last comma. The only concession the Kremlin has made to national sentiment is to permit its decrees to be translated into the national languages—usually to have them better understood.

6. The Theory of Social-Fascism.   One of Stalin's important additions to the heritage of Lenin was his doctrine of social-fascism. It played an important role in splitting the working-class movement in the West and contributed heavily to the triumph of Fascism in Germany and Spain. Once "socialism in one country" had been proclaimed as the primary goal of the Soviet Union, it was of the first importance to enlist the workers of the West as its defenders against any possible intervention from without. Communist parties abroad, therefore, were ordered to concentrate their energies in achieving hegemony over the working class and to coordinate their political activities with the foreign policy needs of the Soviet Union. To do this successfully the influence of the Social-Democratic organizations had to be destroyed —all the more so because the latter sometimes participated in Western coalition governments. Despite the fact that the Social-Democratic parties were working-class parties and despite the fact that the rising Fascist movement was a deadly threat to *all* working-class parties, Stalin declared that the Social-Democrats "were the moderate wing of fascism. These organizations [Fascist and Social-Democratic] do not negate but supplement each other. They are not antipodes: they are twins."

At the very time that Hitler was looming on the horizon of Western Europe this theory became the official doctrine of all Communist parties. Stalin underestimated the likelihood of Hitler's coming to power and apparently took the calculated risk that if he did achieve power he would lead Germany to a war of *revanche* against France and her allies—a war which the Soviet Union would sit out. Under the aegis of the theory of social-fascism, a terrific campaign was unloosed against the Social-Democratic Party in Germany and elsewhere which made impossible any genuine united front activity against the growing danger of Fascism. On several crucial occasions, e.g., in the referendum initiated by the Nazis against the Socialist government of Prussia and in the Berlin subway strike, the Communists openly cooperated with the Nazis. All this contributed strongly to Hitler's triumph. Even after Hitler was in power the main enemy in Communist eyes was not the Nazis or the capitalist order but the Social-Democrats. The heroic resistance of the Austrian Socialists against the clerical Fascism of Dollfuss brought no turn. The line was the same in every country. Even in New York a socialist protest meeting against the repressions of the Dollfuss regime held in Madison Square Garden was violently broken up by the Communists. Not until it became clear that Hitler was contemplating an attack on the Soviet Union did Stalin change course, abandon the theory of social-fascism, and launch the slogans for a Popular Front at the Seventh Congress of the Communist International. At the same time, as a form of insurance, Stalin made secret overtures to the Hitler regime for a possible rapprochement. After the Munich Pact, from which the Soviet Union was excluded, these overtures brought fruit in the Stalin-Hitler Pact of 1939. This prefaced the Second World War in which until June 22, 1941, when Hitler invaded Russia, Stalin, although technically a neutral, actively aided Nazi Germany with moral and material support and bitterly denounced the democratic Western powers as warmongering imperialists responsible for the conflict.

After the Second World War, Stalin used the Red Army to set up Communist satellite states in Central Europe in which all genuinely socialist parties were ruthlessly destroyed.

7. The Triumph of Stalinism. As we have seen, implicit in some of Lenin's theories and practices, although he appeared unconscious of it, is a conception of a totalitarian society whose executive power is vested in a small number of individuals, in effect responsible to no one but themselves and in whose hands is centered an absolute monopoly of all means of production, education, and coercion. During the long years of his reign, Stalin brought the elements to explicit expression, destroying at the same time certain other features of Leninism which might have led to a less undemocratic fruition.

Even during Lenin's life, it was apparent that no legal

political opposition on the part of any non-socialist group would be tolerated. By the time Lenin died, he had, in essence, outlawed all other socialist parties. Since by definition only the Communist Party could properly grasp and defend the true interests of the working class, the programs of all other working-class parties must lead to disaster. In consequence they were all "objectively" counter-revolutionary. Nonetheless, at certain times some differences of opinion were permitted within the Communist Party itself. Although its actual organization was never democratic, since it was controlled from above, freedom of debate and inter-party discussion were not unusual even in periods of crisis. Once decisions were taken (almost always Lenin's), there were no reprisals against the persons of the participants or their families. Nor were their careers ended if they were on the losing side of an argument. Inasmuch as the separation between the Party and Soviet was a legal fiction, the only avenue through which any differences of opinion in the Soviet Union could be aired was the Communist Party.

After Stalin consolidated his power this avenue was closed. Differences were settled no longer by discussion but by fiat, followed by recantations, purges, public-show trials (in which defendants vied with each other in self-debasement), deportation to concentration camps, and executions. All of Lenin's surviving lieutenants, save Stalin, were pictured as spies, wreckers, and schemers of capitalist restoration from the very beginning of the October Revolution.[1] All this was accompanied by organized campaigns, unparalleled even under Czarism, of the most fulsome flattery of Stalin. He was personally credited with revolutionary advances in all the arts and sciences. On holiday occasions he was endowed with divine attributes of omniscience and foresight. By the time Stalin died the Soviet Union had become transformed into a full-scale totalitarian state and the model for all its satellite countries.

8. **Stalin's Achievements.** For good or for ill, under Stalin's leadership the Soviet Union reached the first rank of the world powers. From being one of the most

---

[1] *Cf.* the Report of the Commission of Inquiry, headed by John Dewey, the American philosopher, on the Moscow Trials: *Not Guilty* (New York, 1938).

backward countries in the world, the Soviet Union became one of the most highly industrialized. Although agricultural productivity per capita is not much higher than it was in pre-Revolutionary days, it is more reliable. Poor harvests no longer give rise to famine. Great strides have been made in wiping out illiteracy. Educational facilities have been enormously developed and, where questions of political reliability and social origins do not enter, careers are open to talents. Women are treated as equals of men even in respect to the most backbreaking and onerous work in mines and factories. Except for citizens who run afoul of the secret police because of their criticism of the regime, their failure to perform the tasks set for them, their social origins or their family associations with those proscribed under these categories, all have an opportunity to work. They are free to criticize themselves and each other for not doing enough work. But they are not free to criticize the government.

Under Stalin not only did the Soviet Union grow economically but geographically. Impressive explorations have been undertaken in the Arctic and new lands have been settled with captive peoples as well as native elements uprooted from their local regions. In area and population the Soviet Union has increased beyond any point attained in the past. It has the largest military force on earth. It no longer need fear armed intervention from without. The entire non-Communist world now lives in fear of it.

For these achievements the Soviet peoples have paid a price in blood and tears and loss of freedom immeasurably greater than that paid by any other nation for its modernization.

Stalin's accomplishments as a thinker have been much more modest even if no questions are raised about the authenticity of the writings which have appeared under his name. Although the narrowest political motivations explain his revision of traditional Marxism, he has, to some extent, corrected the Utopianism of Marx's ideas concerning the state, the existence of a classless society, and the principles of socialist distribution. In each case, however, his revisions go beyond the moderate realism required to bring the democratic socialist ideas of Marx into consonance with the facts of experience.

At the time Stalin died it would hardly be an exaggeration to say that Marx's classless society was being more nearly achieved under capitalism than in the Soviet Union. Conversely, the inequalities and exploitation associated with early capitalist society mark contemporary Soviet society much more than they do the mixed economies of the West.

— 9 —

MARXISM TODAY

Whether the Soviet Union should be called a Marxist state and the Communist movement a Marxist movement depends upon how we define and interpret the word "Marxism." In social and political affairs the use of words is not an arbitrary matter, for some words are charged with penumbral emotive associations. As such they play a powerful role in human life. People have died for "Socialism" or "Freedom" who would not have died for the specific things designated by the terms. This is particularly true with respect to the Soviet Union and the Communist movement. Despite their totalitarian character, by labeling themselves "Marxist" they still rally to their standard many for whom the term "Marxist" suggests a democratic movement everywhere embattled in behalf of the exploited and oppressed.

Historically it is not an unusual phenomenon for a term to refer to a group whose members may differ more significantly with each other than with those outside the group. The differences among those called "Christians" approximate the differences among those called "Marxists." Tolstoy and Loyola regarded themselves as Christians. Yet Tolstoy shared more in common with Gandhi, the non-Christian, than with Loyola and many other

Christians. Similarly, the differences in aspiration, feeling, and democratic commitment which separate Marx, Engels, Kautsky, Plekhanov, Bernstein, Jaurès, and Luxemburg from Lenin and Stalin seem incomparably greater than the difference between the regimes of the latter and those of Hitler, Mussolini, and Franco.

The kinship between Marxism and present-day Communism is not to be found on the plane of social philosophy but rather on the plane of historical doctrine. And here, as we have seen, a most paradoxical and ironical relationship exists. For despite their invocations of Marxism, the Communists have decisively refuted by their very actions the orthodox Marxist theory of social development and the more comprehensive theory of historical materialism of which it is a part.

If the analysis is valid, then, independently of the question of whether the so-called scientific socialism of Marx and Engels is sound, this socialism does not guide, and never has guided, Communist action. The Communists are neither historical nor economic determinists. Marxism in the Soviet Union functions strictly in the way Marx defined an ideology, i.e., as a "false consciousness" which masks from the protagonists themselves the causes, ground, and motives of action.

The actual guiding doctrine of the Communist regime, as distinct from its official ideology of Marxism, is a kind of latter-day Utopianism, a social engineering whose goals recognize no limits except physical and biological impossibility and whose means are improvised in an opportunistic spirit. The goals are fixed—a world society, hierarchically organized, planned throughout, with power centered in the Kremlin—pursued with unrelenting fanaticism and never tested by the consequences of the means employed to achieve them. Prediction of Communist political behavior is much more likely to be accurate if it is based on the Communist theory, strategy, and tactics of world domination. Those who believe that the Communist slogan of "peaceful coexistence" is anything more than a device to lull the democratic world into a false security while the Soviet Union and its satellites gather strength for the final kill will probably live long enough to recognize their error.

The very nature of the social system of the Soviet Union defies analysis in terms of the concepts of classical capitalism and socialism. To a considerable degree this is also true of the social systems of Great Britain and the United States. Nonetheless, to the extent that the economy of a culture can be distinguished from the political forms under which it functions, then, since the instruments of production are not owned by private individuals but by the collectivity, the economy of the Soviet Union may legitimately be called socialist *from the standpoint of the orthodox Marxist classification of cultures*. Just as *the* problem of evil exists only for those who accept God's governance of the world, so the problem of the socialist character of the Soviet economy exists only for orthodox Marxists. For others the economy can be labeled *totalitarian* to indicate that the distinctions between economy, culture, and politics no longer exist in this kind of society. To the extent that they do, the "key" or "basic" factor is no longer the economic organization of society, but its political character.

Although the existence of the Soviet Union refutes the Marxian theory of historical materialism—since the basic economic changes were achieved through political action—it may be argued in a not recondite sense that the humanistic aspect of Marx's social philosophy has been vindicated by the grim facts of the Soviet experience. In declaring it impossible to build a socialist economy where the objective conditions were absent Marx was mistaken. But his conception of man assumed that there were certain basic human needs and moral values which would guide political action in a civilized society, which would limit what human beings would be prepared to do to other human beings and what they would tolerate at the hands of each other. That men cannot build a socialist economy in a backward country except at a morally prohibitive cost—morally prohibitive to man as Marx conceived him to be in the nineteenth century—is the sense of his socialist humanism. If we are completely indifferent to questions of human cost and suffering, only physical and biological necessities limit our action. We can make even a desert bloom into a garden if we are prepared to fertilize it with human corpses and water it with rivers of blood.

Lenin, Stalin, and their followers have helped to destroy the traditional historical determinism which set too narrow limits on what human will and action can achieve. But they therefore have shown, as in different ways have all forms of twentieth-century totalitarianism, that political ideals and institutions have an independent role, and sometimes a *primary* role, in the influences which determine social life. The history of Marxism has brought home to reflective men everywhere the centrality of moral choice and responsibility in historical affairs generally.

This does not mean that everything in Marxism must be abandoned, any more than, because Darwin's views about the mechanisms of evolution have been superseded, his basic insights must be abandoned. It does mean that there is no longer any justification for embracing Marxism as a special school of thought or doctrine. Whatever Marx's valid contributions, they can be readily incorporated in contemporary scientific study of man and society.

Socialism as a philosophy is more inclusive than the theories of Marx and Marxism. These were a set of doctrines about the conditions under which and the means by which socialism was to be introduced. Having abandoned many of these doctrines in the light of their consequences, socialism today as a current of thought claims to represent a fusion of the ideals of modern democracy and modern scientific intelligence.

All socialist movements today which clearly differentiate their orientation from that of Communist and other forms of totalitarianism consider themselves basically ethical in character. (*See Reading No. 24.*) They believe that, although "the individual" and "the social" cannot be separated, human personality takes precedence over the accumulation of material goods and values; that all social institutions including the economic ones should be judged by their effects on the workaday lives of persons; that all proposals for social change should be justified by their fruits in contributing to the individual growth and to the enrichment of the quality of personal experience here and now. They believe that opportunities should be open to talents irrespective of differences in race, color, sex, or religion; that no one has a moral right to social goods and services, once he has developed beyond the age of dependence, who makes no contribution to society or, more simply, that no ablebodied person should live off

the labor of other people; that labor itself should be
humanized not only in the obvious sense of making
conditions of labor less onerous but in the sense of
making it, where possible, a means of creative expression and, where not, a preface to a leisure in which the
best in thought and art and recreation may be enjoyed.
They believe in the importance of democratic participation and ultimate democratic control of social institutions on all levels in order to insure and strengthen
political, intellectual, and cultural freedom. They believe
that the community must manifest an *equality of concern* for all persons to develop their individual differences, a concern expressed in institutional provisions
for equality of treatment. They interpret equality of
treatment not to mean identical prescriptions of goods
and services for all any more than equality of medical
treatment means to them identical prescriptions of
drugs for all. The principle which John Dewey enun-
ciated for education they seem to have taken as a guide
to everything else. "What the best and wisest parent
wants for his own child, that must the community want
for all its children."

It is in the light of these ideals that democratic socialist movements advocate planned programs for full
employment, adequate housing, social security, and
other measures of public welfare. By and large, they
no longer seem to regard any particular form of property as essential to the achievement of their purpose.
Their most authoritative spokesmen make the claim that
all they require of any form of property is that it
permit the liberation of human energies without making
the quality of human life dependent upon arbitrary
decisions. That is why belief in the indispensability of
democracy is affirmed as the primary commitment of
all socialists. And that is why in the present juncture
of world history *socialists no longer regard the key issue
to be the mode of economic production but the mode of
political decision*.

The liberation of nuclear energy and other technological discoveries may solve the problem of poverty under
any political system. But they cannot solve the problems
of keeping society free. This, democratic socialists tell
us, is the unending task to which modern socialism
devotes itself.

It would be both unjust and untrue to assert that the aims of socialism so conceived and so expressed are the concern only of those who call themselves "Socialists." Therefore, socialism as a *political* party or movement in a democracy can distinguish itself from other democratic parties only by the *specific* program it proposes to meet *specific* problems. This means that the differences among them is one of degree, not of kind.

Class struggles will continue, but so long as they are resolved by the democratic process, democratic socialists acknowledge that they cannot literally become class wars. The only class "war" which they are prepared unqualifiedly to wage is the defense of democracy against the enemies of freedom.

Democratic socialists deny that this viewpoint means "the bankruptcy" of the socialist movement. They say, on the contrary, that it represents the diffusion and triumph of their ideas. In their eyes, the embarrassments which flow from the successes of their movement are experienced in two ways. First, a clear-cut, comprehensive program no longer separates them from their erstwhile opponents. They are still in the vanguard of movements of social reform, but it is hard for them to distinguish where the socialist vanguard ends and the main body of non-socialist public opinion begins. The second embarrassment arises from the fact that the old slogans and formulations are reiterated in situations which demand new ones. The immediate reforms that were appended to the *Communist Manifesto* as an agenda for socialist action were largely outmoded in the lifetime of its authors. Each generation of intelligent socialists has been compelled to set up a schedule of new measures for adoption based upon a common consensus of acceptance of the old. At any definite moment, a glance backward in every country where political freedom has been preserved, even where capitalist forms have been retained, will reveal the headway made by the ideas and ideals of democratic socialism. Democratic socialists assert, perhaps with some justification, that they have inspired measures of reform even among the groups who are still terrified of the name "socialism." Today whether it is a proposal for labor co-determination in industry or for an annual guaranteed wage, they claim it to be traceable to the socialist principle that whatever form property takes its use must be responsibly controlled by those whom its power affects.

Democratic socialists insist that, once we peel away the rhetoric, it can be more truly said now than in the past, "We are all socialists now." Stripped of slogans and catchwords, the differences among democratic parties are not reducible to the question of *either* socialism *or* capitalism but of *more* or *less*. The program of the recently revived Socialist International is thoroughly imbued with this spirit.

By a strange doctrinal shift the orthodox Marxist theory of historical materialism seems to have found converts among a small but highly articulate academic group of opponents of socialism. They confidently predict that a planned socialist economy, or any kind of planned economy, must result in the loss of democracy and the rise of totalitarianism. In this view, the mode of economic production, at least in a socialist society, uniquely determines the political system of society. Political action is presumably capable of affecting the operation of a free market economy, but political action in a planned economy is ruled out except as a whip to enforce the grim decrees of planning boards. Nonetheless, the prediction that the growth in responsible economic control and planning is certain to lead to the erosion of political freedom is dubious on logical as well as historical grounds. Logically, it overlooks the plural forms of political control which are compatible with any given economic system. Historically, it does not give sufficient weight to the fact that in countries where planning goes hand in hand with dictatorship, democracy was destroyed *before* a planned economy was introduced and not in consequence of its introduction.

To some it may appear that all the historical content of the traditional socialist movement has been dissolved in the formal abstractions of democracy. From the standpoint of the democratic socialist movement this would be a profound error, for such a charge identifies democracy merely with the mechanisms of registering consent. But when democratic socialists speak of "democracy" today they refer to much more than electoral procedures. They believe that it embraces entire sets of institutional practices in social, ethnic, legal and educational life, in addition to a functioning Bill of Rights for the defense of minorities. The term "democracy" has in consequence acquired in their writings a connotation broader, richer, and more complex than it has ever had in the past. It designates not so much an electoral procedure but a way of life. In former centuries the conception of "democracy as a way of life" would have been unintelligible. It is still vague today. But its implications in any concrete context are sufficiently clear to suggest a direction if not a specific program of activity. Democratic socialists assert that there is no valid socialist claim which is excluded from the conception of democracy as a way of life.

Have democratic socialists substituted one form of Utopianism for another? Have they abandoned their nineteenth-century dogmas of inevitability, which at least had the virtue of concreteness, for vacuous abstractions about democracy, for the glorification of unrealizable ideals? It must be admitted that democratic institutions in practice have fallen far short of the democratic ideal. Nonetheless with all their imperfections they have proved to be a more viable medium for social reconstruction than most Marxists in the past have assumed. The agitator's question: "Can the worker 'eat' democracy?" has been emphatically answered by the worker's own experience. That experience has shown that, under a government based on the principle of individual liberty, the worker has not only retained and extended his freedoms but that he "eats" far better than in any society in which a dictatorship rules, especially where a dictatorship rules in his name. His experience has also shown that the workers have a stronger vested interest in democracy than has management. In a dictatorship, free trade-unionism is impossible, whereas management can always come to terms with the holders of power. Even the wretched securities promised by the totalitarian states to the workers are dependent upon bureaucratic caprice and are forfeited by any show of critical independence. In such states where workers are denied the freedoms they possess in a democratic society, security becomes slavery; vocation, forced labor; privacy, concealment; the family, a hutch for breeding; the school, an outpost of the state; social intelligence, a technique of rationalization; art and literacy, weapons to impose conformity; the person, a subject. This is true independently of the forms of property relationship—and independently of whether they are called socialist or capitalist or feudal or bureaucratic.

For all these reasons socialists conclude that what remains perennially valid in the ambiguous legacy of Marxism is the dedication to scientific spirit and the democratic faith. This is denied by those who, accepting capitalism as a social philosophy, insist that all forms of socialism sooner or later must lead to the abridgment of freedom. To this, socialists reply that such a view is doctrinaire and contributes to strengthening the forces of totalitarianism opposed not only to American democracy but to free society everywhere.

The last word in this continuing debate has not been spoken. Historical events of the new scientific age are sure to challenge the solutions which appeared adequate for earlier practical and theoretical problems. Each reader must therefore interpret the legacy of Marx and the Marxists for himself. Whether he rejects it, accepts it or modifies it, his decision cannot be wise unless it is informed. The sole aim of this study has been to aid him in making a wise decision.

Part II

SELECTED READINGS

— Reading No. 1 —

MARX AND ENGELS: THE COMMUNIST MANIFESTO[1]

Both friend and foe regard the Communist Manifesto
*(1848) as one of the most effective and influential politi-
cal pamphlets ever written. Its context, style, and prophetic
passion represent Marx at his best as thinker, writer, and
man of action.*

⤸   ⤸   ⤸

A spectre is haunting Europe—the spectre of Communism. All the Powers of old Europe have entered into
a holy alliance to exorcise this spectre: Pope and Czar,
Metternich and Guizot, French Radicals and German
police-spies.

Where is the party in opposition that has not been de-
cried as Communistic by its opponents in power? Where
the Opposition that has not hurled back the branding re-
proach of Communism, against the more advanced opposition parties, as well as against its reactionary adver-
saries?

Two things result from this fact.

I. Communism is already acknowledged by all European Powers to be itself a Power.

II. It is high time that Communists should openly, in
the face of the whole world, publish their views, their
aims, their tendencies, and meet this nursery tale of the
Spectre of Communism with a Manifesto of the party
itself. . . .

[1] Translated by Samuel Moore and revised by Frederich
Engels.

I

BOURGEOIS AND PROLETARIANS

The history of all hitherto existing society is the history of class struggles.

Freeman and slave, patrician and plebeian, lord and serf, guild-master and journeyman, in a word, oppressor and oppressed, stood in constant opposition to one another, carried on an uninterrupted, now hidden, now open fight, a fight that each time ended, either in a revolutionary reconstitution of society at large, or in the common ruin of the contending classes.

In the earlier epochs of history, we find almost everywhere a complicated arrangement of society into various orders, a manifold gradation of social rank. In ancient Rome we have patricians, knights, plebeians, slaves; in the Middle Ages, feudal lords, vassals, guild-masters, journeymen, apprentices, serfs; in almost all of these classes, again, subordinate gradations.

The modern bourgeois society that has sprouted from the ruins of feudal society has not done away with class antagonisms. It has but established new classes, new conditions of oppression, new forms of struggle in place of the old ones.

Our epoch, the epoch of the bourgeoisie, possesses, however, this distinctive feature: it has simplified the class antagonisms. Society as a whole is more and more splitting up into two great hostile camps, into two great classes directly facing each other: Bourgeoisie and Proletariat. . . .

The bourgeoisie, historically, has played a most revolutionary part.

The bourgeoisie, wherever it has got the upper hand, has put an end to all feudal, patriarchal, idyllic relations. It has pitilessly torn asunder the motley feudal ties that bound man to his "natural superiors," and has left remaining no other nexus between man and man than naked self-interest, than callous "cash payment." It has drowned the most heavenly ecstasies of religious fervour, of chivalrous enthusiasm, of philistine sentimentalism, in the icy water of egotistical calculation. It has resolved personal worth into exchange value, and in place of the numberless indefeasible chartered freedoms, has set up that single, unconscionable freedom—Free Trade. In one word, for exploitation, veiled by religious and political illusions, it has substituted naked, shameless, direct, brutal exploitation.

The bourgeoisie has stripped of its halo every occupation hitherto honoured and looked up to with reverent awe. It has converted the physician, the lawyer, the priest, the poet, the man of science, into its paid wage-labourers.

The bourgeoisie has torn away from the family its sentimental veil, and has reduced the family relation to a mere money relation.

The bourgeoisie . . . has been the first to show what man's activity can bring about. It has accomplished wonders far surpassing Egyptian pyramids, Roman aqueducts, and Gothic cathedrals; it has conducted expeditions that put in the shade all former Exoduses of nations and crusades.

The bourgeosie cannot exist without constantly revolutionising the instruments of production, and thereby the relations of productions, and with them the whole relations of society. . . .

The need of a constantly expanding market for its products chases the bourgeoisie over the whole surface of the globe. It must nestle everywhere, settle everywhere, establish connexions everywhere. . . .

The bourgeoisie, during its rule of scarce one hundred years, has created more massive and more colossal productive forces than have all preceding generations together. Subjection of Nature's forces to man, machinery, application of chemistry to industry and agriculture, steam-navigation, railways, electric telegraphs, clearing of whole continents for cultivation, canalisation of rivers, whole populations conjured out of the ground—what earlier century had even a presentiment that such productive forces slumbered in the lap of social labour?

We see then: the means of production and of exchange, on whose foundation the bourgeoisie built itself up, were generated in feudal society. At a certain stage in the development of these means of production and of ex-change, the conditions under which feudal society produced and exchanged, the feudal organisation of agriculture and manufacturing industry, in one word, the feudal relations of property became no longer compatible with the already developed productive forces; they became so many fetters. They had to be burst asunder; they were burst asunder.

Into their place stepped free competition, accompanied by a social and political constitution adapted to it, and by the economical and political sway of the bourgeois class.

A similar movement is going on before our own eyes. Modern bourgeois society with its relations of production, of exchange and of property, a society that has conjured up such gigantic means of production and of exchange, is like the sorcerer, who is no longer able to control the powers of the nether world whom he has called up by his spells. For many a decade past the history of industry and commerce is but the history of the revolt of modern productive forces against modern conditions of production, against the property relations that are the conditions for the existence of the bourgeoisie and of its rule. It is enough to mention the commercial crises that by their periodical return put on its trial, each time more threateningly, the existence of the entire bourgeois society. In these crises a great part not only of the existing products, but also of the previously created productive forces, are periodically destroyed. In these crises there breaks out an epidemic that, in all earlier epochs, would have seemed an absurdity—the epidemic of over-production. Society suddenly finds itself put back into a state of momentary barbarism; it appears as if a famine, a universal war of devastation, had cut off the supply of every means of subsistence; industry and commerce seem to be destroyed; and why? Because there is too much civilisation, too much means of subsistence, too much industry, too much commerce. The productive forces at the disposal of society no longer tend to further the development of the conditions of bourgeois property; on the contrary, they have become too powerful for these conditions, by which they are fettered, and so soon as they overcome these fetters, they bring disorder into the whole of bourgeois society, endanger the existence of bourgeois property. The conditions of bourgeois society are too narrow to comprise the wealth created by them. And how does the bourgeoisie get over these crises? On the one hand by enforced destruction of a mass of productive forces; on the other, by the conquest of new markets, and by the more thorough exploitation of the old ones. That is to say, by paving the way for more extensive and more destructive crises, and by diminishing the means whereby crises are prevented.

The weapons with which the bourgeoisie felled feudalism to the ground are now turned against the bourgeoisie itself.

But not only has the bourgeoisie forged the weapons that bring death to itself; it has also called into existence the men who are to wield those weapons, the modern working class—the proletarians. . . .

The proletariat goes through various stages of development. With its birth begins its struggle with the bourgeoisie. At first the contest is carried on by individual labourers, then by the work-people of a factory, then the operatives of one trade, in one locality, against the individual bourgeois who exploits them. . . .

But with the development of industry the proletariat not only increases in number; it becomes concentrated in greater masses, its strength grows, and it feels that strength more. The various interests and conditions of life within the ranks of the proletariat are more and more equalised, in proportion as machinery obliterates all distinctions of labour, and nearly everywhere reduces wages to the same low level. . . . The workers begin to form combinations (Trades' Unions) against the bourgeois; they club together in order to keep up the rate of wages; they found permanent associations in order to make provision beforehand for these occasional revolts. Here and there the contest breaks out into riots.

Now and then the workers are victorious, but only for a time. The real fruit of their battle lies, not in the immediate result, but in the ever-expanding union of the workers. . . .

Finally, in times even the class-struggle nears the decisive hour, the process of dissolution going on within the ruling-class, in fact within the whole range of old society, assumes such a violent, glaring character, that a small section of the ruling class cuts itself adrift, and joins the revolutionary class, the class that holds the future in its hands. Just as, therefore, at an earlier period, a section of the nobility went over to the bourgeoisie, so now a portion of the bourgeoisie goes over to the proletariat, and in particular, a portion of the bourgeois ideologists, who have raised themselves to the level of comprehending theoretically the historical movement as a whole. . . .

All the preceding classes that got the upper hand sought to fortify their already acquired status by subjecting society at large to their conditions of appropriation. The proletarians cannot become masters of the productive forces of society, except by abolishing their own previous mode of appropriation, and thereby also every other previous mode of appropriation. They have nothing of their own to secure and to fortify; their mission is to destroy all previous securities for, and insurances of, individual property.

All previous historical movements were movements of minorities, or in the interest of minorities. The proletarian movement is the self-conscious, independent movement of the immense majority, in the interest of the immense majority. The proletariat, the lowest stratum of our present society, cannot stir, cannot raise itself up, without the whole superincumbent strata of official society being sprung into the air. . . .

In depicting the most general phases of the development of the proletariat, we traced the more or less veiled civil war, raging within existing society, up to the point where that war breaks out into open revolution, and where the violent overthrow of the bourgeoisie lays the foundation for the sway of the proletariat.

Hitherto, every form of society has been based, as we have already seen, on the antagonism of oppressing and oppressed classes. But in order to oppress a class, certain conditions must be assured to it under which it can, at least, continue its slavish existence. The serf, in the period of serfdom, raised himself to membership in the commune, just as the petty bourgeois, under the yoke of feudal absolutism, managed to develop into a bourgeois. The modern labourer, on the contrary, instead of rising with the progress of industry, sinks deeper and deeper below the conditions of existence of his own class. He becomes a pauper, and pauperism develops more rapidly than population and wealth. And here it becomes evident, that the bourgeoisie is unfit any longer to be the ruling class in society, and to impose its conditions of existence upon society as an overriding law. It is unfit to rule because it is incompetent to assure an existence to its slave within his slavery, because it cannot help letting him sink into such a state, that it has to feed him, instead of being fed by him. Society can no longer live under this bourgeoisie, in other words, its existence is no longer compatible with society.

The essential condition for the existence, and for the sway of the bourgeois class, is the formation and augmentation of capital; the condition for capital is wage-labour. Wage-labour rests exclusively on competition between the labourers. The advance of industry, whose involuntary promoter is the bourgeoisie, replaces the isolation of the labourers, due to competition, by their revolutionary combination, due to association. The development of Modern Industry, therefore, cuts from under its feet the very foundation on which the bourgeoisie produces and appropriates products. What the bourgeoisie, therefore, produces, above all, are its own grave-diggers. Its fall and the victory of the proletariat are equally inevitable. . . .

— Reading No. 2 —

KARL MARX: HISTORICAL MATERIALISM[2]

This is Marx's own classic statement of how he reached historical materialism and his summary of the position.

[2] From the preface to *A Contribution to the Critique of Political Economy* (1859).

✔   ✔   ✔

. . . . The proceedings of the Rhenish Landtag on thefts of wood and parcelling of landed property, the official polemic which Herr von Schaper, then *Oberpräsident* of the Rhine Province, opened against the *Rheinische Zeitung* on the conditions of the Moselle peasantry, and finally debates on free trade and protective tariffs provided the first occasions for occupying myself with economic questions. On the other hand, at that time when the good will "to go further" greatly outweighed knowledge of the subject, a philosophically weakly tinged echo of French Socialism and Communism made itself audible in the *Rheinische Zeitung*. I declared myself against this amateurism, but frankly confessed at the same time in a controversy with the *Allgemeine Augsburger Zeitung* that my previous studies did not permit me even to venture any judgment on the content of the French tendencies. Instead, I eagerly seized on the illusion of the managers of the *Rheinische Zeitung*, who thought that by a weaker attitude on the part of the paper they could secure a remission of the death sentence passed upon it, to withdraw from the public stage into the study. The first work which I undertook for a solution of the doubts which assailed me was a critical review of the Hegelian philosophy of right, a work the introduction to which appeared in 1844 in the *Deutsch-Französische Jahrubücher*, published in Paris. My investigation led to the result that legal relations as well as forms of state are to be grasped neither from themselves nor from the so-called general development of the human mind, but rather have their roots in the material conditions of life, the sum total of which Hegel, following the example of the Englishmen and Frenchmen of the eighteenth century, combines under the name of "civil society," that however the anatomy of civil society is to be sought in political economy. The investigation of the latter, which I began in Paris, I continued in Brussels, whither I had emigrated in consequence of an expulsion order of M. Guizot.

The general result at which I arrived and which, once won, served as a guiding thread for my studies, can be briefly formulated as follows: In the social production of their life, men enter into definite relations of production which correspond to a definite stage of development of their material productive forces. The sum total of these relations of production constitutes the economic structure of society, the real foundation, on which rises a legal and political superstructure and to which correspond definite forms of social consciousness. The mode of production of material life conditions (*bedingt*) the social, political, and intellectual life process in general. It is not the consciousness of men that determines (*bestimmt*) their being, but, on the contrary, their social being that determines their consciousness. At a certain stage of their development, the material productive forces of society come in conflict with the existing relations of production, or—what is but a legal expression for the same thing—with the property relations within which they have been at work hitherto. From forms of development of the productive forces these relations turn into their fetters. Then begins an epoch of social revolution. With the change of the economic foundation the entire immense superstructure is more or less rapidly transformed. In considering such transformations a distinction should always be made between the material transformation of the economic conditions of production, which can be determined with the precision of natural science, and the legal, political, religious, esthetic or philosophic—in short, ideological forms in which men become conscious of this conflict and fight it out. Just as our opinion of an individual is not based on what he thinks of himself, so can we not judge of such a period of transformation by its own consciousness; on the contrary, this consciousness must be explained rather from the contradictions of material life, from the existing conflict between the social productive forces and the relations of production. No social order ever perishes before all the productive forces for which there is room in it have developed; and new, higher relations of production never appear before the material conditions of their existence have matured in the womb of the old society itself. Therefore mankind always sets itself only such tasks as it can solve; since, looking at the matter more closely, it will always be found that the task itself arises only when the material conditions for its solution already exist or are at least in the process of formation. In broad outlines Asiatic, ancient, feudal, and modern bourgeois modes of production can be designated as progressive epochs in the economic formation of society. The bourgeois relations of production are the last antagonistic form of the social process of production—antagonistic not in the sense of individual antagonism, but of one arising from the social conditions of life of the individuals; at the same time the productive forces developing in the womb of bourgeois society create the material conditions for the solution of that antagonism. This social formation brings, therefore, the prehistory of human society to a close. . . .

— Reading No. 3 —

KARL MARX: THE FETISHISM OF THE COMMODITY AND ITS SECRET[3]

This is one of the key passages in Marx's sociological interpretation of economic categories in which he seeks to establish that commodities, products of men's hands, are in the saddle and ride him according to their own laws.

A commodity appears, at first sight, a trivial thing, self-understood. Its analysis shows that it is a very complicated thing, abounding in metaphysical subtleties and

[3] From *Capital*, vol. 1 ch. 1. sec. 4, English trans. by Ernest Untermann (Chicago: Charles Kerr & Co., 1906).

theological quirks. So far as it is a value in use, there is nothing mysterious about it, whether I consider it from the point of view that by its properties it is capable of satisfying human wants, or from the point of view that those properties are the product of human labour. It is clear as noon-day, that man, by his industry, changes the forms of the materials furnished by nature, in such a way as to make them useful to him. The form of wood, for instance, is altered, by making a table out of it. Yet, for all that the table continues to be that common, every-day thing, wood. But, so soon as it steps forth as a commodity, it is changed into something transcendent. It not only stands with its feet on the ground, but, in relation to all other commodities, it stands on its head, and evolves out of its wooden brain grotesque ideas, far more wonderful than "table-turning" ever was.

The mystical character of commodities does not originate, therefore, in their use-value. Just as little does it proceed from the nature of the determining factors of value. For, in the first place, however varied the useful kinds of labour, or productive activities, may be, it is a physiological fact, that they are functions of the human organism, and that each such function, whatever may be its nature or form, is essentially the expenditure of human brain, nerves, muscles, &c. Secondly, with regard to that which forms the groundwork for the quantitative determination of value, namely the duration of that expenditure, or the quantity of labour, it is quite clear that there is a palpable difference between its quantity and quality. In all states of society, the labour-time that it costs to produce the means of subsistence must necessarily be an object of interest to mankind, though not of equal interest in different stages of development. And lastly, from the moment that men in any way work for one another, their labour assumes a social form.

Whence, then, arises the enigmatical character of the product of labour, so soon as it assumes the form of commodities? Clearly from this form itself. The quality of all sorts of human labour is expressed objectively by their products all being equally values; the measure of the expenditure of labour-power by the duration of that expenditure takes the form of the quantity of value of the products of labour; and finally, the mutual relations of the producers, within which the social character of their labour affirms itself, take the form of a social relation between the products.

A commodity is therefore a mysterious thing, simply because in it the social character of men's labour appears to them as an objective character stamped upon the product of that labour; because the relation of the producers to the sum total of their own labour is presented to them as a social relation, existing not between themselves, but between the products of their labour. This is the reason why the products of labour become commodities, social things whose qualities are at the same time perceptible and imperceptible by the senses. In the same way the light from an object is perceived by us not as the subjective excitation of our optic nerve, but as the objective form of something outside the eye itself. But, in the act of seeing, there is at all events, an actual passage of light from one thing to another, from the external object to the eye. There is a physical relation between physical things. But it is different with commodities. There, the existence of the things *quâ* commodities, and the value relation between the products of labour which stamps them as commodities, have absolutely no connection with their physical properties and with the material relations arising therefrom. There it is a definite social relation between men, that assumes, in their eyes, the fantastic form of a relation between things. In order, therefore, to find an analogy, we must have recourse to the mist-enveloped regions of the religious world. In that world the productions of the human brain appear as independent beings endowed with life, and entering into relation both with one another and the human race. So it is in the world of commodities with the products of men's hands. This I call the Fetishism which attaches itself to the products of labour, so soon as they are produced as commodities, and which is therefore inseparable from the production of commodities.

This Fetishism of commodities has its origin, as the foregoing analysis has already shown, in the peculiar social character of the labour that produces them.

As a general rule, articles of utility become commodities, only because they are products of the labour of private individuals or groups of individuals who carry on their work independently of each other. The sum total of the labour of all these private individuals forms the aggregate labour of society. Since the producers do not come into social contact with each other until they exchange their products, the specific social character of each producer's labour does not show itself except in the act of exchange. In other words, the labour of the individual asserts itself as a part of the labour of society, only by means of the relations which the act of exchange establishes directly between the products, and, indirectly through them, between the producers. To the latter, therefore, the relations connecting the labour of one individual with that of the rest appear, not as direct social relations between individuals at work, but as what they really are, material relations between persons and social relations between things. It is only by being exchanged that the products of labour acquire, as values, one uniform social status, distinct from their varied forms of existence as objects of utility. This division of a product into a useful thing and a value becomes practically important, only when exchange has acquired such an extension that useful articles are produced for the purpose of being exchanged, and their character as values has therefore to be taken into account, beforehand, during production. From this moment the labour of the individual producer acquires socially a two-fold character. On the one hand, it must, as a definite useful kind of labour, satisfy a definite social want, and thus hold its place as part and parcel of the collective labour of all, as a branch of a social division of labour that has sprung up spontaneously. On the other hand, it can satisfy the manifold wants of the individual producer himself, only in so far as the mutual exchangeability of all kinds of useful private labour is an established social fact, and therefore the private useful labour of each producer ranks on an equality with that of all others. The equalization of the most different kinds of labour can be the result only of an abstraction from their inequalities, or of reducing them to their common denominator, viz., expenditure of human labour power or human labour in the abstract. The two-fold social character of the labour of the individual appears to him, when reflected in his brain, only under those forms which are impressed upon that labour in everyday practice by the exchange of products. In this way, the character that his own labour possesses of being socially useful takes the form of the condition, that the product must be not only useful, but useful for others, and the social character that his particular labour has of being the equal of all other particular kinds of labour, takes the form that all the physically different articles that are the products of labour, have one common quality, viz., that of having value.

Hence, when we bring the products of our labour into relation with each other as values, it is not because we see in these articles the material receptacles of homogeneous human labour. Quite the contrary; whenever, by an exchange, we equate as values our different products, by that very act, we also equate, as human labour, the different kinds of labour expended upon them. We are not aware of this, nevertheless we do it. Value, therefore, does not stalk about with a label describing what it is. It is value, rather, that converts every product into a social hieroglyphic. Later on, we try to decipher the hieroglyphic, to get behind the secret of our own social products; for to stamp an object of utility as a value, is just as much a social product as language. The recent scientific discovery, that the products of labor, so far as they are values, are but material expressions of the human labour spent in their production, marks, indeed, an epoch in the history of the development of the human race, but, by no means, dissipates the mist through which the social character of labour appears to us to be an objective character of the products themselves. The fact, that in the particular form of production with which we are dealing, viz., the production of commodities, the specific social character of private labour carried on independently, consists in the equality of every kind of that labour, by virtue of its being human labour, which character, therefore, assumes in the product the form of value—this fact appears to the producers, notwithstanding the discovery above referred to, to be just as real and final, as the fact, that, after the discovery by science of the component gases of air, the atmosphere itself remained unaltered.

What, first of all, practically concerns producers when they make an exchange, is the question; how much of some other product they get for their own? in what proportions the products are exchangeable? When these proportions have, by custom, attained a certain stability, they appear to result from the nature of the products, so that, for instance, one ton of iron and two ounces of gold appear as naturally to be of equal value as a pound of gold and a pound of iron in spite of their different physical and chemical qualities appear to be of equal weight. The character of having value, when once impressed upon products, obtains fixity only by reason of their acting and re-acting upon each other as quantities of value. These quantities vary continually, independently of the will, foresight and action of the producers. To them their own social action takes the form of the action of objects, which rule the producers instead of being ruled by them. It requires a fully developed production of commodities before, from accumulated experience alone, the scientific conviction springs up, that all the different kinds of private labour, which are carried on independently of each other, and yet as spontaneously developed branches of the social division of labour, are continually being reduced to the quantitive proportions in which society requires them. And why? Because, in the midst of all the accidental and ever fluctuating exchange-relations between the products, the labour-time socially necessary for their production forcibly asserts itself like an over-riding law of nature. The law of gravity thus asserts itself when a house falls about our ears. The determination of the magnitude of value by labour-time is therefore a secret, hidden under the apparent fluctuations in the relative values of commodities. Its discovery, while removing all appearance of mere accidentality from the determination of the magnitude of the values of products, yet in no way alters the mode in which that determination takes place.

Man's reflections on the forms of social life, and consequently, also, his scientific analysis of those forms, take a course directly opposite to that of their actual historical development. He begins, post festum, with the results of the process of development ready to hand before him. The characters that stamp products as commodities, and whose establishment is a necessary preliminary to the circulation of commodities, have already acquired the stability of natural, self-understood forms of social life, before man seeks to decipher, not their historical character, for in his eyes they are immutable, but their meaning. Consequently it was the analysis of the prices of commodities that alone led to the determination of the magnitude of value, and it was the common expression of all commodities in money that alone led to the establishment of their characters as values. It is, however, just this ultimate money form of the world of commodities that actually conceals, instead of disclosing, the social character of private labour, and the social relations between the individual producers. When I state that coats or boots stand in a relation to linen, because it is the universal incarnation of abstract human labour, the absurdity of the statement is self-evident. Nevertheless, when the producers of coats and boots compare those articles with linen, or what is the same thing with gold or silver, as the universal equivalent, they express the relation between their own private labour and the collective labour of society in the same absurd form.

The categories of bourgeois economy consist of such like forms. They are forms of thought expressing with social validity the conditions and relations of a definite, historically determined mode of production, viz., the production of commodities. The whole mystery of commodities, all the magic and necromancy that surrounds the products of labour as long as they take the form of commodities, vanishes therefore, so soon as we come to other forms of production.

— Reading No. 4 —

KARL MARX: HISTORICAL TENDENCY OF CAPITALIST ACCUMULATION [4]

This selection gives Marx's prediction of the economic development and ultimate dénouement of a commodity producing society.

✓   ✓   ✓

What does the primitive accumulation of capital, *i.e.,* its historical genesis, resolve itself into? In so far as it is not immediate transformation of slaves and serfs into wage-labourers, and therefore a mere change of form, it only means the expropriation of the immediate producers, *i.e.,* the dissolution of private property based on the labour of its owner.

The private property of the labourer in his means of production is the foundation of petty industry; petty industry, again, is an essential condition for the development of social production and of the free individuality of the labourer himself. Of course, this petty mode of production exists also under slavery, serfdom, and other states of dependence. But it flourishes, it lets loose its whole energy, only where the labourer is the private owner of his own means of labour set in action by himself: the peasant of the land which he cultivates, the artisan of the tool which he handles as a virtuoso. This mode of production presupposes parcelling of the soil, and scattering of the other means of production. . . . At a certain stage of development it brings forth the material agencies for its own dissolution. From that moment new forces and new passions spring up in the bosom of society, but the old social organisation fetters them and

⁴ From *Capital,* vol. I, ch. XXXII, English trans. by Ernest Untermann (Chicago: Charles Kerr & Co., 1906).

keeps them down. It must be annihilated; it is annihilated.

Its annihilation, the transformation of the individualised
and scattered means of production into socially concentrated ones, of the pigmy property of the many into the
huge property of the few, the expropriation of the great
mass of the people from the soil, from the means of subsistence and from the means of labour, this fearful and
painful expropriation of the mass of people forms the
prelude to the history of capital. Self-earned private property, that is based, so to say, on the fusing together of the
isolated, independent labourer with the conditions of his
labour, is supplanted by capitalistic private property,
which rests on exploitation of the nominally free labour
of others, *i.e.*, on wages-labour.

As soon as this process of transformation has sufficiently decomposed the old society from top to bottom,
as soon as the labourers are turned into proletarians, their
means of labour into capital, as soon as the capitalist
mode of production stands on its own feet, then the
further socialisation of labour and the further transformation of the land and other means of production, as well as
the further expropriation of private proprietors, takes a
new form. That which is now to be expropriated is no
longer the labourer working for himself, but the capitalist
exploiting many labourers. This expropriation is accomplished by the action of the immanent laws of capitalistic
production itself, by the centralisation of capital. One
capitalist always kills many.

Hand in hand with this centralisation, or this expropriation of many capitalists by few, develops, on an ever
extending scale, the cooperative form of the labour-
process, the conscious technical application of science, the
economising of all means of production by combined,
socialised labour, the entanglement of all peoples in the
net of the world-market, and with this, the international
character of the capitalistic regime.

Along with the constantly diminishing number of the
magnates of capital, who usurp and monopolise all advantages of this process of transformation, grows the mass
of misery, oppressions, slavery, degradation, exploitation,
but with this too grows the revolt of the working-class,

always increasing in numbers, and disciplined, united, organised by the very mechanism of the process of capitalist production itself. The monopoly of capital becomes a fetter upon the mode of production, which has sprung up and flourished along with, and under it. Centralisations of the means of production and socialisation of labour at last reach a point where they become incompatible with their capitalist integument. This integument is burst asunder. The knell of capitalist private property sounds. The expropriators are expropriated. . . .

— Reading No. 5 —

KARL MARX: RELIGION AND ECONOMICS [5]

In this selection Marx applies historical materialism to religion.

✔   ✔   ✔

The religious world is but the reflex of the real world. And for a society based upon the production of commodities, in which the producers in general enter into social relations with one another by treating their products as commodities and values, whereby they reduce their individual private labour to the standard of homogeneous human labour—for such a society, Christianity with its *cultus* of abstract man, more especially in its bourgeois developments, Protestantism, Deism, &c., is the most fit-

[5] From *Capital*, vol. 1 ch. 1. sec. 4. English trans. by Ernest Untermann (Chicago: Charles Kerr & Co., 1906).

ting form of religion. In the ancient Asiatic and other ancient modes of production, we find that the conversion of men into producers of commodities holds a subordinate place, which, however, increases.in importance as the primitive communities approach nearer and nearer to their dissolution. Trading nations, properly so called, exist in the ancient world only in its interstices, like the gods of Epicurus in the Intermundia, or like Jews in the pores of Polish society. Those ancient social organisms of production are, as compared with bourgeois society extremely simple and transparent. But they are founded either on the immature development of man individually, who has not yet severed the umbilical cord that unites him with his fellow men in a primitive tribal community, or upon direct relations of subjection. They can arise and exist only when the development of the productive power of labour has not risen beyond a low stage, and when, therefore, the social relations within the sphere of material life, between man and man, and between man and Nature, are correspondingly narrow. This narrowness is reflected in the ancient worship of Nature, and in the other elements of the popular religions. The religious reflex of the real world can, in any case, only then finally vanish, when the practical relations of everyday life offer to man none but perfectly intelligible and reasonable relations with regard to his fellowmen and to nature.

The life-process of society, which is based on the process of material production, does not strip off its mystical veil until it is treated as production by freely associated men, and is consciously regulated by them in accordance with a settled plan. This, however, demands for society a certain material ground-work or set of conditions of existence which in their turn are the spontaneous product of a long and painful process of development.

KARL MARX: ON TRADITION, PERSONALITY, AND CLASS-FORCES[6]

Following are a few key passages from one of Marx's historical writings, The 18th Brumaire of Louis Napoleon, *in which Marx applies his theory of history to an important contemporary event. The first two paragraphs are from the preface to the second edition; the rest from the body of the text.*

✓   ✓   ✓

Of the writings dealing with the same subject approximately *at the same time* as mine, only two deserve notice: Victor Hugo's *Napoleon the Little* and Proudhon's *Coup d'État.*

Victor Hugo confines himself to bitter and witty invective against the responsible publisher of the *coup d'état.* The event itself appears in his work like a bolt from the blue. He sees in it only the violent act of a single individual. He does not notice that he makes this individual great instead of little by ascribing to him a personal power of initiative such as would be without parallel in world history. Proudhon, for his part, seeks to represent the *coup d'état* as the result of an antecedent historical development. Unnoticeably, however, his historical construction of the *coup d'état* turns into a historical *apologia* for its hero. Thus he falls into the error of our so-called *objective* historians. I, on the contrary, demonstrate how the *class struggle* in France created circumstances and relationships that made it possible for a grotesque mediocrity to play a hero's part.

[6] Marx-Engels, *Selected Works,* English trans. (Foreign Language Publishing House: Moscow, 1950), vol. I, pp. 221 ff.

*   *   *

Hegel remarks somewhere that all facts and person-
ages of great importance in world history occur, as it
were, twice. He forgot to add: the first time as tragedy,
the second as farce. Caussidière for Danton, Louis Blanc
for Robespierre, the *Montagne* of 1848 to 1851 for the
Montagne of 1793 to 1795, the Nephew for the Uncle.
And the same caricature occurs in the circumstances at-
tending the second edition of the eighteenth Brumaire!

Men make their own history, but they do not make it
just as they please; they do not make it under circumstances chosen by themselves, but under circumstances
directly encountered, given and transmitted from the
past. The tradition of all the dead generations weighs
like a nightmare on the brain of the living. And just
when they seem engaged in revolutionizing themselves
and things, in creating something that has never yet
existed, precisely in such periods of revolutionary crisis
they anxiously conjure up the spirits of the past to their
service and borrow from them names, battle cries and
costumes in order to present the new scene of world history in this time-honoured disguise and this borrowed
language. Thus Luther donned the mask of the Apostle
Paul, the Revolution of 1789 to 1814 draped itself alter-
nately as the Roman republic and the Roman empire,
and the Revolution of 1848 knew nothing better to do
than to parody, now 1789, now the revolutionary tradition of 1793 to 1795. In like manner a beginner who
has learnt a new language always translates it back into
his mother tongue, but he has assimilated the spirit of
the new language and can produce freely in it only when
he finds his way in it without recalling the old and forgets his native tongue in the use of the new.

Consideration of this conjuring up of the dead of
world history reveals at once a salient difference. Camille
Desmoulins, Danton, Robespierre, Saint-Just, Napoleon,
the heroes as well as the parties and the masses of the
old French Revolution, performed the task of their time
in Roman costume and with Roman phrases, the task of
unchaining and setting up modern *bourgeois* society. The
first ones knocked the feudal basis to pieces and mowed

off the feudal heads which had grown on it. The other created inside France the conditions under which alone free competition could be developed, parcelled landed property exploited, and the unchained industrial productive power of the nation employed; and beyond the French borders he everywhere swept the feudal institutions away, so far as was necessary to furnish bourgeois society in France with a suitable up-to-date environment on the European Continent. The new social formation once established, the antediluvian Colossi disappeared and with them resurrected Romanity—the Brutuses, Gracchi, Publicolas, the tribunes, the senators, and Caesar himself. Bourgeois society in its sober reality had begotten its true interpreters and mouthpieces in the Says, Cousins, Royer-Collards, Benjamin Constants and Guizots; its real military leaders sat behind the office desks, and the hog-headed Louis XVIII was its political chief. Wholly absorbed in the production of wealth and in peaceful competitive struggle, it no longer comprehended that ghosts from the days of Rome had watched over its cradle. But unheroic as bourgeois society is, it nevertheless took heroism, sacrifice, terror, civil war and battles of peoples to bring it into being. And in the classically austere traditions of the Roman republic its gladiators found the ideals and the art forms, the self-deceptions that they needed in order to conceal from themselves the bourgeois limitations of the content of their struggles and to keep their enthusiasm on the high plane of the great historical tragedy. Similarly, at another stage of development, a century earlier, Cromwell and the English people had borrowed speech, passions and illusions from the Old Testament for their bourgeois revolution. When the real aim had been achieved, when the bourgeois transformation of English society had been accomplished, Locke supplanted Habakuk.

Bourgeois revolutions, like those of the eighteenth century, storm swiftly from success to success; their dramatic effects outdo each other; men and things seem set in sparkling brilliants; ecstasy is the everyday spirit; but they are short-lived; soon they have attained their zenith, and a long crapulent depression lays hold of society before it learns soberly to assimilate the results of its storm-and-stress period. On the other hand, proletarian revolutions, like those of the nineteenth century, criticize themselves constantly, interrupt themselves continually in their own course, come back to the apparently accomplished in order to begin it afresh, deride with unmerciful thoroughness the inadequacies, weaknesses and paltrinesses of their first attempts, seem to throw down their adversary only in order that he may draw new strength from the earth and rise again, more gigantic, before them, recoil ever and anon from the indefinite prodigiousness of their own aims, until a situation has been created which makes all turning back impossible, and the conditions themselves cry out:

Hic Rhodus, hic salta! (Here is Rhodes: do your stuff here and now!)

. . . The Constitution, the National Assembly, the dynastic parties, the blue and the red republicans, the heroes of Africa, the thunder from the platform, the sheet lightning of the daily press, the entire literature, the political names and the intellectual reputations, the civil law and the penal code, the liberté, égalité, fraternité and the second Sunday in May 1852—all has vanished like a phantasmagoria before the spell of a man whom even his enemies do not make out to be a magician. Universal suffrage seems to have survived only for a moment, in order that with its own hand it may make its last will and testament before the eyes of all the world and declare in the name of the people itself: All that exists deserves to perish.

It is not enough to say, as the French do, that their nation was taken unawares. A nation and a woman are not forgiven the unguarded hour in which the first adventurer that came along could violate them. The riddle is not solved by such turns of speech, but merely formulated differently. It remains to be explained how a nation of thirty-six millions can be surprised and delivered unresisting into captivity by three high-class swindlers.

. . . under the absolute monarchy, during the first Revolution, under Napoleon, bureaucracy was only the means of preparing the class rule of the bourgeoisie. Under the Restoration, under Louis Philippe, under the parliamentary republic, it was the instrument of the ruling class, however much it strove for power of its own.

Only under the second Bonaparte does the state seem to have made itself completely independent. . . .

And yet the state power is not suspended in midair. Bonaparte represents a class, and the most numerous class of French society at that, the *small-holding peasants*. . . .

The small-holding peasants form a vast mass, the members of which live in similar conditions but without entering into manifold relations with one another. Their mode of production isolates them from one another instead of bringing them into mutual intercourse. The isolation is increased by France's bad means of communication and by the poverty of the peasants. Their field of production, the small holding, admits of no division of labour in its cultivation, no application of science and, therefore, no diversity of development, no variety of talent, no wealth of social relationships. Each individual peasant family is almost self-sufficient; it itself directly produces the major part of its consumption and thus acquires its means of life more through exchange with nature than in intercourse with society. A small holding, a peasant and his family; alongside them another small holding, another peasant and another family. A few score of these make up a village, and a few score of villages make up a Department. In this way, the great mass of the French nation is formed by simple addition of homologous magnitudes, much as potatoes in a sack form a sack of potatoes. In so far as millions of families live under economic conditions of existence that separate their mode of life, their interests and their culture from those of the other classes, and put them in hostile opposition to the latter, they form a class. In so far as there is merely a local interconnection among these small-holding peasants, and the identity of their interests begets no community, no national bond and no political organization among them, they do not form a class. They are consequently incapable of enforcing their class interest in their own name, whether through a parliament or through a convention. They cannot represent themselves, they must be represented. Their representative must at the same time appear as their master, as an authority over them, as an unlimited governmental power that protects them against the other classes and sends them rain and sunshine from above. The political influence of the small-holding peasants, therefore, finds its final expression in the executive power subordinating society to itself.

Historical tradition gave rise to the belief of the French peasants in the miracle that a man named Napoleon would bring all the glory back to them. And an individual turned up who gives himself out as the man because he bears the name of Napoleon, in consequence of the *Code Napoléon,* which lays down that *la recherche de la paternité est interdite. . . .*

. . . The Bonaparte dynasty represents not the revolutionary, but the conservative peasant that strikes out beyond the condition of his social existence, the small holding, not the country folk who, linked up with the towns, want to overthrow the old order through their own energies, but on the contrary those who, in stupefied seclusion within this old order, want to see themselves and their small holdings saved and favoured by the ghost of empire. It represents not the enlightenment, but the superstition of the peasant; not his judgment, but his prejudice; not his future, but his past. . . .

— Reading No. 7 —

FREDERICK ENGELS: "SCIENTIFIC" VERSUS "UTOPIAN" SOCIALISM[7]

These passages give Engels' more prosaic and detailed version of some of Marx's leading ideas with special reference to what distinguished Marx and Engels, in their own minds, from all varieties of Utopianism.

↗   ↗   ↗

. . . The Utopians' mode of thought has for a long time governed the Socialist ideas of the nineteenth century, and still governs some of them. Until very recently all French and English Socialists did homage to it. The earlier German Communism, including that of Weitling, was of the same school. To all these Socialism is the expression of absolute truth, reason, and justice, and has only to be discovered to conquer all the world by virtue of its own power. And as absolute truth is independent of time, space, and of the historical development of man, it is a mere accident when and where it is discovered. With all this, absolute truth, reason, and justice are different with the founder of each different school. And as each one's special kind of absolute truth, reason, and justice is again conditioned by his subjective understanding, his conditions of existence, the measure of his knowledge and his intellectual training, there is no other ending possible in this conflict of absolute truths than that they shall be mutually exclusive one of the other. Hence, from this nothing could come but a kind of eclectic, average Socialism, which, as a matter of fact, has up to the present time dominated the minds of most of

[7] Marx-Engels, *Selected Works*, English trans. (Foreign Language Publishing House: Moscow, 1950), vol. 2, pp. 117-118, 125-6, 137-8.

the socialist workers in France and England. Hence, a mish-mash allowing of the most manifold shades of opinion; a mish-mash of such critical statements, economic theories, pictures of future society by the founders of different sects, as excite a minimum of opposition; a mish-mash which is the more easily brewed the more the definite sharp edges of the individual constituents are rubbed down in the stream of debate, like rounded pebbles in a brook.

To make a science of Socialism, it had first to be placed upon a real basis. . . .

The materialist conception of history starts from the proposition that the production of the means to support human life and, next to production, the exchange of things produced, is the basis of all social structure; that in every society that has appeared in history, the manner in which wealth is distributed and society divided into classes or orders is dependent upon what is produced, how it is produced, and how the products are exchanged. From this point of view the final causes of all social changes and political revolutions are to be sought, not in men's brains, not in man's better insight into eternal truth and justice, but in changes in the modes of production and exchange. They are to be sought, not in the *philosophy*, but in the *economics* of each particular epoch. The growing perception that existing social institutions are unreasonable and unjust, that reason has become unreason, and right wrong, is only proof that in the modes of production and exchange changes have silently taken place with which the social order, adapted to earlier economic conditions, is no longer in keeping. From this it also follows that the means of getting rid of the incongruities that have been brought to light must also be present, in a more or less developed condition, within the changed modes of production themselves. These means are not to be invented by deduction from fundamental principles, but are to be discovered in the stubborn facts of the existing system of production.

What is, then, the position of modern Socialism in this connection?

The present structure of society—this is now pretty generally conceded—is the creation of the ruling class of to-day, of the bourgeoisie. The mode of production peculiar to the bourgeoisie, known, since Marx, as the capitalist mode of production, was incompatible with the feudal system, with the privileges it conferred upon individuals, entire social ranks and local corporations, as well as with the hereditary ties of subordination which constituted the framework of its social organisation. The bourgeoisie broke up the feudal system and built upon its ruins the capitalist order of society, the kingdom of free competition, of personal liberty, of the equality, before the law, of all commodity owners, of all the rest of the capitalist blessings. Thenceforward the capitalist mode of production could develop in freedom. Since steam, machinery, and the making of machines by machinery transformed the older manufacture into modern industry, the productive forces evolved under the guidance of the bourgeoisie developed with a rapidity and in a degree unheard of before. But just as the older manufacture, in its time, and handicraft, becoming more developed under its influence, had come into collision with the feudal trammels of the guilds, so now modern industry, in its more complete development, comes into collision with the bounds within which the capitalist mode of production holds it confined. The new productive forces have already outgrown the capitalistic mode of using them. And this conflict between productive forces and modes of production is not a conflict engendered in the mind of man, like that between original sin and divine justice. It exists, in fact, objectively, outside us, independently of the will and actions even of the men that have brought it on. Modern Socialism is nothing but the reflex, in thought, of this conflict in fact; its ideal reflection in the minds, first of the class directly suffering under it, the working class. . . .

Whilst the capitalist mode of production more and more completely transforms the great majority of the population into proletarians, it creates the power which, under penalty of its own destruction, is forced to accomplish this revolution. Whilst it forces on more and more the transformation of the vast means of production, already socialised, into State property, it shows itself the way to accomplishing this revolution. *The proletariat seizes political power and turns the means of production into State property.*

But, in doing this, it abolishes itself as a proletariat, abolishes all class distinctions and class antagonisms, abolishes also the State as State. Society thus far, based upon class antagonisms, had need of the State. That is, of an organization of the particular class which was *pro tempore* the exploiting class, an organisation for the purpose of forcibly keeping the exploited classes in the condition of oppression corresponding with the given mode of production (slavery, serfdom, wage-labor). The State was the official representative of society as a whole; the gathering of it together into a visible embodiment. But it was this only in so far as it was the State of that class which itself represented, for the time being, society as a whole: in ancient times, the State of slaveowning citizens; in the Middle Ages, the feudal lords; in our own time, the bourgeoisie. When at last it becomes the real representative of the whole of society, it renders itself unnecessary. As soon as there is no longer any social class to be held in subjection; as soon as class rule, and the individual struggle for existence based upon our present anarchy in production, with the collisions and excesses arising from these, are removed, nothing more remains to be repressed, and a special repressive force, a State, is no longer necessary. The first act by virtue of which the State really constitutes itself the representative of the whole of society—the taking possession of the means of production in the name of society—this is, at the same time, its last independent act as a State. State interference in social relations becomes, in one domain after another, superfluous, and then dies out of itself; the government of persons is replaced by the administration of things, and by the conduct of processes of production. The State is not "abolished." It withers away. . . .

— Reading No. 8 —

KARL KAUTSKY: THE INFLUENCE OF THE MODE OF PRODUCTION [8]

Kautsky defends historical materialism and clarifies its leading assumptions especially the expression that the mode of production—the substructure—"ultimately" or "in the last analysis" determines ideology—the super-structure—of society.

✓   ✓   ✓

We must distinguish among the ideas of any given generation between the old which it has inherited from its predecessors and the new which it brings forth itself. The new do not necessarily have to elbow out the old. They can adapt themselves to it and enrich the spiritual life. Not everything which our ancestors thought or knew is regarded by us as an error. Many old ideas remain intact. But of course only those which are compatible, at least to some extent compatible, with the new situation. Otherwise they would never be able to maintain themselves, they would be surrendered either explicitly or in actual fact, that is to say, they would cease to exercise a practical effect on the behavior of man and therefore not require to be formally repudiated.

The rise of new ideas under the influence of new material conditions, the adaptation of old ideas to new relations, the struggle against the old ideas which have shown themselves incompatible with the new and their final elimination—that is the content of the spiritual struggle of every generation in which a new technique or economy arises. The impulse to this movement is ex-

[8] From *Die Materialistische Geschichtsauffsassung* (Berlin, 1927), vol. I, pp. 818-19, 830, 836.

clusively provided by the economy. The ideology follows it after some delay.

But in order to understand the ideas which the given generation has inherited from an earlier time, I must not only investigate them but also the previous epoch. I must determine which among its ideas were then new and which not. We will further find that only a part were newly developed—and only such ideas can be explained in terms of the economic relations of the time. For the explanation of the others I must go still further back. In this fashion, in order to grasp the total ideology of our time, we must go back to the most distant periods. Only in that way can we be successful in laying bare all their economic origins. But we will always find, if we dig deep enough, that all ideas are rooted in economic relations.

This is the meaning of the metaphor of substructure and superstructure. The relationships between the two factors are not as simple as they seem at first glance.

Let us take as an illustration of what has been said, Christianity. Among the ideas which determine the spiritual life of our time it is still of great significance. . . . Yet it would be completely in vain to try to derive the ideas of Christianity from existing economic conditions. If we want to understand it we must go back to the time in which it appeared in world history as a new phenomenon. We must investigate its origins during the first centuries of our era when the democracy of antiquity broke down and an all powerful Caesarism arose. The economic relations of the time and their consequences, the impoverishment of the masses, the concentration of wealth in a few hands, loss of population, constant civil war between the holders of power who thanks to their accumulations of plunder could support large armies, the cessation of allpolitical activity among the people, for the impoverished masses became corrupted and could be bought while the rich sunk themselves in debauchery:—this was the real basis out of which Christianity arose and make it explicable.

But by no means completely—only that which was distinctively new to it—the longing for peace, scorn of the world, disgust with life, lack of confidence in oneself and one's surroundings, etc. . . .

Yet besides these features Christianity includes many other ideas which it did not newly produce but which it already found as long dominant, which it took from the life out of which it arose. . . .

We have seen that the degree to which new and old elementes are combined in the political, philosophical, religious, artistic ideology of a period, a class, a party can be very different depending upon circumstances.

No ideology, not even the most radical or revolutionary, can be built only out of new elements. That is completely impossible for everyone stands on the shoulders of his predecessors and has learned from them, often, sad to say, not enough . . .

A history of the ideas of a period, written from the standpoint of the materialistic conception of history, should not limit itself to bringing these ideas in relation to be given economic relations. It will never succeed in explaining the entire spiritual and cultural life of a period in terms of its economy.

As Engels repeatedly proclaimed economic relations are the decisive factor in world history only in the *last analysis*. . . . This is correct but we must supplement this with the recognition of the necessity of distinguishing among the Constitutions, forms of law, theories, etc. of a given period between those it has acquired from its predecessors and those it newly produces.

Only the last are erected on the economic conditions of the time. The traditional cultural forms belong, on the other hand, not to the consequences, not to the superstructure, but to the conditions themselves, to the substructure of the new economy just as much as the new forms of consciousness which corresponds to that economy. . . . Let us therefore not forget: only in the *last analysis* is the whole juristic, political, ideological complex to be regarded as a superstructure upon an economic substructure. For any individual phenomenon in history, whether it be of an economic, ideological, or any other kind, it is not necessarily valid. In some of its relations it functions as substructure, in others as superstructure.

Only for the actually *new* appearance in history is the Marxist proposition about the relation between the substructure and superstructure unconditionally valid.

KARL KAUTSKY: ON THE AGRICULTURAL PROGRAM[9]

Claiming to be faithful to Marx and Engels' views on agriculture, Kautsky applies them in such a way that they are substantially modified. "Orthodoxy" learns.

✓   ✓   ✓

Is the large-scale undertaking superior and more productive in agriculture than it is in industry, and is this the type of organisation which should be aimed at in order to provide the population with cheap food and to ensure more leisure and greater wealth to the agricultural labourer with the same, or with an increased, volume of production?

A generation ago this question was hotly discussed in our ranks. Since then, however, interest has somewhat waned. Marx and Engels held that with modern agricultural methods and practice large holdings show the same advantages as big industry, this being the only type of organisation in which modern methods of production can be utilised to the full. They considered that the peasant small-holder was a relic of barbarian times, doomed to disappear, and that it was no task of ours to encourage his survival. This view was borne out by a series of events, and became particularly manifest during the great agricultural crisis in the two final decades of the last century. The other members of the Party came forward, the most famous being Eduard David, who declared that the rule with regard to the superiority of large-scale undertakings did not apply to agriculture in the same way as it did to industry, but that, on the contrary, small peasant holdings were preferable, the future

[9] Karl Kautsky, *Bolshevism at a Deadlock,* English trans. (New York, 1931), pp. 34 ff.

being with them. In agriculture, unlike industry, the wage system cannot be dispensed with by socializing large-scale enterprises, but would result from their disintegration and division into small family holdings which can be worked by the husband, the wife, and the younger children without the aid of hired labor.

This discussion induced me to deal with the matter thoroughly in my book *The Agrarian Question* (1899). . . .

The main conclusion which I formed in 1899 was that I had to agree in some points with David, and had to give up the view held by Marx and Engels, only, however, to cling to the essential points of the latter far more firmly. I had to agree that the progress of large-scale production in agriculture, noticed by Marx and Engels, had stopped, and that it had never really made much headway. On the other hand, I could not observe a progressive replacement of large-scale undertakings by small holdings, but noticed that the relative sizes of the undertakings remained stable. The one or the other gains ground in turn, but the movement is always very slow, and never continues for long in the same direction. Generally speaking, the relationship between the relative sizes of the holdings alters little, if only influenced by purely economic factors and not by external forces. It is difficult to define precisely the superiority of large-scale agriculture as compared with small holdings or vice versa; sometimes one, sometimes the other proves to be more profitable, all according to the social conditions prevailing.

Marx and Engels had already recognised this. They did not consider that every large holding was necessarily superior to the small, but only included those which had at their disposal all the appliances provided by modern technique and modern agrarian science, which are partly inaccessible and partly inapplicable to small holdings.

Where large and small holdings are worked with the same appliances and the same knowledge, the small holdings always prove to be superior, for the interest of the peasant in the output from his holding is far deeper than the interest of the hired labourer in the working of large holdings. Only the better appliances and greater knowledge used in the large holdings can counterbalance this

superiority of the small holdings. Moreover, large-scale
agricultural undertakings developed on lines which very
strongly resisted the application of highly developed
machinery and knowledge; this is an important difference
between large-scale operations in agriculture and in
industry. This is pointed out here, as little attention has
been paid to it.

Big estates originated very differently from capitalistic
big industry. The latter is of relatively recent date, being
only a few centuries old, whereas big estates and large
holdings are already found at the beginning of written
history. Capitalistic big industry develops as a result of
the economic and technical advantages which it offers
over handicraft. The low prices which it makes possible
are its irresistible weapons.

Landlordism, on the other hand, is the product of
force, of conquest. . . .

There was no great change when forced labour was
replaced by hired labour on the big estates. The educational facilities and possibilities of organising to obtain
proper wages, housing, and hours and conditions of work
are inferior in the country to those in the large town. It
is, therefore, especially difficult for the farm labourer to
attain that degree of intelligence, independence, and
interest in his work without which the successful application of modern technique and science in agriculture is
far less possible than in industry. The work is not always
carried on under the same conditions requiring the same
handling as in a factory, but is done in the open fields
where conditions change very quickly, and where machinery and methods of modern agriculture must be adapted
accordingly. Modern large-scale organisation, in agriculture then, demands a higher degree of intelligence
and independence from the paid worker than most
branches of big industry. The social conditions under
which the big estates have been managed hitherto make
it more difficult than in the towns for the paid labourer
to acquire more knowledge, to get accustomed to independent thinking and acting, to form big organisations
and to influence the process of production through
them. This is the mainreason why large-scale agriculture

has not yet attained that economic superiority which is due to it by virtue of modern technique and biological discoveries.

— Reading No. 9 —

GEORGI PLEKHANOV: THE INDIVIDUAL IN HISTORY[10]

Here is Plekhanov's "sophisticated" yet orthodox defence of the monistic interpretation of history in which "ultimately" the mode of economic production and not personality, no matter how outstanding, decides. In this connection Kautsky's chapter in Vol. II of his Materialistic Interpretation of History (1927) *and Trotsky's discussion in the* History of the Russian Revolution (1932), *Vol. I. should be consulted. Cf. also chapter V of my* The Hero in History: A Study in Limitation and Possibility *for a critique.*

↗   ↗   ↗

Sainte-Beuve thought that had there been a sufficient number of minor and dark causes of the kind that he had mentioned, the outcome of the French Revolution would have been the *opposite* of what we know it to have been. This is a great mistake. No matter how intricately the minor psychological and physiological factors causes may have been interwoven, they would not under

[10] G. V. Plekhanov, *The Role of the Individual in History* (1898), English trans. (Foreign Language Publishing House: Moscow, 1944), pp. 37-41.

any circumstances have eliminated the great social needs that gave rise to the French Revolution; and as long as these needs remained unsatisfied the revolutionary movement in France would have continued. To make the outcome of this movement the opposite of what it was, the needs that gave rise to it would have had to be the opposite of what they were; and this, of course, no combination of minor causes would ever be able to bring about.

The causes of the French Revolution lay in the character of *social relations;* and the minor causes assumed by Sainte-Beuve could lie only in the *personal qualities of individuals.* The final cause of social relationships lies in the state of productive forces. This depends on the qualities of individuals, perhaps, only in the sense that these individuals possess more or less talent for making technical improvements, discoveries and inventions. Sainte-Beuve did not have these qualities in mind. No other qualities, however, enable individuals directly to influence the state of productive forces, and hence, the social relations which they determine, i.e., *economic relations.* No matter what the qualities of the given individual may be, they cannot eliminate the given economic relations if the latter conform to the given state of productive forces. But the personal qualities of individuals make them more or less fit to satisfy those social needs which arise out of the given economic relations, or to prevent such satisfaction. The urgent social need of France at the end of the Eighteenth Century was the substitution for the obsolete political institutions of new institutions that would conform more to her economic system. The most prominent and useful public men of that time were those who were more capable than others of helping to satisfy this most urgent need. We will assume that Mirabeau, Robespierre, and Napoleon were men of this type. What would have happened had premature death not removed Mirabeau from the political stage? The constitutional monarchist party would have retained their considerable power for a longer period; its resistance to the republicans would, therefore, have been more energetic. But that is all. No Mirabeau could, at that time, have averted the triumph of the republicans. Mirabeau's power rested entirely on the sympathy and confidence of the people; but the people wanted a republic, as the Court irritated them by its obstinate defence of the old order. As soon as the people became convinced that Mirabeau did not sympathize with their republican strivings they would have ceased to sympathize with him; and then the great orator would have lost nearly all influence, and in all probability would have fallen a victim to the very movement that he would vainly have tried to check. Approximately the same thing may be said about Robespierre. Let us assume that he was an absolutely indispensable force in his party; but at all events, he was not the only force. If the accidental fall of a brick had killed him, say, in January 1793, his place would, of course, have been taken by somebody else, and although this person might have been inferior to him in every respect, nevertheless, events would have taken *the same course* as they did when Robespierre was alive. For example, even under these circumstances the Gironde would probably not have escaped defeat; but it is possible that Robespierre's party would have lost power somewhat earlier and we would now be speaking not of the Thermidor reaction, but of the Floréal, Prairial or Messidor reaction. Perhaps some will say that with his inexorable terror, Robespierre did not delay but hastened the downfall of his party. We will not stop to examine this supposition here; we will accept it as if it were quite sound. In that case we must assume that Robespierre's party would have fallen not in Thermidor, but in Fructidor, Vendémaire, or Brumaire. In short, it may have fallen sooner or perhaps later, but it certainly would have fallen, because the section of the people which supported Robespierre's party was totally unprepared to hold power for a prolonged period. At all events, results "opposite" to those which arose from Robespierre's energetic action are out of the question.

Nor could they have arisen even if Bonaparte had been struck down by a bullet, let us say, at the battle of Arcole. What he did in the Italian and other campaigns other generals would have done. Probably, they would not have displayed the same talent as he did, and would not have achieved such brilliant victories; nevertheless, the French Republic would have emerged victorious from the wars it waged at the time because its soldiers were incomparably the best in Europe. As for the 18th of Brumaire and its influence on the internal life of France, here, too, *in essence,* the general course and outcome of events would probably have been the same as they were under Napoleon. The Republic, mortally wounded by the events of the 9th of Thermidor, was slowly dying. The Directoire was unable to restore order which the bourgeoisie, having rid itself of the rule of the higher estates, now desired most of all. To restore order a *"good sword,"* as Sieyes expressed it, was needed. At first it was thought that General Joubert would serve in this virtuous role, but when he was killed at Novi, the names of Moreau, MacDonald, and Bernadotte were mentioned. Bonaparte was only mentioned later: and had he been killed, like Joubert, he would not have been mentioned at all, and some other "sword" would have been put forward. It goes without saying that the man whom events had elevated to the position of dictator must have been tirelessly aspiring to power himself, energetically pushing aside and ruthlessly crushing all who stood in his way. Bonaparte was a man of iron energy and was remorseless in the pursuit of his goal. But there were not a few energetic, talented, and ambitious egoists in those days, besides him. The place Bonaparte succeeded in occupying would, probably, not have remained vacant. Let us assume that the other general who had secured this place would have been more peaceful than Napoleon, that he would not have roused the whole of Europe against himself, and therefore, would have died in the Tuileries and not on the Island of St. Helena. In that case the Bourbons would not have returned to France at all; for them, such a result would certainly have been the "opposite" of what it was. In its relation to the internal life of France as a whole, however, this result would have differed little from the actual result. After the "good sword" had restored order and had consolidated the power of the bourgeoisie, the latter would have tired soon of its barrack-room habits and despotism. A liberal movement would have arisen, similar to the one

that arose after the Restoration; the fight would have
gradually flared up, and as "good swords" are not distinguished for their yielding nature, the virtuous Louis-
Philippe would, perhaps have ascended the throne of his
dearly beloved kinsmen not in 1830 but in 1820, or in
1825. All such changes in the course of events might,
to some extent, have influenced the subsequent political,
and through it, the economic life of Europe. Nevertheless, under no circumstances would the final outcome of
the revolutionary movement have been the *"opposite"*
of what it was. Owing to the specific qualities of their
minds and characters influential individuals can change
the *individual features of events and some of their par-*
ticular consequences, but they cannot change their general *trend,* which is determined by other forces.

— Reading No. 10 —

DANIEL DE LEON: INDUSTRIAL UNIONISM AND THE SOCIALIST REPUBLIC [11]

Daniel De Leon's simple and straightforward concep-
tion of the goal—the American Socialist Republic—and
the method by which it is to be won.

✓   ✓   ✓

Capitalism is the last expression of Class Rule. The
economic foundation of Class Rule is the private owner-

[11] An editorial from the *Daily People* of January 20, 1913,
    reprinted with the permission of Arnold Peterson, Na-
    tional Secretary of the Socialist Labor Party.

ship of the necessaries for production. The social structure, or garb, of Class Rule is the political State—that social structure in which Government is an organ separate and apart from production, with no vital function other than the maintenance of the supremacy of the Ruling Class.

The overthrow of Class Rule means the overthrow of the political State, and its substitution with the Industrial Social Order, under which the necessaries for production are collectively owned and operated by and for the people.

Goals determine methods. The goal of social evolution being the final overthrow of Class Rule, its methods must fit the goal.

As in Nature, where optical illusions abound, and stand in the way of progress until cleared, so in society.

The fact of economic despotism by the Ruling Class raises, with some, the illusion that the economic organization and activity of the despotized Working Class is all-sufficient to remove the ills complained of.

The fact of political despotism by the Ruling Class raises, with others, the illusion that the political organization and activity of the despotized Working Class is all-sufficient to bring about redress.

The one-legged conclusion regarding economic organization and activity fatedly abuts, in the end, in pure and simple bombism, as exemplified in the A. F. of L., despite its Civic Federation and Militia of Christ affiliations, as well as by the Anarcho-Syndicalist so-called Chicago I. W. W.,—the Bakouninism, in short, against which the genius of Marx struggled and warned.

The one-legged conclusion regarding political organization and activity as fatedly abuts, in the end, in pure and simple ballotism, as already numerously and lamentably exemplified in the Socialist party—likewise struggled and warned against by Marx as "parliamentary idiocy."

Industrial Unionism, free from optical illusions, is clear upon the goal—the substitution of the political State with the Industrial Government. Clearness of vision renders Industrial Unionism immune both to the Anarch self-deceit of the "No Government!" slogan, together with all the mischief that flows therefrom, and to the politician's "parliamentary idiocy" of looking to legislation for the overthrow of class rule.

The Industrial Union grasps the principle: "No Government, no organization; no organization, no co-operative labor; no co-operative labor, no abundance for all without arduous toil, hence, no Freedom."—Hence, the Industrial Union aims at a democratically centralized Government, accompanied by the democratically requisite "local self-rule."

The Industrial Union grasps the principle of the political state—central and local authorities disconnected from productive activity; and it grasps the requirement of the Government of Freedom—the central and local administrative authorities of the productive capabilities of the people.

The Industrial Union hearkens to the command of Social Evolution to cast the Nation, and, with the Nation, its Government, in a mold different from the mold in which Class Rule casts Nations and existing Governments. While Class Rule casts the Nation, and, with the Nation, its Government, in the mold of territory, Industrial Unionism casts the Nation in the mold of useful occupations, and transforms the Nation's Government into the representations from these. Accordingly, Industrial Unionism organizes the useful occupations of the land into constituencies of Future Society.

In performing this all-embracing function, Industrial Unionism, the legitimate offspring of civilization, comes equipped with all the experience of the Age.

Without indulging in the delusion that its progress will be a "dress parade"; and, knowing that its program carries in its fold that acute stage of all evolutionary processes known as Revolution, the Industrial Union connects with the achievements of the Revolutionary Fathers of the country, the first to frame a constitution that denies the perpetuity of their own social system, and that, by its amendment clause, legalizes Revolution. Connecting with that great achievement of the American Revolution, fully aware that the Revolution, which it is big with, being one that concerns the masses and that needs the masses for its execution, excludes the bare idea of conspiracy, and imperatively commands an open and above board

agitational, educational and organizing activity; finally, its
path lighted by the beacon tenet of Marx that none but
the bona fide Union can set on foot the true political
party of Labor;—Industrial Unionism bends its efforts
to unite the Working Class upon the political as well as
the industrial field,—on the industrial field because, without the integrally organized Union of the Working Class,
the revolutionary act is impossible; on the political field,
because on none other can be proclaimed the revolutionary purpose, without consciousness of which the Union
is a rope of sand.

Industrial Unionism is the Socialist Republic in the
making; and the goal once reached, the Industrial Union
is the Socialist Republic in operation.

Accordingly, the Industrial Union is at once the batter-
ing ram with which to pound down the fortress of Capitalism, and the successor of the capitalist social structure
itself.

A key paragraph from De Leon's *The Burning Question of Trades Unionism* (1903): Civilized society will
know no such ridiculous thing as geographic constituencies. It will only know industrial constituencies. The
parliament of civilization in America will consist, not of
Congressmen from geographic districts, but of representatives of trades throughout the land, and their legislative
work will not be the complicated one which a society of
conflicting interests, such as capitalism, requires but the
easy one which can be summed up in the statistics of the
wealth needed, the wealth producible, and the work required—and that any average set of workingmen's representatives are fully able to ascertain, infinitely better than
our modern rhetoricians in Congress.

EDWARD BERNSTEIN: SOCIALIST IDEALS, FACTS, AND EXPERIENCE[12]

This is a typical passage from the classic of common sense Socialist reformism which unloosed an ideological crusade in behalf of the orthodox faith. It is reprinted from the concluding chapter of Edward Bernstein's epoch-making book, Die Voraussetzungen des Sozialismus und die Aufgaben der Sozialdemokratie, *which gave expression and additional impetus to the revisionist movement in Germany and elsewhere.*

✓   ✓   ✓

. . . Tradition is a very widespread phenomenon from which no party, no literary or artistic line of thought, is free, and which penetrates deeply even into most of the sciences. It will probably never be quite rooted out. A certain interval of time must always pass before men so far recognise the inconsistency of tradition with what exists as to put the former on the shelf. Until this happens tradition usually forms the most powerful means of linking those together whom no strong, constant, effective interest or external pressure knits together. Hence the intuitive preference of all men of action, however revolutionary they may be in their aims, for tradition. "Never swap horses whilst crossing a stream." This motto of old Lincoln is rooted in the same thought as Lassalle's well-known anathema against the "nagging spirit of liberalism, the complaint of individual opining and wanting to know better." Whilst tradition is essentially conservative, criticism is almost always destructive. At the moment of important action, therefore, criticism,

[12] *Evolutionary Socialism,* English trans. (New York, 1909), pp. 200-05.

even when most justified by facts, can be an evil, and therefore be reprehensible.

To recognise this is, of course, not to call tradition sacred and to forbid criticism. Parties are not always in the midst of rapids when attention is paid to one task only.

For a party which has to keep up with a real evolution, criticism is indispensable and tradition can become an oppressive burden, a restraining fetter.

But men in very few cases willingly and fully account for the importance of the changes which take place in their traditional assumptions. Usually they prefer to take into account only such changes as are concerned with undeniable facts and to bring them into unison as far as can be with the traditional catchwords. The method is called pettifogging, and the apologies and explanations for it are called cant.

Cant—the word is English, and is said to have been first used in the sixteenth century as a description of the saintly sing-song of the Puritans. In its more general meaning it denotes an unreal manner of speech, thoughtlessly imitative, or used with the consciousness of its untruth, to attain any kind of object, whether it be in religion, politics, or be concerned with theory or actuality. In this wider meaning cant is very ancient. . . . Every nation, every class and every group united by theory or interest has its own cant. It has partly become such a mere matter of convention, of pure form, that no one is any longer deceived by its emptiness, and a fight against it would be shooting idly at sparrows. But this does not apply to the cant that appears in the guise of science and the cant which has become a political battle cry.

My proposition, "To me that which is generally called the ultimate aim of socialism is nothing, but the movement is everything," has often been conceived as a denial of every definite aim of the socialist movement. . . .

When eight years ago I reviewed the Schulze-Gävernitz book . . . I expressed the conviction that with the continuance of free development, the English working classes would certainly increase their demands, but would desire nothing that could not be shown each time to be necessary and attainable beyond all doubt. That is at the bottom nothing else than what I say to-day. . . .

No socialist capable of thinking dreams to-day in England of an imminent victory for socialism by means of a violent revolution—none dreams of a quick conquest of Parliament by a revolutionary proletariat. But they rely more and more on work in the municipalities and other self-governing bodies. The early contempt for the trade union movement has been given up; a closer sympathy has been won for it and, here and there also, for the co-operative movement.

And the ultimate aim? Well, that just remains an ultimate aim. "The working classes have no fixed and perfect Utopias to introduce by means of a vote of the nation. They know that in order to work out their own emancipation—and with it that higher form of life which the present form of society irresistibly makes for by its own economic development—they, the working classes, have to pass through long struggles, a whole series of historical processes, by means of which men and circumstances will be completely transformed. They have no ideals to realise, they have only to set at liberty the elements of the new society which already have been developed in the womb of the collapsing bourgeois society." So writes Marx in *Civil War in France*. I was thinking of this utterance, not in every point, but in its fundamental thought in writing down the sentence about the ultimate aim. For after all what does it say but that the movement, the series of processes, is everything, whilst every aim fixed beforehand in its details is immaterial to it. I have declared already that I willingly abandon the form of the sentence about the ultimate aim as far as it admits the interpretation that every general aim of the working class movement formulated as a principle should be declared valueless. But the preconceived theories about the drift of the movement which go beyond such a generally expressed aim, which try to determine the direction of the movement and its character without an ever-vigilant eye upon facts and experience, must necessarily always pass into Utopianism, and at some time or other stand in the way, and hinder the real theoretical and practical progress of the movement. . . .

JEAN JAURÈS: IDEALISM AND HISTORY [13]

This is Jaurès' typical argument that economics can explain everything about man except what is distinctively human.

⸸　　　⸸　　　⸸

Humanity is the product of a long physiological evolution which precedes historical evolution. When man in the course of this long physiological evolution emerged from the lower animals, there was already implanted in the first human brain certain predispositions and tendencies.

What are they?

There is to begin with the capacity for what I call disinterested sensations. One can observe that as animals rise in the scale of life the purely egoistic senses are gradually subordinated to the aesthetic and disinterested senses. In the lower ranges of animal life sight and hearing are poorly developed but the sense of odor and taste and the faculty of grasping are well developed, that is to say, the senses which are aroused by the presence of the prey and which stimulate physical and egoistic appetite. On the other hand, as animals develop there is a corresponding development of the sense of hearing and sight. Of course it is quite true that not only do the images of the prey to be seized reach the animal through its eye but also at the same time other images which do not stir the animal appetites. Similarly, through the ear the animal receives the sounds which enable it to get on the track of the prey and to avoid danger; but there also reaches it

[13] From *"L'idealisme de l'histoire,"* lecture delivered in 1894, from *Pages Choisies* (Paris, 1922), pp. 368-70.

harmonies that have no immediate relation to the animal's physical appetite and the conditions of its security. Sight is overwhelmed by images which transcend the immediate sensibility of the animal, and hearing is assailed by tones which transcend its immediate needs. In this way the universe makes itself felt in animal nature in a form quite other than that of a struggle for existence. . . .

Besides this original predisposition which the human animal brings to the long process of economic evolution, he has the further faculty, already awakened among the animals themselves, of grasping the universal in the particular, the species in the individual, of discerning the general resemblances in the diversities of things. . . .

In summary, I agree with Marx that all development ultimately is a reflection of economic phenomena in the brain but on the condition that we say that there is already in the brain, in virtue of its aesthetic sense, imaginative sympathy, and need for unitary understanding, fundamental forces which influence economic life.

Please note that I am not juxtaposing intellectual faculties with economic forces (as if they were external to each other) . . . No, I do not wish to present them in juxtaposition but I say it is impossible that observed economic phenomena can affect the human brain without setting into operation the original powers I have just analyzed. And that is why I cannot agree with Marx that religious, political, and moral conceptions are nothing but a reflection of economic phenomena. Man represents such a fusion of what is human in him and his economic environment that it is impossible to dissociate economic life from moral life. To subordinate one to the other it is first necessary to separate them from each other. But this separation is impossible. One can no more cut man in two and dissociate his organic life from his consciousness than one can cut historical humanity in two and dissociate its life of ideas and ideals from its economic life. That is my thesis whose partial confirmation I find in Greek Philosophy.

— Reading No. 13 —

N. LENIN: STATE AND REVOLUTION [14]

Following are some key passages from an important work of Lenin written on the eve of the Communist coup d'etat against the democratic Provisional Government of Russia.

✓　　　　✓　　　　✓

The state is the product and the manifestation of the irreconcilability of class antagonisms. When, where, and to what extent the State arises, depends directly on when, where, and to what extent the class antagonisms of a given society cannot be objectively reconciled. And conversely the existence of the state proves that the class antagonisms are irreconcilable . . .

The substitution of a proletarian for the capitalist State is impossible without a violent revolution, while the abolition of the proletarian State, that is, of all States, is only possible through "withering away" . . .

Marx excluded England [and the U.S.] where a revolution, even a people's revolution, could be imagined, and was then possible *without* the preliminary condition of the destruction "of the available ready machinery of the State."

To-day in 1917, in the epoch of the first great imperialist war, this distinction of Marx's becomes unreal, and England and America, the greatest and last representatives of Anglo-Saxon "liberty," in the sense of the absence of militarism and bureaucracy, have to-day completely rolled down into the dirty, bloody morass of

[14] N. Lenin, *The State and Revolution,* edition Socialist Labor Press (Glasgow, 1919), pp. 11, 26, 40, 91.

military-bureaucratic institutions common to all Europe, crushing all else under themselves. To-day, both in England and America, the "preliminary condition of any real people's revolution" is the break-up, the shattering of the "available ready machinery of the State" (perfected in those countries between 1914 and 1917, up to the "European" general imperialist standard) . . .

We are not Utopians, we do not indulge in "dreams" of how best to do away *immediately* with all management, with all subordination: these are anarchist dreams based upon a want of understanding of the tasks of a proletarian dictatorship . . . No, we want the Socialist revolution with human nature as it is now; human nature cannot itself do without subordination, without control, without managers and clerks. But there must be submission to the armed vanguard of all the exploited and laboring classes. . . .

. . . It is constantly forgotten that the destruction of the State involves also the destruction of democracy; that the withering away of the State also means the withering away of Democracy. At first sight such a statement seems exceedingly strange and incomprehensible. Indeed, perhaps someone or other may begin to fear lest we be expecting the advent of such an order of society in which the principle of majority rule will not be expected—for is not a Democracy just a recognition of this principle?

No, Democracy is not identical with majority rule. No, Democracy is a *State* which recognizes the subjection of the minority to the majority, that is, an organization for the systematic use of *violence* by one class against another, by one part of the population against another.

Democracy for an insignificant minority, democracy for the rich—that is the democracy of capitalist society. . . .

The dictatorship of the proletariat . . . cannot produce merely an expansion of democracy. *Together* with an immense expansion of democracy—for the first time becoming democracy for the poor—the dictatorship of the proletariat will produce a series of restrictions of liberties in the case of oppressors, exploiters and capitalists. We must crush them in order to free humanity from

wage-slavery; their resistance must be broken by force.
It is clear that where there is suppression there must also
be violence, and there cannot be liberty and democracy.

— Reading No. 13a —

N. LENIN: THE WORKER, THE DAY AFTER THE COMMUNISTS TAKE POWER [15]

This extract, from The State and Revolution, *gives Lenin's pre-revolutionary conception of some features of the transitional period to Communism particularly as far as "equality" is concerned.*

✓   ✓   ✓

. . . In this connection the special measures adopted
by the Commune and emphasized by Marx are particularly noteworthy: the abolition of all representative al-
lowances, and of all special salaries in the case of
officials; and the lowering of the payment of *all* servants
of the State to the level of the *workmen's wages.* Here is
shown, more clearly than anywhere else, the *break*—
from a bourgeois democracy to a proletarian democracy;
from the democracy of the oppressors to the democracy
of the oppressed; from the domination of a "special
force" for the suppression of a given class to the suppression of the oppressors by the whole force of the
majority of the nation—the proletariat and the peasants.

[15] N. Lenin, *The State and Revolution,* edition British Socialist
    Party (Glasgow, England, October, 1919).

And it is precisely on this most obvious point, perhaps the most important so far as the problem of the State is concerned, that the teachings of Marx have been forgotten. It is entirely neglected in all the innumerable popular commentaries. It is not "proper" to speak about it as if it were a piece of old-fashioned *"naiveté";* just as the Christians, having attained the position of a State religion "forget" the *"naiveté"* of primitive Christianity, with its revolutionary democratic spirit.

The lowering of the pay of the highest State officials seems simply a naive, primitive demand of democracy. One of the "founders" of the newest Opportunism, the former Social-Democrat, E. Bernstein, has more than once exercised his talents in the repetition of the vulgar capitalist jeers at "primitive" Democracy. Like all opportunists, like the present followers of Kautsky, he quite failed to understand that, first of all, the transition from Capitalism to Socialism is impossible without "return," in a measure, to "primitive" Democracy. How can we otherwise pass on to the discharge of all the functions of Government by the majority of the population and by every individual of the population? And, secondly, he forgot that "primitive Democracy" on the basis of Capitalism and capitalist culture is not the same primitive Democracy as in pre-historic or pre-capitalist times. Capitalist culture has created industry on a large scale in the shape of factories, railways, posts, telephones and so forth: and *on this basis* the great majority of functions of "the old State" have become enormously simplified and reduced, in practice, to very simple operations such as registration, filing and checking. Hence they will be quite within the reach of every literate person, and it will be possible to perform them for the usual "working man's wage." This circumstance ought, and will, strip them of all their former glamour as "Government," and, therefore, privileged service.

The control of all officials, without exception, by the unreserved application of the principle of election and, *at any time,* re-call; and the approximation of their salaries to the "ordinary pay of the workers"—these are simple and "self-evident" democratic measures, which harmonise completely the interests of the workers and the majority of peasants; and, at the same time, serve as a bridge, leading from Capitalism to Socialism. These measures refer to the State, that is, to the purely political reconstruction of society; but, of course, they only acquire their full meaning and importance when accompanied by the "expropriation of the expropriators" or at least by the preliminary steps towards it, that is, by the passage from capitalist private ownership of the means of production to social ownership.

> The Commune [wrote Marx] realised that ideal of all bourgeois revolutions, cheap Government, by eliminating the two largest items of expenditure—the army and the bureaucracy.

From the peasantry, as from other sections of the lower middle class, only an insignificant minority "rise to the top," and "enter society," make a career in a bourgeois sense, that is, become transformed either into propertied members of the upper middle class, or into secure and privileged officials. The great majority of peasants in all capitalist countries where the peasant class does exist (and the majority of capitalist countries are of this kind) are oppressed by the Government and long for its overthrow, in the hope of a "cheap" Government. This hope can only be realised by the proletariat; and by the fact of realising it, the proletariat makes a step forward at the same time towards the Socialist reconstruction of the State.

— Reading No. 14 —

N. LENIN: COMMUNIST ORGANIZATION AND STRATEGY [16]

The following are the famous "twenty-one" conditions laid down as binding upon all Communist Parties throughout the world, a year after the founding of the Communist International, and subsequently rigorously enforced. For a systematic exposition of the details of Communist strategy and tactics, see P. Selznick, The Organizational Weapon, (New York, 1952).

✓ ✓ ✓

The Second Congress of the Communist International rules that the conditions for joining the Communist International shall be as follows:

1. The general propaganda and agitation should bear a really Communist character, and should correspond to the program and decisions of the Third International. The entire party press should be edited by reliable Communists who have proved their loyalty to the cause of the proletarian revolution. The dictatorship of the proletariat should not be spoken of simply as a current hackneyed formula, it should be advocated in such a way that its necessity should be apparent to every rank-and-file workingman and workingwoman, to each soldier and peasant, and should emanate from every-day facts, systematically recorded by our press day by day.

All periodical and other publications, as well as all party publications and editions, are subject to the control

[16] From *Blueprints for World Conquest as Outlined by the Communist International* (Washington, 1946), pp. 65-72

of the presidium of the party, independently of whether the party is legal or illegal. It should in no way be permitted that the publishers abuse their autonomy and carry on a policy not fully corresponding to the policy of the party.

Wherever the followers of the Third International have access, and whatever means of propaganda are at their disposal, whether the columns of newspapers, popular meetings, labor unions or co-operatives,—it is indispensable for them not only to denounce the bourgeoisie, but also its assistants and agents—reformists of every color and shade.

2. Every organization desiring to join the Communist International shall be bound systematically and regularly to remove from all the responsible posts in the labor movement (party organization, editorship, labor unions, parliamentary factions, co-operatives, municipalities, etc.) all reformists and followers of the "centre," and to have them replaced by Communists, even at the cost of replacing at the beginning "experienced" opportunists by rank-and-file workingmen.

3. The class struggle in almost every country of Europe and America is entering the phase of civil war. Under such conditions the Communists can have no confidence in bourgeois laws. They should create everywhere a parallel illegal apparatus, which at the decisive moment should be of assistance to the party to do its duty toward the revolution. In every country where, in consequence of martial law or of other exceptional laws, the Communists are unable to carry on their work legally, a combination of legal and illegal work is absolutely necessary.

4. Persistent and systematic propaganda and agitation must be carried on in the army, where Communist groups should be formed in every military organization. Wherever owing to repressive legislation agitation becomes impossible, it is necessary to carry on such agitation illegally. But refusal to carry on or participate in such work should be considered equal to treason to the revolutionary cause, and incompatible with affiliation to the Third International.

5. A systematic and regular propaganda is necessary in the rural districts. The working class can gain no victory unless it possesses the sympathy and support of at least part of the rural workers and of the poor peasants, and unless other sections of the population are equally utilized. Communist work in the rural districts is acquiring a predominant importance during the present period. It should be carried on through Communist workmen of both city and country who have connections with the rural districts. To refuse to do this work, or to transfer such work to untrustworthy half reformists, is equal to renouncing the proletarian revolution.

6. Every party desirous of affiliating to the Third International should renounce not only avowed social patriotism, but also the falsehood and the hypocrisy of social pacifism: It should systematically demonstrate to the workers that without a revolutionary overthrow of capitalism no international arbitration, no talk of disarmament, no democratic reorganization of the League of Nations will be capable of saving mankind from new imperialist wars.

7. Parties desirous of joining the Communist International must recognize the necessity of a complete and absolute rupture with reformism and the policy of the "centrists," and must advocate this rupture amongst the widest circles of the party membership, without which condition a consistent Communist policy is impossible. The Communist International demands unconditionally and peremptorily that such rupture be brought about with the least possible delay . . .

8. In the Colonial question and that of the oppressed nationalities, there is necessary an especially distinct and clear line of conduct of the parties of countries where the bourgeoisie possesses such colonies or oppresses other nationalities. Every party desirous of belonging to the Third International should be bound to denounce without any reserve all the methods of "its own" imperialists in the colonies, supporting not in words only but practically a movement of liberation in the colonies. It should demand the expulsion of its own imperialists from such

colonies, and cultivate among the workmen of its own country a truly fraternal attitude towards the working population of the colonies and oppressed nationalities, and carry on a systematic agitation in its own army against every kind of oppression of the colonial population.

9. Every party desirous of belonging to the Communist International should be bound to carry on systematic and persistent Communist work in the labor unions, co-operatives and other organizations of working masses. It is necessary to form Communist nuclei within these organizations, which by persistent and lasting work should win over labor unions to Communism. These nuclei should constantly denounce the treachery of the social patriots and of the fluctuations of the "centre." These Communist nuclei should be completely subordinated to the party in general.

10. Any party belonging to the Communist International is bound to carry on a stubborn struggle against the Amsterdam "International" of the yellow labor unions. It should propagate insistently amongst the organized workers the necessity of a rupture with the yellow Amsterdam International. It should support by all means in its power the International Unification of Red Labor Unions joining to the Communist International.

11. Parties desirous of joining the Third International shall be bound to inspect the personnel of their parliamentary factions, to remove all unreliable elements therefrom, to control such factions, not only verbally but in reality, to subordinate them to the Central Committee of the party, and to demand from each Communist representative in parliament to subject his entire activity to the interests of real revolutionary propaganda, and agitation.

12. All the parties belonging to the Communist International should be formed on the basis of the principle of democratic centralization. At the present time of acute civil war the Communist Party will only be able fully to do its duty when it is organized in a sufficiently centralized manner; when it possesses an iron discipline and when its party centre enjoys the confidence of the party

membership and is endowed with complete power, authority and ample rights.

13. The Communist parties of those countries where the Communist activity is legal should clean out their members from time to time, as well as those of the party organizations, in order to systematically free the party from the petty bourgeois elements which penetrate into it.

14. Each party desirous of affiliating to the Communist International should be obliged to render every possible assistance to the Soviet Republics in their struggle against all counter-revolutionary forces. The Communist parties should carry on a precise and definite propaganda to induce the workers to refuse to transport any kind of military equipment intended for fighting against the Soviet Republics, and should also by legal or illegal means carry on a propaganda amongst the troops sent against the workers' republics, etc.

15. All those parties which up to the present moment have stood upon the old social democratic programs should within the shortest time possible draw up a new Communist program in conformity with the special conditions of their country, and in accordance with the resolutions of the Communist International . . .

16. All the resolutions of the congresses of the Communist International, as well as the resolutions of the Executive Committee are binding for all parties joining the Communist International. The Communist International, operating under the conditions of most acute civil warfare, should be centralized in a better manner than the Second International. At the same time, the Communist International and the Executive Committee are naturally bound in every form of their activity to consider the variety of conditions under which the different parties have to work and struggle, and generally binding resolutions should be passed only on such questions upon which such resolutions are possible.

17. In connection with the above, all parties desiring to join the Communist International should alter their names. Each party desirous of joining the Communist International should bear the following name: Communist Party of such and such a country, section of the Third

Communist International. The question of the party name is not only a formal one, but is a political question of great importance. The Communist International has declared a decisive war against the entire bourgeois world, and all the yellow Social Democratic parties. It is indispensable that every rank-and-file worker should be able clearly to distinguish between the Communist parties and the old official "Social-Democratic" or "Socialist" parties, which have betrayed the cause of the working class.

18. All the leading organs of the press of every party are bound to publish all the most important documents of the Executive Committee of the Communist International.

19. All parties which have joined the Communist International as well as those which have expressed a desire to do so are obliged in as short a space of time as possible, and in no case later than four months after the Second Congress of the Communist International, to convene an Extraordinary Congress in order to discuss these conditions. In addition to this, the Central Committees of these parties should take care to acquaint all its local organizations with the regulations of the Second Congress.

20. All those parties which at the present time are willing to join the Third International, but have so far not changed their tactics in any radical manner, should, prior to their joining the Third International, take care that not less than two-thirds of their committee members and of all their central institutions should be composed of comrades who have made an open and definite declaration prior to the convening of the Second Congress, as to their desire that the party should affiliate to the Third International. Exceptions are permitted only with the consent of the Executive Committee of the Third International. . . .

21. Those members of the party who reject in principle the conditions and the theses of the Third International, are liable to be excluded from the party. . . .

N. LENIN: ON SHOOTING CRITICS OUT OF SEASON [17]

The following selection, showing Lenin's application of terrorism to socialist critics, is taken from his speech before the Eleventh Congress of the Russian Communist Party, 1922.

✓ ✓ ✓

. . . The other day I read an article by Comrade Rakosi in No. 20 of the *Communist International* on a new book by Otto Bauer (who was our teacher at one time, but who, like Kautsky, became a miserable philistine after the war). Bauer now writes: "They are now retreating to capitalism; we have always said that the revolution is a bourgeois revolution."

And the Mensheviks and Socialist-Revolutionaries, all of whom preach this sort of thing, are astonished when we say that we shall shoot those people who say such things. They are amazed; but surely it is clear. When an army is in retreat, a hundred times more discipline is required than when the army is advancing, because during an advance everybody presses forward. If everybody started rushing back now, that would spell disaster—immediate and inevitable.

Precisely at such a moment, the most important thing is to retreat in good order, to fix the precise limits of the retreat, and not to give way to panic. And when a Menshevik says, "You are now retreating; I have been advocating retreat all the time, I agree with you, I am your man, let us retreat together," we say in reply, "For the public advocacy of Menshevism our revolutionary courts

[17] N. Lenin, *Selected Works* (Foreign Languages Publishing House: Moscow, 1951), vol. II, pt. 2, pp. 648-9.

must pass sentence of death, otherwise they are not our courts, but God knows what."

They cannot understand this and exclaim, "What dictatorial manners these people have!" They still think we are persecuting the Mensheviks because they fought us in Geneva. But had we followed them we would have been unable to hold power for two months. Indeed, the sermons which Otto Bauer, the leaders of the Second and Two-and-a-half Internationals, the Mensheviks and Social-Revolutionaries preach express their true nature: "The revolution has gone too far. What you are saying now we have been saying all the time; permit us to say it again." But we say in reply: "Permit us to put you before a firing squad for saying that. Either you refrain from expressing your views, or, if you insist on expressing your political views publicly in the present circumstances, when our position is far more difficult than it was when the Whiteguardists were directly attacking us, we shall treat you as the worst and most pernicious White Guard elements." We must never forget this. . . .

N. LENIN: ON COMMUNIST MORALITY [18]

Lenin frankly avows that Communist morality is completely subordinated to the interests of the class struggle of the proletariat. This passage is taken from an address to the Communist Youth League, 1920.

✓   ✓   ✓

Here, first of all, I will deal with the question of communist ethics.

You must train yourselves to be Communists. The task of the Youth League is to organize its practical activities in such a way that by learning, organizing, uniting, and fighting, its members should train themselves and all who look to it as a leader; it should train Communists. The whole object of training, educating, and teaching the youth of today should be to imbue them with communist ethics.

But is there such a thing as communist ethics? Is there such a thing as communist morality? Of course, there is. It is often made to appear that we have no ethics of our own; and very often the bourgeoisie accuse us Communists of repudiating all ethics. This is a method of shuffling concepts, of throwing dust in the eyes of the workers and peasants.

In what sense do we repudiate ethics and morality?

In the sense in which it is preached by the bourgeoisie, who derived ethics from God's Commandments. . . .

We repudiate all morality taken apart from human society and classes. We say that it is a deception, a fraud, a befogging of the minds of the workers and peasants by the landlords and capitalists.

[18] N. Lenin, *Selected Works* (Foreign Languages Publishing House: Moscow, 1951), vol. II, pt. 2, pp. 482-84.

We say that our morality is entirely subordinated to the interests of the class struggle of the proletariat. Our morality is derived from the interests of the class struggle of the proletariat.

The old society was based on the oppression of all the workers and peasants by the landlords and capitalists. We had to destroy this, we had to overthrow them; but for this we had to create unity. . . .

This unity could be provided only by factories and workshops, only by the proletariat, trained and aroused from its long slumber . . . We now say, on the basis of experience, that only the proletariat could have created that compact force which the disunited and scattered peasantry are following and which has withstood all the onslaughts of the exploiters. Only this class can help the toiling masses to unite, rally their ranks, and finally defend, finally consolidate and finally build up communist society.

That is why we say that there is no such thing as morality apart from human society; it is a fraud. Morality for us is subordinated to the interests of the class struggle of the proletariat . . .

. . . When people talk to us about morality, we say: for the Communist morality lies entirely in this solid, united discipline and conscious mass struggle against the exploiters. . . . The basis of communist morality is the struggle for the consolidation and completion of Communism. That, too, is the basis of communist training, education, and teaching. . . .

N. LENIN: ON COMMUNIST WORK IN TRADE-UNIONS[19]

There can be no doubt that Messrs. Gompers, Henderson, Jouhaux, and Legien are very grateful to "Left" revolutionaries, who, like the German opposition "on principle" (heaven preserve us from such "principles"!) or like some of the revolutionaries in the American Industrial Workers of the World, advocate leaving the reactionary trade unions and refusal to work in them. There need be no doubt that these gentlemen, the "leaders" of opportunism, will resort to every trick of bourgeois diplomacy, to the aid of bourgeois governments, the priests, the police, and the courts, to prevent Communists joining the trade unions, to force them out by every means, to make their work in the trade unions as unpleasant as possible, to insult, bait and persecute them. We must be able to withstand all this, to agree to all and every sacrifice, and even—if need be—to resort to various stratagems, artifices, illegal methods, to evasion and subterfuges only so as to get into the trade unions, to remain in them, and to carry on communist work in them at all costs.

[19] N. Lenin, *Selected Works* (Foreign Languages Publishing House: Moscow, 1951), vol. II, pt. 2, pp. 378-79.

— Reading No. 14d —

J. STALIN: HOW TO MAKE OFFENCE LOOK LIKE DEFENCE [20]

The Communist justification of violent overthrow of democratic regimes is that it is a measure of defence *against the anticipated reaction of opponents of their program who presumably would not abide by a peaceful democratic change in power. The following comment of Stalin on the use the Communists made of the slogan of defence under the democratic Kerensky regime throws an interesting light on their claim.*

⚹　　　⚹　　　⚹

An original peculiarity of the revolutionary tactics of this period must be pointed out. This peculiarity consists therein that the revolution attempted to carry out every, or almost every step of its attack under the appearance of defence. There is no doubt that the refusal to permit the transfer of troops was a serious aggressive act of the revolution; nevertheless this attack was undertaken under the slogan of the defence of Petrograd against a possible attack of the external enemy. There is no doubt that the formation of the revolutionary military committee was a still more serious step in the attack against the Provisional Government; nevertheless it was carried out under the slogan of the organisation of the Soviet control over the activities of the military staff. There is no doubt that the open going over of the garrison to the revolutionary military committee and the organisation of the network of Soviet commissioners indicated the beginning of the insurrection; nevertheless these steps were taken under the slogan of the defence of the Petrograd Soviets against possible attacks of the counter-revolution.

[20] From "Leninism or Trotskyism," *The Errors of Trotskyism,* English trans. (London, 1925), pp. 225-26.

It is as though the revolution had hidden its acts of aggression under the cloak of defence so as to attract all the more easily the undecided elements into its sphere of influence. This must also explain the apparent defensive character of the speeches, articles and slogans of this period, which none the less, in their intrinsic value, bore a thoroughly offensive character.

— Reading No. 15 —

LEON TROTSKY: THE PERMANENT REVOLUTION[21]

Written in 1906, Trotsky outlines the future program which Lenin and the Bolshevik Party were to adopt in 1917. At the time Trotsky wrote this, he was practically alone in his stand which represented a profound abandonment of Marxian historical materialism. It is significant that the work from which the following is extracted was republished by the Communist International in Moscow 1921, while Lenin was alive, and translated into foreign languages as well.

✓   ✓   ✓

. . . Every political party deserving the name, strives to capture political power and thus place the State at the service of the class whose interests it reflects. The Social-democrats being a proletarian party naturally strive for the political domination of the working class.

[21] From *A Review and Some Perspectives*, English trans. (Communist International: Moscow, 1921), pp. 35-40.

The proletariat grows and becomes stronger with the growth of capitalism. In this sense the development of capitalism is also the development of the proletariat towards dictatorship. But the day and the hour on which power will be transferred to the working class directly depends, not upon the level of the productive forces, but on the relations of the class struggle, on the international situation, and on the traditions, the initiative and the fighting preparedness of the workers.

It is possible for the workers to come into power in economically backward countries sooner than in advanced countries. In 1871 the workers took power in their hands in petty bourgeois Paris—true it lasted for only two months, but in highly developed capitalist England or the United States the workers have never held power for a single hour. To imagine that the dictatorship of the proletariat is in some way automatically dependent on the technical development of a country is reducing "economic" materialism to absurdity. This point of view has nothing in common with Marxism.

In our view the Russian Revolution will create conditions in which power will pass into the hands of the workers—and in the event of the victory of the revolution, it must pass into the hands of the workers—before the bourgeoisie is able to develop their ability to govern.

. . . There is no doubt that the concentration, the culture, and the political importance of the industrial proletariat depends on the extent of development of capitalist industry. But this dependence is not direct. Between the productive forces of a country and the political strength of its classes there are various social political factors which divert and sometimes completely change the form of political relations. In spite of the fact that the productivity of the United States is ten times greater than that of Russia, nevertheless the political role of the Russian proletariat, its influence on the politics of the country, and its possibility of influencing the politics of the world is incomparably greater than that of the proletariat of the United States.

. . . Does not all this give us reason to assume that the Russian "man" will take power sooner than his "master"?

There can be two forms of political optimism. One can exaggerate one's strength and advantages in a revolutionary situation and undertake tasks which are not justified by the given relation of forces. On the other hand one may optimistically put a limit to the revolutionary tasks beyond which however we shall be driven by the logic of our position.

It is possible to reduce all the questions of the revolution to a minor scale by the assertion that our revolution is bourgeois in its aims and therefore in its inevitable results, closing one's eyes to the fact that the chief actor in this bourgeois revolution is the proletariat, all the time pressing forward to power.

One may reassure oneself that in a bourgeois revolution the domination of the proletariat can only be a transitional episode, forgetting that once the proletariat has taken power in its hands it will not give it up without a desperate resistance or until it has been torn from its hands by armed force.

One may reassure oneself that the social conditions of Russia are not ripe for socialism, without thinking that the proletariat, taking power, by the very logic of its position, must inevitably press forward the introduction of State management of industry. The general sociological term bourgeois revolution by no means solves the politico-tactical problems, contradictions, and difficulties, which the mechanics of a given bourgeois revolution throw up.

In the bourgeois revolution at the end of the XVIII. century which aimed at the domination of capital, the dictatorship of the Sansculottes was found to be possible. This dictatorship was not simply a passing episode, it left its impress upon the ensuing century, in spite of the fact that it was very quickly crushed against the enclosing barriers of the bourgeois revolution. In the revolutions commencing in the XXth century, the direct aim of which is also bourgeois, we observe the growth of the inevitable, or perhaps only the probable political domin tion of the proletariat. The proletariat itself will see to it that the domination does not become a passing "episode" as some realist philistines hope. But we can at once ask ourselves: "Is it inevitable that the proletarian dicta-

torship should be crushed against the barriers of the
bourgeois revolution, or is it possible that in a given set
of world historical conditions, the prospects of victory
may open wide before it, and that it may break the barriers of the bourgeois revolution? Here we are confronted
by a question of tactics: should we consciously work for
a working class government during the period that the
revolution is developing towards this stage,—or must we
at that moment regard political power as a misfortune
which the bourgeois revolution will thrust upon the workers, and which it would be better to avoid?

— Reading No. 16 —

KARL KAUTSKY: TERRORISM AND COMMUNISM [22]

*Written in 1919, Kautsky charges the Communists with
having betrayed the principles of Marxism, socialism,
and democracy. At the time it was composed, the Communist terror was getting under way. Compared to subsequent actions, it was relatively mild, not yet unleashed
in its full fury against all opponents including workers,
peasants, socialists, and dissident Communists. (For a
Bolshevik reply see Reading No. 16a.)*

✓   ✓   ✓

Many revolutionaries of the West point triumphantly
to the fact that Bolshevism is still in power, and apparently, even at the time when these lines are being written

[22] Karl Kautsky, *Terrorism and Communism,* English trans.
    (National Labor Press: London, 1920), pp. 198, 215,
    202 ff.

(May, 1919) is still outwardly intact; yet the critics of Bolshevism at the very beginning of its rule prophesied a speedy collapse. This collapse would have actually taken place long ago, if the Bolsheviks had been true to their programme. They have merely kept themselves going by discarding one after another some part of their programme, so that finally they have achieved the very contrary to that which they set out to obtain. For instance, in order to come into power they threw overboard all their democratic principles. In order to keep themselves in power they have had to let their Socialist principles go the way of the democratic. They have maintained themselves as individuals; but they have sacrificed their principles, and have proved themselves to be thorough-going opportunists.

Bolshevism has, up to the present, triumphed in Russia, but Socialism has already suffered a defeat. We have only to look at the form of society which has developed under the Bolshevik regime, and which was bound so to develop, as soon as the Bolshevik method was applied. . . .

Originally they were whole-hearted protagonists of a National Assembly, elected on the strength of a universal and equal vote. But they set this aside, as soon as it stood in their way. They were thorough-going opponents of the death penalty, yet they established a bloody rule. When democracy was being abandoned in the State they became fiery upholders of democracy within the proletariat, but they are repressing this democracy more and more by means of their personal dictatorship. They abolished the piece-work system, and are now reintroducing it. At the beginning of their regime they declared it to be their object to smash the bureaucratic apparatus, which represented the means of power of the old State; but they have introduced in its place a new form of bureaucratic rule. They came into power by dissolving the discipline of the army, and finally the army itself. They have created a new army, severely disciplined. They strove to reduce all classes to the same level, instead of which they have called into being a new class distinction. They have created a class which stands on a lower level than the proletariat, which latter they have raised to a privileged class; and over and above this they have caused still another class to appear, which is in receipt of large incomes and enjoys high privileges. . . .

The absolutism of the old bureaucracy has come again to life in a new but, as we have seen, by no means improved form; and also alongside of this absolutism are being formed the seeds of a new capitalism, which is responsible for direct criminal practices, and which in reality stands on a much lower level than the industrial capitalism of former days. It is only the ancient feudal land estate which exists no more. For its abolition conditions in Russia were ripe. But they were not ripe for the abolition of capitalism. . . . Moreover, this loss of liberty is not compensated for by increase of prosperity. . . .

The economic, and with it also the moral, failure of Bolshevik methods is inevitable. It can only be veiled over if it should end in a military collapse. No world revolution, no help from without could hinder the economic failure of Bolshevik methods. The task of European Socialism, as against Communism, is quite different, namely, to take care that the moral catastrophe resulting from a particular *method* of Socialism shall not lead to the catastrophe of Socialism in general; and, further, to endeavour to make a sharp distinction between these methods and the Marxist method, and bring this distinction to the knowledge of the masses. Any Radical-Socialist Press must ill understand the interests of social revolution, if it really imagines it serves those interests by proclaiming to the masses the identity of Bolshevism and Socialism, making them believe that the present form of the Soviet Republic, just because it is sailing under the flag of omnipotence of the working-classes and of Socialism itself. . . .

Among the phenomena for which Bolshevism has been responsible, terrorism, which begins with the abolition of every form of freedom of the Press, and ends in a system of wholesale execution, is certainly the most striking and the most repellant of all. It is that which gave rise to the greatest hatred against the Bolsheviks. . . .

Shooting—that is the Alpha and Omega of Communist

government wisdom. Yet does not Lenin himself call upon the "intelligentsia" to help him in the struggle against the rogues and the adventurers? Certainly he does; only he withholds from them the one and only means that can help, namely the *freedom of the Press*. The control exercised by the Press, in every respect free and unimpeded, alone can keep in check those rogues and adventurers who inevitably fasten on to any Government which is unlimited in its powers and uncontrolled. Indeed, often through the very lack of the freedom of the Press these parasites thrive the more. . . .

— Reading No. 16a —

LEON TROTSKY: IN DEFENCE OF TERRORISM [23]

This is Trotsky's reply to Kautsky and other socialists. The same logic which he uses to justify terrorism against "capitalists" was subsequently used to justify terrorism against all those, including workers and peasants, who opposed the Communist party leadership. It was, at a still later time, applied to followers of Trotsky.

✓   ✓   ✓

. . . Kautsky, in spite of all the happenings in the world to-day, completely fails to realize what war is in general, and the civil war in particular. He does not understand that every, or nearly every, sympathizer with

[23] L. Trotsky, *Dictatorship vs. Democracy* (New York: Workers Party of America, 1922), pp. 54-55, 57-59.

Thiers in Paris was not merely an "opponent" of the Communards in ideas, but an agent and spy of Thiers, a ferocious enemy ready to shoot one in the back. The enemy must be made harmless, and in wartime this means that he must be destroyed.

The problem of revolution, as of war, consists in breaking the will of the foe, forcing him to capitulate and to accept the conditions of the conqueror. The will, of course, is a fact of the physical world, but in contradistinction to a meeting, a dispute, or a congress, the revolution carries out its object by means of the employment of material resources—though to a less degree than war. The bourgeoisie itself conquered power by means of revolts, and consolidated it by the civil war. In the peaceful period, it retains power by means of a system of repression. As long as class society, founded on the most deep-rooted antagonisms, continues to exist, repression remains a necessary means of breaking the will of the opposing side.

Even if, in one country or another, the dictatorship of the proletariat grew up within the external framework of democracy, this would by no means avert the civil war. The question as to who is to rule the country, *i.e.*, of the life or death of the bourgeoisie, will be decided on either side, not by references to the paragraphs of the constitution, but by the employment of all forms of violence.

. . . The degree of ferocity of the struggle depends on a series of internal and international circumstances. The more ferocious and dangerous is the resistance of the class enemy who have been overthrown, the more inevitably does the system of repression take the form of a system of terror.

. . . The Russian proletariat was the first to enter the path of the social revolution, and the Russian bourgeoisie, politically helpless, was emboldened to struggle against its political and economic expropriation only because it saw its elder sister in all countries still in power, and still maintaining economic, political, and, to a certain extent, military supremacy.

If our November revolution had taken place a few months, or even a few weeks, after the establishment of the rule of the proletariat in Germany, France, and England, there can be no doubt that our revolution would have been the most "peaceful," the most "bloodless" of all possible revolutions on this sinful earth. But this historical sequence—the most "natural" at the first glance, and, in any case, the most beneficial for the Russian working class—found itself infringed—not through our fault, but through the will of events. Instead of being the last, the Russian proletariat proved to be the first. It was just this circumstance, after the first period of confusion, that imparted desperation to the character of the resistance of the classes which had ruled in Russia previously, and forced the Russian proletariat, in a moment of the greatest peril, foreign attacks, and internal plots and insurrections, to have recourse to severe measures of State terror. No one will now say that those measures proved futile. But, perhaps, we are expected to consider them "intolerable"?

The working class, which seized power in battle, had as its object and its duty to establish that power unshakeably, to guarantee its own supremacy beyond question, to destroy its enemies' hankering for a new revolution, and thereby to make sure of carrying out Socialist reforms. Otherwise there would be no point in seizing power.

The revolution "logically" does not demand terrorism, just as "logically" it does not demand an armed insurrection. What a profound commonplace! But the revolution does require of the revolutionary class that it should attain its end by all methods at its disposal—if necessary, by an armed rising; if required, by terrorism. A revolutionary class which has conquered power with arms in its hands is bound to, and will, suppress, rifle in hand, all attempts to tear the power out of its hands. Where it has against it a hostile army, it will oppose to it its own army. Where it is confronted with armed conspiracy, attempt at murder, or rising, it will hurl at the heads of its enemies an unsparing penalty. Perhaps Kautsky has invented other methods? Or does he reduce the whole question to the *degree* of repression, and recommend in all circumstances imprisonment instead of execution?

The question of the form of repression, or of its degree, of course, is not one of "principle." It is a question of expediency. In a revolutionary period, the party which has been thrown from power, which does not reconcile itself with the stability of the ruling class, and which proves this by its desperate struggle against the latter, cannot be terrorized by the threat of imprisonment, as it does not believe in its duration. It is just this simple but decisive fact that explains the widespread recourse to shooting in a civil war.

Or, perhaps, Kautsky wishes to say that execution is not expedient, that "classes cannot be cowed." This is untrue. Terror is helpless—and then only "in the long run"—if it is employed by reaction against a historically rising class. But terror can be very efficient against a reactionary class which does not want to leave the scene of operations. *Intimidation* is a powerful weapon of policy, both internationally and internally. War, like revolution, is founded upon intimidation. A victorious war, generally speaking, destroys only an insignificant part of the conquered army, intimidating the remainder and breaking their will. The revolution works in the same way: it kills individuals, and intimidates thousands. In this sense, the Red Terror is not distinguishable from the armed insurrection, the direct continuation of which it represents. The State terror of a revolutionary class can be condemned "morally" only by a man who, as a principle, rejects (in words) every form of violence whatsoever—consequently, every war and every rising. For this one has to be merely and simply a hypocritical Quaker.

"But, in that case, in what do your tactics differ from the tactics of Tsarism?" we are asked, by the high priests of Liberalism and Kautskianism.

You do not understand this, holy men? We shall explain to you. The terror of Tsarism was directed against the proletariat. The gendarmerie of Tsarism throttled the workers who were fighting for the Socialist order. Our Extraordinary Commissions shoot landlords, capitalists, and generals who are striving to restore the capitalist order. Do you grasp this . . . distinction? Yes? For us Communists it is quite sufficient.

— Reading No. 17 —

ROSA LUXEMBURG: SOCIALISM AND THE DEMOCRATIC PROCESS [24]

Here are some characteristic passages from Rosa Luxemburg's critique of the Russian Revolution in which she limns with prescience the consequences of Bolshevik theory and practice on Soviet life.

✓ ✓ ✓

. . . Socialism in life demands a complete spiritual transformation in the masses degraded by centuries of bourgeois class rule. Social instincts in place of egotistical ones, mass initiative in place of inertia, idealism which conquers all suffering, etc., etc. No one knows this better, describes it more penetratingly; repeats it more stubbornly than Lenin. But he is completely mistaken in the means he employs. Decree, dictatorial force of the factory overseer, draconic penalties, rule by terror—all these things are but palliatives. The only way to a rebirth is the school of public life itself, the most unlimited, the broadest democracy and public opinion. It is the rule by terror which demoralizes.

When all this is eliminated, what really remains? In place of the representative bodies created by general, popular elections, Lenin and Trotsky have laid down the soviets as the only true representation of the laboring masses. But with the repression of political life in the land as a whole, life in the soviets must also become more and more crippled. Without general elections, without unrestricted freedom of press and assembly, without a free struggle of opinion, life dies out in every public

[24] Rosa Luxemburg, *The Russian Revolution*, English trans. by Bertram D. Wolfe (Workers Age Publishers: 1940), pp. 47-48, 52-54.

institution, becomes a mere semblance of life, in which
only the bureaucracy remains as the active element. Public life gradually falls asleep, a few dozen party leaders
of inexhaustible energy and boundless experience direct
and rule. Among them, in reality only a dozen outstanding heads do the leading and an elite of the working class
is invited from time to time to meetings where they are
to applaud the speeches of the leaders, and to approve
proposed resolutions unanimously—at bottom, then, a
clique affair—a dictatorship, to be sure, not the dictatorship of the proletariat, however, but only the dictatorship
of a handful of politicians, that is a dictatorship in the
bourgeois sense, in the sense of the rule of the Jacobins.
. . . Yes, we can go even further: such conditions must
inevitably cause a brutalization of public life: attempted
assassinations, shooting of hostages, etc. . . .

The basic error of the Lenin-Trotsky theory is that
they, too, just like Kautsky, oppose dictatorship to democracy. "Dictatorship *or* democracy" is the way the question is put by Bolsheviks and Kautsky alike. The latter
naturally decides in favor of "democracy," that is, of
bourgeois democracy, precisely because he opposes it to
the alternative of the socialist revolution. Lenin and
Trotsky, on the other hand, decide in favor of dictatorship in contradistinction to democracy, and thereby, in
favor of the dictatorship of a handful of persons, that
is, in favor of dictatorship on the bourgeois model. They
are two opposite poles, both alike being far removed
from a genuine socialist policy. The proletariat, when it
seizes power, can never follow the good advice of Kautsky, given on the pretext of the "unripeness of the country," the advice being to renounce the socialist revolution
and devote itself to democracy. . . .

"As Marxists," writes Trotsky, "we have never been
idol worshippers of formal democracy." Surely, we have
never been idols of formal democracy. Nor have we
ever been idol worshippers of socialism or Marxism
either. . . .

"We have never been idol worshippers of formal
democracy." All that really means is: we have always
distinguished the social kernel from the political form of

bourgeois democracy; we have always revealed the hard kernel of social inequality and lack of freedom hidden under the sweet shell of formal equality and freedom— not in order to reject the latter but to spur the working class into not being satisfied with the shell, but rather, by conquering political power, to create a socialist democracy to replace bourgeois democracy—not to eliminate democracy altogether.

But socialist democracy is not something which begins only in the promised land after the foundations of socialist economy are created; it does not come as some sort of Christmas present for the worthy people who, in the interim, have loyally supported a handful of socialist dictators. Socialist democracy begins simultaneously with the beginnings of the destruction of class rule and of the construction of socialism. It begins at the very moment of the seizure of power by the socialist party. It is the same thing as the dictatorship of the proletariat.

Yes, dictatorship! But this dictatorship consists in the *manner of applying democracy,* not in its *elimination,* in energetic, resolute attacks upon the well-entrenched rights and economic relationships of bourgeois society, without which a socialist transformation cannot be accomplished. But this dictatorship must be the work of the *class* and not of a little leading minority in the name of the class—that is, it proceed step by step out of the active participation of the masses; it must be under their direct influence, subjected to the control of complete public activity; it must arise out of the growing political consciousness of the mass of the people. . . .

JOSEPH STALIN: THE GENERALIZATION OF THE PERMANENT REVOLUTION [25]

Stalin accepts the thesis of the permanent revolution in terms of Lenin's formulation. This should be compared carefully with Reading No. 15.

✓   ✓   ✓

. . . Where will the revolution begin? Where, in what country, can the front of capital be pierced first?

Where industry is more developed, where the proletariat constitutes the majority, where there is more culture, where there is more democracy—that was the reply usually given formerly.

No, objects the Leninist theory of revolution; *not necessarily where industry is more developed,* and so forth. The front of capital will be pierced where the chain of imperialism is weakest, for the proletarian revolution is the result of the breaking of the chain of the world imperialist front at its weakest link; and it may turn out that the country which has started the revolution, which has made a breach in the front of capital, is less developed in a capitalist sense than other, more developed, countries, which have, however, remained within the framework of capitalism.

In 1917 the chain of the imperialist world front proved to be weaker in Russia than in the other countries. It was there that the chain gave way and provided an outlet for the proletarian revolution. Why? Because in Russia a great popular revolution was unfolding, and at its head marched the revolutionary proletariat, which had

[25] J. Stalin, *Problems of Leninism* (Foreign Languages Publishing House: Moscow, 1953), pp. 37-38.

such an important ally as the vast mass of the peasantry who were oppressed and exploited by the landlords. Because the revolution there was opposed by such a hideous representative of imperialism as tsarism, which lacked all moral prestige and was deservedly hated by the whole population. The chain proved to be weaker in Russia, although that country was less developed in a capitalist sense than, say, France or Germany, England, or America.

Where will the chain break in the near future? Again, where it is weakest. It is not precluded that the chain may break, say, in India. Why? Because that country has a young, militant, revolutionary proletariat, which has such an ally as the national liberation movement—an undoubtedly powerful and undoubtedly important ally. Because there the revolution is confronted by such a well-known foe as foreign imperialism, which lacks all moral credit and is deservedly hated by the oppressed and exploited masses of India.

It is also quite possible that the chain will break in Germany. Why? Because the factors which are operating, say, in India are beginning to operate in Germany as well; but, of course, the enormous difference in the level of development between India and Germany cannot but stamp its imprint on the progress and outcome of a revolution in Germany. . . .

JOSEPH STALIN: ON THE DICTATORSHIP OF THE PROLETARIAT [26]

Stalin restates Lenin in catechetical form.

✓   ✓   ✓

From this theme I take the three fundamental questions:

a) the dictatorship of the proletariat as the instrument of the proletarian revolution;

b) the dictatorship of the proletariat as the rule of the proletariat over the bourgeoisie:

c) the Soviet power as the state form of the dictatorship of the proletariat.

1. *The dictatorship of the proletariat as the instrument of the proletarian revolution.* The question of the proletarian dictatorship is above all a question of the main content of the proletarian revolution. The proletarian revolution, its movement, its sweep and its achievements acquire flesh and blood only through the dictatorship of the proletariat. The dictatorship of the proletariat is the instrument of the proletarian revolution, its organ, its most important mainstay, brought into being for the purpose of, firstly, crushing the resistance of the overthrown exploiters and consolidating the achievements of the proletarian revolution, and, secondly, carrying the proletarian revolution to its completion, carrying the revolution to the complete victory of socialism. The revolution can vanquish the bourgeoisie, can overthrow its power, without the dictatorship of the proletariat. But the revolution will be unable to crush the resistance of the bour-

[26] J. Stalin, *Problems of Leninism* (Foreign Languages Publishing House: Moscow, 1953), pp. 46-52.

geoisie, to maintain its victory and to push forward to the final victory of socialism unless, at a certain stage of its development, it creates a special organ in the form of the dictatorship of the proletariat as its principal mainstay.

"The fundamental question of every revolution is the question of power." (*Lenin.*) Does this mean that all that is required is to assume power, to seize it? No, it does not. The seizure of power is only the beginning. For many reasons the bourgeoisie that is overthrown in one country remains for a long time stronger than the proletariat which has overthrown it. Therefore, the whole point is to retain power, to consolidate it, to make it invincible. What is needed to attain this? To attain this it is necessary to carry out at least the three main tasks that confront the dictatorship of the proletariat "on the morrow" of victory.

a) to break the resistance of the landlords and capitalists who have been overthrown and expropriated by the revolution, to liquidate every attempt on their part to restore the power of capital;

b) to organize construction in such a way as to rally all the labouring people around the proletariat, and to carry on this work along the lines of preparing for the liquidation, the abolition of classes;

c) to arm the revolution, to organize the army of the revolution for the struggle against foreign enemies, for the struggle against imperialism. . . .

2. *The dictatorship of the proletariat as the rule of the proletariat over the bourgeoisie.* From the foregoing it is evident that the dictatorship of the proletariat is not a mere change of personalities in the government, a change of "cabinet," etc., leaving the old economic and political order intact. The Mensheviks and opportunists of all countries, who fear dictatorship like fire and in their fright substitute the concept "conquest of power" for the concept "dictatorship," usally reduce the "conquest of power" to a change of "cabinet," to the accession to power of a new cabinet made up of people like Scheidemann and Noske, MacDonald and Henderson. It is hardly necessary to explain that these and similar cabinet

changes have nothing in common with the dictatorship of the proletariat, with the conquest of real power by the real proletariat. The MacDonalds and Scheidemanns in power, while the old bourgeois order is allowed to remain, their so-called governments cannot be anything else than an apparatus serving the bourgeoisie, a screen to hide the ulcers of imperialism, a weapon in the hands of the bourgeoisie against the revolutionary movement of the oppressed and exploited masses. Capital needs such governments as a screen when it finds it inconvenient, unprofitable, difficult to oppress and exploit the masses without the aid of a screen. . . .

The dictatorship of the proletariat arises not on the basis of the bourgeois order, but in the process of the breaking up of this order after the overthrow of the bourgeoisie, in the process of the expropriation of the landlords and capitalists, in the process of the socialization of the principal instruments and means of production, in the process of violent proletarian revolution. The dictatorship of the proletariat is a revolutionary power based on the use of force against the bourgeoisie.

The state is a machine in the hands of the ruling class for suppressing the resistance of its class enemies. *In this respect* the dictatorship of the proletariat does not differ essentially from the dictatorship of any other class, for the proletarian state is a machine for the suppression of the bourgeoisie. But there is one *substantial* difference. This difference consists in the fact that all hitherto existing class states have been dictatorships of an exploiting minority over the exploited majority, whereas the dictatorship of the proletariat is the dictatorship of the exploited majority over the exploiting minority.

Briefly: *the dictatorship of the proletariat is the rule—unrestricted by law and based on force—of the proletariat over the bourgeoisie,* a rule enjoying the sympathy and support of the labouring and exploited masses. (Lenin, *The State and Revolution.*)

From this follow two main conclusions:

First conclusion: The dictatorship of the proletariat cannot be "complete" democracy, democracy for *all,* for the rich as well as for the poor; the dictatorship of the proletariat "must be a state that is democratic *in a new way* (*for* the proletariat and nonpropertied in general) and dictatorial *in a new way* (*against*[27] the bourgeoisie)" (See Vol. XXI, p. 393.) The talk of Kautsky and Co. about universal equality, about "pure" democracy, about "perfect" democracy, and the like, is a bourgeois of the indubitable fact that the equality between exploited and exploiters is impossible. The theory of "pure" democracy is the theory of the upper stratum of the working class, which has been broken in and is being fed by the imperialist robbers. It was brought into being for the purpose of concealing the ulcers of capitalism, of touching up imperialism and lending it moral strength in the struggle against the exploited masses. Under capitalism there are no real "liberties" for the exploited, nor can there be, if for no other reason than that the premises, printing plants, paper supplies, etc., indispensable for the actual enjoyment of "liberties" are the privilege of the exploiters. Under capitalism the exploited masses do not, nor can they ever, really participate in the administration of the country, if for no other reason than that, even under the most democratic regime, under conditions of capitalism, governments are not set up by the people but by the Rotschilds and Stinneses, the Rockefellers and Morgans. Democracy under capitalism is *capitalist* democracy, the democracy of the exploiting minority, based on the restriction of the rights of the exploited majority and directed against this majority.

Second conclusion: The dictatorship of the proletariat cannot emerge as the result of the peaceful development of bourgeois society and of bourgeois democracy; it can emerge only as the result of the smashing of the bourgeois state machine, the bourgeois army, the bourgeois bureaucratic machine, the bourgeois police. . . .

[27] Author's italics.—*J.St.*

— Reading No. 20 —

JOSEPH STALIN: SOCIALISM IN ONE COUNTRY[28]

Stalin develops the theme of building socialism in one country without relinquishing the objective of international revolution. For a critique of this conception, see Reading No. 22.

✓   ✓   ✓

What do we mean by the *possibility* of the victory of socialism in one country?

We mean the possibility of solving the contradictions between the proletariat and the peasantry with the aid of the internal forces of our country, the possibility of the proletariat assuming power and using that power to build a complete socialist society in our country, with the sympathy and support of the proletarians of other countries, but without the preliminary victory of the proletarian revolution in other countries.

Without such a possibility, building socialism is building without prospects, building without being sure that socialism will be completely built. It is no use engaging in building socialism without being sure that we can build it completely, without being sure that the technical backwardness of our country is not an *insuperable* obstacle to the complete construction of a fully socialist society. To deny such a possibility is to display lack of faith in the cause of building socialism, to abandon Leninism.

What do we mean by the *impossibility* of the complete, final victory of socialism in one country without the victory of the revolution in other countries?

We mean the impossibility of having full guarantees

[28] J. Stalin, *Problems of Leninism* (Foreign Languages Publishing House: Moscow, 1953), pp. 192-93.

against intervention, and consequently against the restoration of the bourgeois order, without the victory of the revolution in at least a number of countries. To deny this indisputable thesis is to abandon internationalism, to abandon Leninism.

"We are living," says Lenin, "not merely in a state, but *in a system of states,* and the existence of the Soviet Republic side by side with imperialist states for a long time is unthinkable. One or the other must triumph in the end. And before that end supervenes, a series of frightful collisions between the Soviet Republic and the bourgeois states will be inevitable. That means that if the ruling class, the proletariat, wants to, and will, hold sway, it must prove its capacity to do so by military organization also.

"We now have before us," says Lenin in another place, "an extremely unstable equilibrium, but an unquestionable, an indisputable, a certain equilibrium nevertheless. Will it last long? I cannot tell; nor, I think, can anyone tell. And therefore we must exercise the greatest possible caution. And the first precept of our policy, the first lesson to be learned from our governmental activities during the past year, the lesson which all the workers and peasants must learn, is that we must be on the alert, we must remember that we are at all times but a hair's breadth from every manner of invasion."

Clear, one would think! . . .

. . . Will it not be more correct to say that it is not the Party but Zinoviev who is sinning against internationalism and the international revolution? For what else is our country, 'the country that is building socialism,' if not the base of the world revolution? But can it be a real base of the world revolution if it is incapable of completing the building of a socialist society? Can it remain the mighty center of attraction for the workers of all countries that it undoubtedly is now, if it is incapable of achieving victory over the capitalist elements in its own economy, the victory of socialist construction? I think not. But does it not follow from this that scepticism regarding the victory of socialist construction, the dissemination of such scepticism, will lead to our country being discredited as the base of the world revolution? And if our country is discredited the world revolutionary movement will be weakened. How did Messrs. the Social-Democrats try to scare the workers away from us? By preaching that 'the Russians will not get anywhere.' What are we beating the Social-Democrats with now, when we are attracting numerous workers' delegations to our country and thereby strengthening the position of communism all over the world? By our successes in building socialism. Is it not obvious, then, that whoever disseminates scepticism regarding our successes in building socialism thereby indirectly helps the Social-Democrats, reduces the sweep of the international revolutionary movement, and inevitably departs from internationalism? . . .

LEON TROTSKY: CRITICISM OF THE THEORY OF SOCIALISM IN ONE COUNTRY [29]

Trotsky proves that just as he and Lenin revised Marx and Engels, Stalin has revised the revision. It is interesting to observe that Trotsky's own revision of traditional Marxism is presented as a correction which history itself carried out. The logic of events, so to speak, corrected the logic of the theory. Stalin could have plausibly argued in the same way instead of denying that he was revising Lenin's position. In any case, the Bolsheviks actually brought the events about whose logic they subsequently cited in justification of their action.

⚹   ⚹   ⚹

. . . In our epoch, which is the epoch of imperialism, i.e., of *world* economy and *world* politics under the hegemony of finance capital, not a single communist party can establish its program by proceeding solely or mainly from conditions and tendencies of developments in its own country. This also holds entirely for the party that wields the state power within the boundaries of the U.S.S.R. On August 4, 1914, the death knell sounded for national programs for all time. The revolutionary party of the proletariat can base itself only upon an international program corresponding to the development and collapse of capitalism. An international communist program is in no case the sum total of national programs or an amalgam of their common features. The international

[29] Leon Trotsky, *The Third International After Lenin* (New York: Pioneer Publishers, 1936), vol. I, pp. 3-4, 16-17, 20-21, 35-36, 66-67.

program must proceed directly from an analysis of the conditions and tendencies of world economy and of the world political system taken as a whole in all its connections and contradictions, that is, with the mutually antagonistic interdependence of its separate parts. In the present epoch, to a much larger extent than in the past, the national orientation of the proletariat must and can flow only from a world orientation and not *vice versa*. Herein lies the basic and primary difference between communist internationalism and all varieties of national socialism.

. . . The international revolution is regarded as an interconnected process which cannot be predicted in all its concreteness, and, so to speak, its order of occurrence, but which is absolutely clearcut in its general historical outline. Unless the latter is understood, a correct political orientation is entirely out of the question.

However, matters appear quite differently if we proceed from the idea of a socialist development which is occurring and is even being completed in one country. We have today a "theory" which teaches that it is possible to build socialism completely in one country and that the correlations of that country with the capitalist world can be established on the basis of "neutralizing" the world bourgeoisie (Stalin). The necessity for the slogan of a United States of Europe falls away, or is at least diminished, if this essentially national-reformist and not revolutionary-internationalist point of view is adopted. But this slogan is, from our viewpoint, important and vitally necessary because there is lodged in it the condemnation of the idea of an isolated socialist development. For the proletariat of every European country, even to a larger measure than the U.S.S.R.—the difference, however, is one of degree only—it will be most vitally necessary to spread the revolution to the neighboring countries and to support insurrections there with arms in hand, not out of any abstract considerations of international solidarity, which in themselves cannot set the classes in motion, but because of those vital considerations which Lenin formulated hundreds of times—namely, that without *timely* aid from the international revolution, we will be unable to hold out. The slogan of the Soviet United States [of Europe] corresponds to the dynamics of the proletarian revolution, which does not break out simultaneously in all countries, but which passes from country to country and requires the closest bond between them, especially on the European arena, both with a view to defense against the most powerful external enemies, and with a view to economic construction.

. . . Immediately after its one-sided characterization of the law of uneven development pointed out by us, the draft program (of the Sixth Congress of the Communist International) says:

"Hence it follows that the international proletarian revolution must not be regarded as a single simultaneous, and universal act. Hence it follows that the victory of socialism is at first possible in a few, or even in one isolated capitalist country."

That the international revolution of the proletariat cannot be a simultaneous act, of this there can of course be no dispute at all among grownup people after the experience of the October Revolution, achieved by the proletariat of a backward country under pressure of historical necessity, without waiting in the least for the proletariat of the advanced countries "to even out the front." Within these limits, the reference to the law of uneven development is absolutely correct and quite in place. But it is entirely otherwise with the second half of the conclusion—namely, the hollow assertion that the victory of socialism is possible "in one isolated capitalist country." To prove its point the draft program simply says: "Hence it follows. . . ." One gets the impression that this follows from the law of uneven development. But this does not follow at all. "Hence follows" something quite the contrary. If the historical process were such that some countries developed not only unevenly but even *independently of each other,* isolated from each other, then from the law of uneven development would indubitably follow the possibility of building socialism in one capitalist country—at first in the most advanced country and then, as they mature, in the more backward ones. Such was the customary and, so to speak, average

idea of the transition to socialism within the ranks of
the pre-war social democracy. This is precisely the idea
that formed the theoretical basis of social-patriotism. Of
course, the draft program does not hold this view. But it
inclines towards it.

. . . Stalin said in November 1926: "The party always
took as its starting point the idea that the victory of
socialism in one country means the possibility to build
socialism in that country, and that this task can be accomplished with the forces of a single country." (*Pravda*,
Nov. 12, 1926.)

We already know that the party *never took this as its
starting point*. On the contrary, "in many of our works, in
all our speeches, and in our entire press," as Lenin said,
the party proceeded from the opposite position, which
found its highest expression in the program of the
C.P.S.U. But one would imagine that at least Stalin himself "always" proceeded from this false view that "socialism can be built with the forces of one country." Let us
check up.

What Stalin's views on this question were in 1905 or
1915 we have absolutely no means of knowing as there
are no documents whatever on the subject. But in 1924,
Stalin outlined Lenin's views on the building of socialism,
as follows:

"The overthrow of the power of the bourgeoisie and
the establishment of a proletarian government in one
country does not yet guarantee the complete victory of
socialism. The main task of socialism—the *organization
of socialist production*—still remains ahead. Can this
task be accomplished, can the final victory of socialism in
one country be attained, without the joint efforts of the
proletariat of several advanced countries? *No, this is
impossible.* To overthrow the bourgeoisie, the efforts of
one country are sufficient—the history of our revolution
bears this out. For the final victory of socialism, *for the
organization of socialist production, the efforts of one
country, particularly of such a peasant country as Russia
are insufficient*. For this the efforts of the proletarians of
several advanced countries are necessary. . . .

"Such, on the whole, are *the characteristic features of the Leninist theory of the proletarian revolution.*" (Stalin, *Lenin and Leninism,* pp. 40f., Russian ed., 1924.)

One must concede that the "characteristic features of the Leninist theory" are outlined here quite correctly. In the later editions of Stalin's book this passage was altered to read in just the opposite way and the "characteristic features of the Leninist theory" were proclaimed within a year as . . . Trotskyism.

. . . The theory of socialism in one country inexorably leads to an underestimation of the difficulties which must be overcome and to an exaggeration of the achievements gained. One could not find a more anti-social and anti-revolutionary assertion than Stalin's statement to the effect that "socialism has already been 90 percent realized in the U.S.S.R." This statement seems to be especially meant for a smug bureaucrat. In this way one can hopelessly discredit the idea of a socialist society in the eyes of the toiling masses. The Soviet proletariat has achieved grandiose successes, if we take into consideration the conditions under which they have been attained and the low cultural level inherited from the past. But these achievements constitute an extremely small magnitude on the scales of the socialist ideal. Harsh truth and not sugary falsehood is needed to fortify the worker, the agricultural laborer, and the poor peasant, who see that in the eleventh year of the revolution, poverty, misery, unemployment, bread lines, illiteracy, homeless children, drunkenness, and prostitution have not abated around them. Instead of telling them fibs about having realized 90% socialism, we must say to them that our economic level, our social and cultural conditions, approximate today much closer to capitalism, and a backward and uncultured capitalism at that, than to socialism. We must tell them that we will enter on the path of *real* socialist construction only when the proletariat of the most advanced countries will have captured power; that it is necessary to work unremittingly for this, using both levers—the short lever of our internal economic efforts and the long lever of the international proletarian struggle.

In short, instead of the Stalinist phrases about socialism which has already been 90% accomplished, we must speak to them the words of Lenin:

"Russia (the land of poverty) will become such a land (the land of plenty) if we cast away all pessimism and phrasemongering; if clenching our teeth, we gather all our might, strain every nerve and muscle, if we understand that salvation is possible *only* along the road of international socialist revolution that we have entered." (*Works,* Vol. XV, p. 165.)

— Reading No. 21 —

JOSEPH STALIN: THE RENEWED BLOSSOMING OF THE STATE [30]

Following is Stalin's justification of the continuation and development of the state power.

✓   ✓   ✓

. . . It is sometimes asked: "We have abolished the exploiting classes; there are no longer any hostile classes in the country; there is nobody to suppress; hence there is no more need for the state; it must die away.—Why then do we not help our socialist state to wither away? Why do we not strive to put an end to it? Is it not time to get rid of the state, as so much lumber?"

Or again: "The exploiting classes have already been

[30] J. Stalin, *Problems of Leninism* (Foreign Languages Publishing House: Moscow, 1953), pp. 790-94.

abolished in our country; socialism has in the main been
built; we are advancing towards communism. Now, the
Marxist doctrine of the state says that there is to be no
state under communism.—Why then do we not help our
socialist state to wither away? Is it not time we relegated
the state to the museum of antiquities?"

These questions show that those who ask them have
conscientiously memorized certain tenets of the doctrine
of Marx and Engels about the state. But they also show
that these comrades have not grasped the essential meaning of this doctrine; that they do not realize in what
historical conditions the various tenets of this doctrine
were elaborated; and, what is more, that they do not
understand present-day international conditions, have
overlooked the capitalist encirclement and the dangers it
entails for the socialist country. These questions not only
betray an underestimation of the capitalist encirclement,
but also an underestimation of the role and significance
of the bourgeois states and their organs, which send spies,
assassins and wreckers into our country and are waiting
for a favourable opportunity to attack it by armed
force. . . .

What could have given rise to this underestimation?

It arose owing to the fact that certain of the general
tenets of the Marxist doctrine of the state were incom-
pletely elaborated and were inadequate. It received currency owing to our unpardonably heedless attitude to
matters pertaining to the theory of the state, in spite
of the fact that we have had twenty years of practical
experience in state affairs which provides rich material for
theoretical generalizations, and in spite of the fact that,
given the desire, we have every opportunity of successfully filling this gap in theory. . . .

Consider, for example, the classical formulation of the
theory of the development of the socialist state given by
Engels:

> "As soon as there is no longer any class of society
> to be held in subjection; as soon as, along with class
> domination and the struggle for individual existence
> based on the anarchy of production hitherto, the col-
> lisions and excesses arising from these have also been

abolished, there is nothing more to be repressed which would make a special repressive force, a state, necessary. The first act in which the state really comes forward as the representative of society as a whole—the taking possession of the means of production in the name of society—is at the same time its last independent act as a state. The interference of the state power in social relations becomes superfluous in one sphere after another, and then ceases of itself. The government of persons is replaced by the administration of things and the direction of the processes of production. The state is not 'abolished,' *it withers away*."

Is this proposition of Engels' correct?

Yes, it is correct, but only on one of two conditions: a) *if* we study the socialist state only from the angle of the internal development of a country, abstracting ourselves in advance from the international factor, isolating, for the convenience of investigation, the country and the state from the international situation; or b) *if* we assume that socialism is already victorious in all countries, or in the majority of countries, that a socialist encirclement exists instead of a capitalist encirclement, that there is no more danger of foreign attack, and that there is no more need to strengthen the army and the state.

Well, but what if socialism has been victorious only in one separate country, and if, in view of this, it is quite impossible to abstract oneself from international conditions—what then? Engels' formula does not furnish an answer to this question. As a matter of fact, Engels did not set himself this question, and therefore could not have given an answer to it. Engels proceeds from the assumption that socialism has already been victorious more or less simultaneously in all countries, or in a majority of countries. Consequently, Engels is not here investigating any specific socialist state of any particular country, but the development of the socialist state in general, on the assumption that socialism has been victorious in a majority of countries—according to the formula: "Assuming that socialism is victorious in a majority of countries, what changes must the proletarian, socialist state undergo?" Only this general and abstract character of the problem can explain why in his investigation of the question of the socialist state Engels completely abstracted himself from such a factor as international conditions, the international situation.

But it follows from this that Engels' general formula about the destiny of the socialist state in general cannot be extended to the particular and specific case of the victory of socialism in one separate country, a country which is surrounded by a capitalist world, is subject to the menace of foreign military attack, cannot therefore abstract itself from the international situation, and must have at its disposal a well-trained army, well-organized penal organs, and a strong intelligence service, consequently, must have its own state, strong enough to defend the conquests of socialism from foreign attack. . . .

— Reading No. 22 —

THE COMMUNIST PARTY LINE IN CULTURE: LITERATURE [31]

Following are a few official declarations illustrating the fruits of party dictatorship in culture. These are only samplings of the different fields from astronomy to zoology in which the Communist party has exercised thought control with all the sanctions of the state ready to enforce

[31] From *The Country of the Blind,* by George S. Counts and Nucia Lodge (Boston: Houghton, Mifflin, 1949), pp. 79-83. With permission of the authors. This book is a treasure trove of official documents on the party-line in culture.

its decrees. The English translations of the official decrees have been made by George S. Counts and Nucia Lodge.

✓   ✓   ✓

. . . The Central Committee of the All-Union Communist Party notes that the literary journals, *Zvezda* and *Leningrad,* published in Leningrad, are conducted in an entirely unsatisfactory manner.

In the journal *Zvezda* in recent times, along with significant and successful works by Soviet writers, ideologically harmful works have appeared. The gross mistake of *Zvezda* is the placing of a literary tribune at the disposal of the writer Zoshchenko, whose works are alien to Soviet literature. The fact is well known to the editors of *Zvezda* that for a long time Zoshchenko has specialized in writing shallow, empty, and vulgar stories, in preaching decadent banality and neutrality in ideology and politics, designed to confuse and poison the consciousness of our youth. The last of Zoshchenko's published stories, "The Adventures of a Monkey" (*Zvezda,* Nos. 5-6, 1946), is a vulgar parody on Soviet life and Soviet people.

. . . The Central Committee notes that the journal *Leningrad,* which has constantly offered its pages to the vulgar and slanderous attacks of Zoshchenko and to the empty and non-political verses of Akhmatova, is especially badly conducted. Just as the editorial board of *Zvezda,* so the editorial board of the journal *Leningrad* has tolerated grievous mistakes by publishing a series of works saturated with the spirit of servility toward everything foreign.

. . . What is the meaning of the mistakes of the editorial boards of *Zvezda* and *Leningrad*?

The leading workers of the journals and in the first instance the editors, Comrades Saianov and Likharev, have forgotten the thesis of Leninism that our journals, whether scientific or literary, cannot be non-political. They have forgotten that our journals are a mighty instrument of the Soviet state in the cause of the education of the Soviet people, and Soviet youth in particular. They must therefore be controlled by the vital foundation of the Soviet order—its politics.

. . . The Central Committee of the All-Union Communist Party resolves:

1. To oblige the editorial board of the journal *Zvezda*, the Administration of the Union of Soviet Writers, and the Administration of Propaganda of the Central Committee of the All-Union Communist Party to undertake measures for the unconditioned removal of the mistakes and shortcomings of the journal mentioned in the present resolution, to correct the line of the journal, and to insure a high ideological and artistic level of the journal, putting a stop to the appearance in the journal of the works of Zoshchenko and Akhmatova and their ilk.

2. In view of the fact that at the present time the necessary conditions for the publication of two literary journals in Leningrad do not exist, to discontinue the publication of the journal *Leningrad*, concentrating the literary forces of *Leningrad* on the journal *Zvezda*.

3. For the purpose of introducing the necessary order into the work of the editorial office of the journal *Zvezda* and of radically improving the content of its pages, to appoint an editor-in-chief and an editorial board. To have the editor-in-chief assume full responsibility for the ideological and political direction of the journal and for the quality of the works published therein.

4. To appoint Comrade A. M. Yegolin as editor-in-chief of the journal *Zvezda* without relieving him of the duties of Acting Director of the Administration of Propaganda of the Central Committee of the All-Union Communist Party.

THE COMMUNIST PARTY LINE IN MUSIC [32]

. . . The Central Committee of the All-Union Communist Party considers the opera *Velikaia Druzhba* (Music by Vano Muradeli, Libretto by G. Mdivani) produced at the Bolshoi Theatre of the USSR on the Thirtieth Anniversary of the October Revolution to be vicious and inartistic in both its music and its subject matter.

The basic defects of the opera lie first of all in the music. The music is feeble and inexpressive. It contains not a single melody or aria to be remembered. It is confused and disharmonious, built on complicated dissonances, on combinations of sound that grate upon the ear. Some lines and scenes with pretensions to melodiousness are suddenly broken by discordant noises wholly strange to the normal human ear and oppressive to the listener. Between the musical accompaniment and the development of the action on the stage there is no organic connection. The vocal part of the opera—the choral, solo, and ensemble singing—produces a miserable impression. As a result of all this, the potentialities of the orchestra and the singers are not exploited.

. . . The Central Committee of the Party holds that the failure of Muradeli's opera is the result of the formalistic path which he has followed—a path which is false and injurious to the creative work of the Soviet composer.

The conference of Soviet musicians, conducted by the Central Committee of the Party, showed that the failure of Muradeli's opera is not an isolated case. It is closely linked with the unsatisfactory state of contemporary

[32] From *The Country of the Blind,* by George S. Counts and Nucia Lodge (Boston: Houghton, Mifflin, 1949), pp. 160-66.

Soviet music, with the spread of a formalistic tendency among Soviet composers.

As far back as 1936, in connection with the appearance of Dmitri Shostakovich's opera *Lady Macbeth of Mtsensk, Pravda*, the organ of the Central Committee of the Party, subjected to sharp criticism the antipopular formalistic perversions in his music and exposed the harm and danger of this tendency to the future of Soviet music. Writing then on instructions from the Central Committee of theParty, *Pravda* formulated clearly the Soviet people's requirements of their composers.

. . . The Central Committee of the All-Union Communist Party resolves:

1. To condemn the formalistic tendency in Soviet music as against the people and as leading actually to the liquidation of music.

2. To propose to the Administration of Propaganda and Agitation of the Central Committee and the Committee on the Arts that they endeavor to correct the situation in Soviet music, liquidate the shortcomings set forth in the present resolution of the Central Committee, and ensure the development of Soviet music in the direction of realism.

. . . 4. To approve organizational measures of the appropriate Party and Soviet organs directed toward the improvement of musical affairs.

— Reading No. 226 —

THE COMMUNIST PARTY LINE IN DRAMA [33]

. . . In discussing the question of the repertoire of the dramatic theatres and measures for its improvement, the Central Committee of the All Union Communist Party recognizes that the condition of the repertoire of the theatres is unsatisfactory.

. . . The Central Committee of the Party holds that the Committee on Artistic Affairs follows an incorrect line by introducing plays of bourgeois foreign dramatists. The publishing house Iskusstvo, in accordance with instructions from the Committee on Artistic Affairs, has published a volume of one-act plays by contemporary English and American dramatists.

. . . The Central Committee of the All-Union Communist Party resolves:

1. To require the president of the Committee on Artistic Affairs, Comrade Khrapchenko, to eliminate in the shortest possible period the grave shortcomings and mistakes noted in the present resolution.

2. Because of the profound significance of the theatre in the Communist education of the people, to require the Committee on Artistic Affairs and the Union of Soviet Writers to concentrate on the creation of a contemporary Soviet repertoire.

[33] From *The Country of the Blind,* by George S. Counts and Nucia Lodge (Boston: Houghton, Mifflin, 1949), pp. 119-22.

THE COMMUNIST PARTY LINE IN BIOLOGY[34]

. . . "Before beginning the concluding address," said Lysenko, "I must respond to a note which has reached the Presidium. I am asked: What is the attitude of the Central Committee of the All-Union Communist Party to the address which I delivered at this session? My answer is: The Central Committee of the All-Union Communist Party examined and approved my address, 'On the Situation in Biological Science.'"

. . . This announcement by the President evoked the general enthusiasm of the members of the session. With one impulse all those present rose from their seats and engaged in a stormy and prolonged ovation in honor of the Central Committee of the Party of Lenin and Stalin, in honor of the wise leader and teacher of the Soviet people, the greatest scholar of our epoch, Comrade Stalin. . . .

In clear and profoundly thoughtful theses Academician T. D. Lysenko exposed the hopeless attempts of various representatives of the reactionary and decadent school of Mendel and Morgan to defend their positions in science. At the same time he outlined the militant tasks of biological science in the immediate future.

"In science," says Academician T. D. Lysenko, "there is no place for chance. Physics and chemistry achieved stupendous successes in their development because they repudiated the explanation of natural phenomena in terms of chance. Biological science must profit from this experience.

[34] From *PRAVDA,* August 10, 1948, quoted in *The Country of the Blind,* by George S. Counts and Nucia Lodge (Boston: Houghton, Mifflin, 1949), pp. 206-08; 211-12.

"The entire idealistic chromosome theory of inheritance is based on chance. The process of fertilization is subject to pure chance. The splitting of hybrids is subject to chance. The causes of hereditary changes are unknown and are also due to chance. Chance reigns everywhere. Such a theory cannot serve as the foundations of biological science. . . .

. . . Fatherly care is shown by the Party and the government for the strengthening and development of the Michurinist tendency in our science, for the removal of all obstacles on the way to its fullest flowering. This obligates us to develop the work yet more widely and deeply for the fulfillment of the command of the Soviet people on arming the state and collective farms with advanced scientific theory.

We must earnestly put science and theory at the service of the people in order to raise ever more swiftly the harvest of the fields and the productivity of livestock, to raise the productivity of labor on state and collective farms.

I call on all academicians, scientific workers, agronomists, and animal breeders in close union with the progressive workers of the socialist rural economy to direct all their energies to the fulfillment of these great and noble tasks. (*Applause.*)

Progressive biological science is indebted to the geniuses of mankind—*Lenin and Stalin*—for this: *the teachings of Michurin entered into the treasure-house of our knowledge, into science as a golden fund.* (*Applause.*)

Long live the teachings of Michurin, the teachings on the transformation of organic nature for the welfare of the Soviet people! (*Applause.*)

Long live the Party of Lenin and Stalin for revealing Michurin to the world and for the creation in our country of all conditions necessary for the flowering of advanced materialistic biology. (*Applause.*)

Glory to our great friend and coryphaeus of science— our leader and teacher, Comrade Stalin!

(*All stand and applaud for a long time.*)

. . . To the Editors of the Newspaper *Pravda:*

I request the publication of the following text of my declaration.

As long as our Party recognized both tendencies in Soviet genetics and as long as debates between them were regarded as a creative discussion of theoretical questions of contemporary science facilitating the discovery of truth, I persistently defended my views which at some points differed from the views of Academician Lysenko. But now, since it has become clear to me that the basic theses of the Michurin school in Soviet genetics are approved by the Central Committee of the All-Union Communist Party, I, as a member of the Party, cannot defend positions which have been declared mistaken by the Central Committee of our Party. (A. R. Zhebrak). . . .

THE COMMUNIST PARTY LINE ON THE CIRCUS [35]

MOSCOW, March 5—The newspaper Soviet Art said today that reactionary "bourgeois tendencies" have been noted in Soviet circuses and that persons responsible for it ought to be exposed.

"Only by full unmasking of the cosmopolite-theoreticians and formalistic directors who have planted in the arenas of Soviet circuses alien bourgeois tendencies can Soviet circus art achieve a new renaissance and become a genuine expression of the spiritual strength of the peoples inhabiting our great fatherland," the newspaper said.

The three-column article, appearing in Soviet Art, organ of the Fine Arts Committee and the Ministry of Cinematography, was signed by Nikolai Barzilovich. It attacked E. Kuznetsov, theoretician and author, declaring that his works "unrestrainedly praised the decayed circus art of capitalist countries which offered ideologically empty numbers and attractions."

[35] From *The New York Times* (by the UNITED PRESS), March 5, 1949: "Russia Accuses Circuses of 'Bourgeois Tendencies.'"

— Reading No. 23 —

R. HILFERDING: STATE CAPITALISM OR TOTALITARIAN STATE ECONOMY [36]

One of the ablest orthodox Marxist economists assesses the nature of the Soviet State.

↗   ↗   ↗

. . . Does the "bureaucracy" really "rule" the (*Soviet*) economy and consequently the people? Bureaucracy everywhere, and particularly in the Soviet Union, is composed of a conglomeration of the most varied elements. To it belong not only government officials in the narrow sense of the word (i.e. from minor employees up to the generals and even Stalin himself) but also the directors of all branches of industry and such functionaries as, for example, the postal and railway employees. How could this variegated lot possibly achieve a unified rule? Who are its representatives? How does it adopt decisions? What organs are at its disposal?

In reality, the "bureaucracy" is not an independent bearer of power. In accordance with its structure as well as function, it is only an instrument in the hands of the real rulers. It is organized as an hierarchy and subordinated to the commanding power. It receives but does not give orders. Any functionary, as Trotsky justly puts it, "can be sacrificed by his superior in the hierarchical system in order to decrease any kind of dissatisfaction." And these are the new masters of production, the substitute for capitalists! Stalin thoroughly exploded this

[36] From the *Modern Review*, June, 1947, originally published in May, 1940, in the *Socialist Courier* (Russian).

myth when, during the last purges, he ordered shot, among others, thousands of industrial managers.

It is not the bureaucracy that rules, but he who gives orders to the bureaucracy. And it is Stalin who gives orders to the Russian bureaucracy. Lenin and Trotsky with a select group of followers who were never able to come to independent decisions as a party but always remained an instrument in the hands of the leaders (the same was true later with the fascist and national-socialist parties) seized power at a time when the old state apparatus was collapsing. They changed the state apparatus to suit their needs as rulers, eliminating democracy and establishing their own dictatorship which in their ideology, but by no means in practice, was identified with the "dictatorship of the proletariat." Thus they created the first totalitarian state—even before the name was invented. Stalin carried on with the job, removing his rivals through the instrument of the state apparatus and establishing an unlimited personal dictatorship.

This is the reality which should not be obscured by construing alleged domination by a "bureaucracy" which is in fact subordinate to the government to the same extent as are the rest of the people. This is true even though some modest crumbs from the master's table may be doled out to it—without, of course, a guarantee that other crumbs are to follow and at the price of constant danger to their very lives. Their material share does not constitute any important portion of the social product. Nevertheless, the psychological effect of such a differentiation may be quite considerable.

Important economic consequences flow from this fact. It is the essence of a totalitarian state that it subjects the economy to its aims. The economy is deprived of its own laws, it becomes a controlled economy. Once this control is effected, it transforms the market economy into a consumers' economy. The character and extent of needs are then determined by the state. The (Nazi) German and (Fascist) Italian economies provide evidence of the fact that such control, once initiated in a totalitarian state, spreads rapidly and tends to become all-embracing as was the case in Russia from the very beginning. Despite great differences in their points of departure, the economic system of totalitarian states are drawing close to each other. In Germany, too, the state, striving to maintain and strengthen its power, determines the character of production and accumulation. Prices lose their regulating function and become merely means of distribution. The economy, and with it the exponents of economic activity, are more or less subjected to the state, becoming its subordinates. The economy loses the primacy which it held under bourgeois society. This does not mean, however, that economic circles do not have great influence on the ruling power in Germany as well as in Russia. But their influence is conditional, has limits and is not decisive in relation to the essence of policy. Policy is actually determined by a small circle of those who are in power. It is their interests, their ideas as to what is required to maintain, exploit, and strengthen their own power that determines the policy which they impose as law upon the subordinated economy. This is why the subjective factor, the "unforeseeable," "irrational" character of political development has gained such importance in politics.

The faithful believe only in heaven and hell as determining forces; the Marxist sectarian only in capitalism and socialism, in classes—bourgeoisie and proletariat. The Marxist sectarian cannot grasp the idea that present-day state power, having achieved independence, is unfolding its enormous strength according to its own laws, subjecting social forces and compelling them to serve its ends for a short or long period of time.

Therefore neither the Russian nor the totalitarian system in general is determined by the character of the economy. On the contrary it is the economy that is determined by the policy of the ruling power and subjected to the aims and purposes of this power. The totalitarian power lives by the economy, but not for the economy or even for the class ruling the economy—as is the case of the bourgeois state, though the latter (as any student of foreign policy can demonstrate) may occasionally pursue aims of its own. An analogy to the totalitarian state may be found in the era of the late Roman Empire, in the regime of the Praetorians and their emperors.

Of course, from a social democratic viewpoint the Bolshevik economy can hardly be called "socialist," for to us socialism is indissolubly linked to democracy. According to our cencept, socialization of the means of production implies freeing the economy from the rule of one class and vesting it in society as a whole—a society which is democratically self-governed. We never imagined that the political form of that "managed economy" which was to replace capitalist production for a free market could be unrestricted absolutism. The correlation between the economic basis and the political structure seemed to us a very definite one: namely, that the socialist society would inaugurate the highest realization of democracy. Even those among us who believed that the strictest application of centralized power would be necessary or inevitable for the period of transition, considered this period only temporary and bound to end after the suppression of the propertied classes. Together with the disappearance of classes, class rule was also to vanish—that class rule which we considered the only possible form of political rule in general. "The state is withering away. . . ."

But history, this "best of all Marxists," has taught us differently. It has taught us that "administering of things," despite Engels' expectations, may turn into unlimited "administering of people," and thus not only lead to the emancipation of the state from the economy but even to the subjection of the economy to the state.

Once subjected to the state, the economy secures the continued existence of this form of government. The fact that such a result flows from a unique situation primarily brought about by war does not exclude a Marxist analysis, but it alters somewhat our rather simplified and schematic conception of the correlation between economy and state and between economy and politics which developed in a completely different period. The emergence of the state as an independent power greatly complicates the economic characterization of a society in which politics (i.e. the state) plays a determining and decisive role.

For this reason the controversy as to whether the economic system of the Soviet Union is "capitalist" or "socialist" seems to me rather pointless. It is neither. It represents a totalitarian state economy, i.e. a system to which the economies of Germany and Italy are drawing closer and closer.

— Reading No. 24 —

THE AIMS AND TASKS OF DEMOCRATIC SOCIALISM

The following statement was adopted by the Socialist International at Frankfurt-on-Main, Germany, 1951. It indicates the renewed emphasis on democracy as integral to the ends and means of socialism.

✦   ✦   ✦

Socialism has become a major force in world affairs. It has passed from propaganda into practice. In some countries the foundations of a socialist society have already been laid. Here the evils of capitalism are disappearing and the community has developed new vigor. The principles of socialism are proving their worth in action.

. . . In many countries, uncontrolled capitalism is giving place to an economy in which state intervention and collective ownership limit the scope of private capitalists. More people are coming to recognize the need for planning. Social security, free trade unionism and industrial democracy are winning ground.

. . . Communism falsely claims a share in the socialist tradition. In fact it has distorted that tradition beyond recognition. It has built up a rigid theology which is incompatible with the critical spirit of Marxism.

. . . International communism is the instrument of a new imperialist state. Wherever it has achieved power it has destroyed freedom or the chance of gaining freedom. It is based on a militarist bureaucracy and a terrorist police. By producing glaring contrasts of wealth and privilege it has created a new class society. Forced labor plays an important part in its economic organization.

. . . Socialists strive to build a new society in freedom and by democratic means.

Without freedom there can be no socialism. Socialism can be achieved only through democracy. Democracy can be fully realized only through socialism.

. . . Democracy requires the right of more than one party to exist and the right of opposition. But democracy has the right and duty to protect itself against those who exploit its opportunities only in order to destroy it. The defense of political democracy is of vital interest to the people. Its preservation is a condition of realizing social and economic democracy.

. . . Every dictatorship, wherever it may be, is a danger to the freedom of all nations and thereby to the peace of the world. Wherever there is unrestrained exploitation of forced labor, whether under private profit or under political dictatorship, there is danger to the living and moral standards of all the people.

Socialism seeks to replace capitalism by a system in which the public interest takes precedence over the interest of private profit. The immediate economic aims of socialist policy are full employment, higher production, a rising standard of life, social security and a fair distribution of incomes and property.

. . . Socialist planning can be achieved by various means. The structure of the country concerned must decide the extent of public ownership and the form of planning to apply.

. . . Public ownership can take the form of the nationalization of existing private concerns or the creation of new public concerns, municipal or regional enterprise, consumers' or producers' cooperatives.

These various forms of public ownership should be regarded not as ends in themselves but as means of controlling basic industries and services on which the economic life and welfare of the community depend, of rationalizing inefficient industries or of preventing private monopolies and cartels from exploiting the public.

. . . Socialist planning does not presuppose public ownership of all the means of production. It is compatible with the existence of private ownership in important fields, for instance in agriculture, handicraft, retail trade and small and middle-sized industries. The state must prevent private owners from abusing their powers. It can and should assist them to contribute towards increased production and well-being within the framework of a planned economy.

. . . While the guiding principle of capitalism is private profit, the guiding principle of socialism is the satisfaction of human needs.

. . . Socialism means far more than an economic and social system. Economic and social progress have moral value to the extent that they serve to liberate and develop the human personality.

Socialism fights to liberate men from the fears and anxieties from which all forms of political and economic insecurity are inseparable. This liberation will open the way to the spiritual development of men conscious of their responsibilities and to the cultural evolution of complete personalities. Socialism is a powerful factor in promoting this cultural development.

. . . Democratic socialism is international because it aims at liberating all men from every form of economic, spiritual and political bondage.

. . . Democratic socialism is international because it recognizes that no nation can solve all its economic and social problems in isolation.

. . . Absolute national sovereignty must be transcended

. . . The new world society for which socialists strive can develop fruitfully in peace only if it is based on voluntary cooperation between nations. Democracy must, therefore, be established on an international scale under an international rule of law which guarantees national freedom and the rights of man.

A SELECTED BIBLIOGRAPHY

Bernstein, E., *Evolutionary Socialism*, English trans. (London and New York, 1907).

Bukharen, N., *Historical Materialism*, English trans. (New York, 1924).

Burnham, J., *The Managerial Revolution* (New York, 1941).

Carew-Hunt, R. N., *The Theory and Practice of Communism* (New York, 1950).

———— *Marxism: Past and Present* (New York, 1954).

Carr, E. H., *The Bolshevik Revolution*, Vols. I-IV (New York, 1952-54).

Counts, G., *Country of the Blind* (Boston, 1949).

DeLeon, D., *Speeches and Editorials*, 2 vols. (New York, 1930).

Deutscher, I., *Stalin* (New York, 1940).

———— *The Prophet Armed: Trotsky* (New York, 1954).

Dewey, J., *Liberalism and Social Action* (New York, 1935).

———— *The Case of Leon Trotsky* (Hearings) New York, 1937).

———— *Not Guilty* (New York, 1938).

———— *Freedom and Culture* (New York, 1940).

Eastman, M., *Marxism: Is it Science?* (New York, 1940).

Eastman, M. and Hook, S., "Debate on Planning and Democracy," *New Leader*, 1945.

Engels, F., *Anti-Duhring*, English trans. (New York and Moscow, 1936).

Foster, W., *Toward Soviet America* (New York, 1932).

Gurian, W., *Rise and Decline of Marxism* (New York, 1938).

Hillquit, M., *From Marx to Lenin* (New York, 1935).

Hook, S., *From Hegel to Marx* (New York, 1935).

———— *Reason, Social Myth and Democracy* (New York, 1940).

——— *The Hero in History* (New York, 1943).

Jaurès, J., *Problems of Socialism,* English trans. (New York, 1904).

Kulski, W., *The Soviet Regime* (Syracuse, 1954).

Kautsky, K., *Ethics and the Materialistic Conception of History,* English trans. (Chicago, 1918).

——— *Thomas More and His Utopia,* English trans. (New York, 1927).

——— *Bolshevism at a Deadlock,* English trans. (New York, 1931).

——— *Communism vs. Social-Democracy,* English trans. (New York, 1946).

Lenin, N., *Selected Works,* Vols. I-XII, English trans. (Moscow and New York, 1935).

Luxemburg, R., *The Accumulation of Capital,* English trans. (New Haven, 1951).

——— *The Russian Revolution,* English trans. (New York, 1940).

Marx, K., *Capital,* English trans., Vol. I (London, 1886): Vols. I-III (Chicago, 1906).

——— *Communist Manifesto,* English trans. (London, 1888).

——— *Introduction to Critique of Political Economy,* English trans. (Chicago, 1904).

Mehring, F., *Karl Marx,* English trans. (New York, 1936).

Mitrany, D., *Marx Against the Peasant* (London, 1951).

Nomad, M., *Apostles of Revolution* (New York, 1941).

Plamenatz, J., *German Marxism and Russian Communism* (New York, 1954).

Plekhanov, G., *The Individual in History,* English trans. (Moscow, 1940).

——— *Fundamental Problems of Marxism,* English trans. (London, 1929).

Radkey, O. H., *The Election to the Russian Constituent Assembly of 1917* (Cambridge, 1950).

Rosenberg, A., *Democracy and Socialism,* English trans. (New York, 1939).

Russell, B., *The Theory and Practice of Bolshevism* (New York, 1920).

Schumpeter, J., *Capitalism, Socialism and Democracy* (New York, 1943).

Serge, V., *Russia After Twenty Years,* English trans. (New York, 1937).

Simkhovitch, V., *Marxism versus Socialism* (New York, 1923).

Souvarine, B., *Stalin,* English trans. (New York, 1940).

Stalin, J., *Problems of Leninism,* English trans. (Moscow, 1953).

———— *Works,* Vols. I-IX, English trans. (Moscow, 1953).

———— *History of the Communist Party of the Soviet Union,* English trans. (Moscow and New York, 1938).

Strachey, J., *Theory and Practice of Socialism* (London, 1936).

Trotsky, L., *History of the Russian Revolution,* English trans. (New York, 1932).

———— *Revolution Betrayed,* English trans. (New York, 1937).

Webb, B. and S., *Soviet Civilization* (London and New York, 1935).

Wolfe, B., *Three Who Made a Revolution* (New York, 1948).

INDEX

VAN NOSTRAND ANVIL BOOKS already published